Knowledge, Belief, and Character

Studies in Epistemology and Cognitive Theory
Series Editor: *Paul K. Moser, Loyola University of Chicago*

Knowledge, Belief, and Character

Readings in Virtue Epistemology

edited by
GUY AXTELL

ROWMAN & LITTLEFIELD PUBLISHERS, INC.
Lanham • Boulder • New York • Oxford

ROWMAN & LITTLEFIELD PUBLISHERS, INC.

Published in the United States of America
by Rowman & Littlefield Publishers, Inc.
4720 Boston Way, Lanham, Maryland 20706
http://www.rowmanlittlefield.com

12 Hid's Copse Road
Cumnor Hill, Oxford OX2 9JJ, England

British Library Cataloguing in Publication Information Available

Library of Congress Cataloging-in-Publication Data

Knowledge, belief, and character : readings in virtue epistemology / [edited by] Guy
  Axtell.
    p. cm. – (Studies in epistemology and cognitive theory)
    Includes bibliographical references and index.
    ISBN: 978-0-8476-9653-6
      1. Knowledge, Theory of. 2. Virtue. 3. Character. I. Axtell, Guy, 1957- II.
    Studies in epistemology and cognitive theory (Unnumbered)
  BD161.K593 2000
  121—dc21   99-059826

Printed in the United States of America

♾™ The paper used in this publication meets the minimum requirements of American
National Standard for Information Sciences—Permanence of Paper for Printed Library
Materials, ANSI/NISO Z39.48–1992.

To a loving and wonderfully supportive family,
Ruthann, Sandra, and Jan

Contents

Acknowledgments

I would like to express special thanks to Ernest Sosa of Brown University for his support of this collection from its inception. I would also like to thank the editors and publishers who gave their permission for articles, book chapters, or revised and expanded versions of previously published papers, to be reprinted here:

Chapter 1 by Alvin Goldman is sections I-III of "Epistemic Folkways and Scientific Epistemology," reprinted from Goldman's *Liaisons: Philosophy Meets the Cognitive and Social Sciences*, 155-175. Cambridge, Mass.: The MIT Press, 1991.

Chapter 2 by Ernest Sosa originally appeared as chapter 8 of Sosa's *Knowledge in Perspective: Selected Essays in Epistemology*. New York: Cambridge University Press, 1991.

Chapter 3 by Ernest Sosa is sections F and G of "Proper Functionalism and Virtue Epistemology," originally published in *NOUS* 27:1, 51-65. Malden, Mass.: Blackwell Publishers, 1993.

Chapter 4 by Hilary Kornblith was originally published in *The Monist* 68, no. 2, 364-376. La Salle, Ill.: The Hegeler Institute, 1985.

Chapter 5 by John Greco is a specially re-edited selection from Greco's *Putting Skeptics in their Place: Skeptical Arguments and Philosophical Inquiry.* New York: Cambridge University Press, 2000.

Chapter 6 by Jonathan Dancy, chapter 7 by Lawrence BonJour, and chapter 8 by Ernest Sosa were originally published in *Philosophical Studies* 78, 189-235. Dordrecht: Kluwer Academic Publishers, 1995.

Chapter 9 by Linda Zagzebski: An earlier version of this paper was published in the *Proceedings of the Twentieth World Congress of Philosophy, Volume 5: Epistemology*. Bowling Green, Ohio: Philosophy Documentation Center, 2000.

Chapter 12 by Christopher Hookway: An earlier version of this paper was published as "Virtues, Sentiments, and Epistemic Rationality" in the *Proceed-*

ings of the Twentieth World Congress of Philosophy, Volume 5: Epistemology. Bowling Green, Ohio: Philosophy Documentation Center, 2000.

Chapter 13 by Richard Paul is chapter 15 of Paul's *Critical Thinking: What Every Person Needs to Survive in a Rapidly Changing World*, edited by Jane Willsen and A.J.A. Binker, 319-332. Sonoma, Calif.: Foundation for Critical Thinking, 1993.

Chapter 14 by Guy Axtell was originally published as "The Role of the Intellectual Virtues in the Reunification of Epistemology," in *The Monist* 81, no. 2 (The Reunification of Epistemology), 488-508. The current chapter has been re-edited with the gracious permission of the Hegeler Institute, 1998.

Chapter 16 by Linda Zagzebski was originally published in *The Rationality of Theism*, edited by Gotehard Bruntrup, 177-194. Dordrecht: Kluwer Academic Publishers, 2000.

Introduction

I

As is familiar to readers of Aristotle's *Nicomachean Ethics*, the venerable Greek philosopher organized much of his philosophical thought around his understanding of two kinds of human "excellence," *ethike arete* and *dianoetike arete*, or the moral and intellectual virtues. Because of Aristotle's emphasis on questions about what kinds of people we ought to be and what kinds of lives we ought to live and his way of explaining his thoughts on these questions through discussions of *arete*, his philosophical approach is typically described as "virtue theory."

It is well acknowledged that a revival of interest in classically-based virtue theory has occurred in recent philosophy, beginning during or even before the 1970s with discussions among ethicists about the role of the ethical virtues in evaluating agents and their actions. The extension of this interest into epistemology dates to 1980, when the suggestion of an account of justified belief (justification) based upon epistemic or intellectual virtues was made by Ernest Sosa in his paper "The Raft and the Pyramid." As a first approximation, intellectual virtues in contemporary virtue epistemology are those "capacities," "powers," "dispositions," and "acquired habits" of persons that contribute to their success in achieving the cognitive aim or aims.[1] That aim most epistemologists agree is truth, and so Sosa understands intellectual virtue as "a quality bound to help maximize one's surplus of truth over error." This introduction will introduce the reader to the study of the intellectual virtues, and to the dialogue both among self-described virtue epistemologists, and between themselves and their critics. I will first provide a brief overview of the initial motivations behind the revival of virtue theory, and explicate some parallels between the approaches taken to philosophical problems in virtue ethics and in virtue epistemology. The second part of the introduction will survey the central epistemological problems that frame the research interests of virtue epistemology, and the major directions taken in contemporary research. The third part will acquaint the reader with each of the authors and exemplary papers that I have selected for this collection. Finally, the fourth part of the introduction briefly raises and answers some queries about the extended sense of the term "character" as it is used in the title of this collection. I distinguish various connotations of the term, and suggest several senses of "intellectual character" that I believe are appropriate to connect with the acknowledged central epistemic topics of knowledge and justified belief. This requires, however, articulating not only the commonalities, but also the differences between contemporary virtue theories and their classical predecessors.

It is widely agreed today that the role of the virtues had been under-emphasized in ethical theory in a period prior to this recent revival in virtue theory. Some would identify this period with the positivist era through mid-twentieth century in Anglo-American philosophy, while others would more broadly implicate the Modern era in philosophy as a whole. This difference is related to the oft-noted distinction between a "theory of the virtues" and a "virtue theory" (see Julia Driver, chapter 10). We can pick up this distinction in the third part of the introduction; we do not need it for the moment since the example of positivist metaethics is quite sufficient as a basis for indicating concerns that led to a revival of virtue theory. During the positivist era ethics had been dominated by concerns with the philosophical analysis of "thin" concepts like ethical "goodness"; the view of philosophic analysis that accompanied this approach sharply separated logic and philosophical analysis from matters of psychology, and thereby discouraged philosophers from doing substantive work in normative ethics. Even those ethicists who persisted in applying theory to practice and in evaluating the ethical rightness or wrongness of actions typically did so by criteria that did not directly involve consideration of the *character* of moral agents themselves. With the revival of interest in virtue theory, the ethical virtues and vices came to be seen as having more important roles to play, roles that make them valuable both for understanding the motivations underlying an agent's actions, and for evaluating agents as praiseworthy or blameworthy. In the period since the revival of virtue ethics, ethical evaluation has come to focus to a greater extent on situated agents themselves and the habits and dispositions that constitute their moral character.

In his 1980 article, Sosa proposed a virtue-centered epistemology analogous to a form of virtue ethics. Soon thereafter, the intellectual virtues (and their pertinence to the epistemic evaluation of agents and their beliefs) were further developed in Sosa's work, and in that of several others, including Lorraine Code, Hilary Kornblith, and Alvin Goldman. Forms of contemporary virtue theory[2] differ in substantial ways from their classical predecessors, as we shall see. But the recent inclusion of intellectual in addition to ethical virtues as a focus of study reintroduces the distinction and relationship between the kinds of virtue that Aristotle identified. This focus on the intellectual virtues and their role in epistemic evaluation also introduces a kind of parity into the approach to ethical and epistemic normativity, a parity that some see as present at least potentially in the classical outlook. That the fields of ethics and epistemology were sharply divided through much of the twentieth century, and that a great deal of the support positivism lent to that sharp division has been undermined by trends in the last quarter of the century, hardly seems debatable today. The plausibility and philosophical advantages of instilling greater parity through a strongly analogical approach to ethical and epistemic evaluation, however, certainly *are* a matter of debate, and part of the background that should concern us.

Sosa's original foray in the conclusion of his article did not get much beyond a proposal for a reorientation of epistemology. Since that time, he and others have developed intellectual virtue-centered epistemologies in substantial detail. His initial proposal and the reasoning behind it remain informative, though, especially when seen in the context of epistemological debate within which it is set. An agent's *actions* are understood to be the result of her virtues or stable dispositions to act, and these dispositions are conceived in turn to embody rules. "Primary ethical justification," that is, the primary meaning of ascribing rightness or wrongness to actions, as Sosa understands it, attaches to (or derives from) virtues or stable dispositions to act, "through their greater contribution of value when compared with alternatives." An analogous strategy, he then suggests, might prove fruitful in epistemology: we might address the question of what confers justification upon an agent's beliefs by a similar strategy. Following Sosa's analogy, primary epistemic justification would attach "to *intellectual* virtues, to stable dispositions for belief acquisition, through their greater contribution towards getting us to the truth."[3]

This places us in a position to identify a defining methodological feature setting virtue epistemology off from its alternatives. John Greco has described this key feature as a *change in the direction of analysis.* Justification, a property of belief, is explained in terms of the belief's source in an intellectual virtue—that is, a property of persons. This parallels the way that virtue theories of ethics understand the normative properties of actions (rightness/wrongness) in terms of the normative properties of moral agents.[4] Using the analogy between determining an act to be "right" and determining a belief to be "justified," one can understand this change in the direction of analysis by saying that virtue theories make rightness (or justifiedness) follow from an action's (or belief's) source in a virtue, rather than the other way around. According to Greco, "Non-virtue theories try to analyze virtuous character in terms of justified belief, defining the former in terms of dispositions to achieve the latter. I am following Sosa's suggestion that we do things the other way around, defining justified belief in terms of virtuous character. Virtuous character is then defined in terms of successful and stable dispositions to form belief."[5] Another of our contributors, Christopher Hookway, also captures this reversal well when he writes, "Justified beliefs are those that issue from the responsible inquiries of virtuous inquirers. It is a mistake to put it the other way round: epistemic virtues are those habits and dispositions that lead us to have justified beliefs. The primary focus is on how we order activities directed at answering questions and assessing methods of answering questions; it is not upon the epistemic status of beliefs."[6]

All forms of virtue epistemology embody this *change in the direction of analysis* that Greco and Hookway define. Virtue epistemologies typically define not only justified belief but also knowledge through essential reference to their source in intellectual virtues. But answers to the question of how, in turn, to define virtuous character have not enjoyed the same level of consensus. The claim Greco makes above (in step with Sosa's proposal) that "virtuous character is then defined in terms of successful and stable dispositions to form belief" is a claim associated with a "reliabilist" virtue epistemology. Contrarily, Hookway's final sentence, which suggests decentralizing questions of the epistemic status of beliefs in favor of questions of agency and inquiry, is a claim associated with a "responsibilist" virtue epistemology. Those authors oriented towards responsibilism typically do not agree with the "consequential" approach Sosa, Greco, Alvin Goldman, and others take to defining the virtues—that is, by their reliable success in producing true belief.

The defining interests and concerns of responsibilists will come into sharper focus later in this introduction. Responsibilist themes are represented in this collection through contributions by Linda Zagzebski, Jonathan Dancy, James Montmarquet, Christopher Hookway, and Richard Paul. In the next section, we will begin by discussing the epistemological problems that frame the research interests of the reliabilist strain of contemporary virtue epistemology that Ernest Sosa inaugurates. After this, following the general arrangement of papers in the collection, we will further elaborate on the epistemological problems that frame the research interests of responsibilist virtue epistemology.[7]

II

Sosa made his initial suggestion for an intellectual virtue-centered account of knowledge and justification in support of externalist or reliabilist epistemology. Indeed he drew his own comparisons with the reliabilist conceptions of justification and the "causal theory of knowing" of Alvin Goldman and others *circa* 1980. A driving force for the development of externalist accounts of knowledge and justification, in turn, has been discussion of Gettier-type problems, which pose a very serious challenge to the traditional conception of knowledge as justified true belief.[8] It merits a brief digression to explain the nature of Gettier-problems and the general character of reliabilist approaches to them.

E. L. Gettier (1963) rocked the traditional conception of knowledge through his framing of specific cases of justified true beliefs that appear *not* to constitute knowledge. This suggests the need for either a new account of justification or else a search for an additional condition (of warrant or positive epistemic status) that, together with justified true belief, constitutes the proper set of necessary and sufficient conditions for knowledge. Gettier-problems have been widely discussed since the mid-1960s without any single clear line of resolution. But one of the striking features of contemporary epistemology since Gettier's influential paper was published has been a broadening consensus on the need to abandon many aspects of the "traditional" conception of knowledge. This is primarily because accounting for the problems raised by his cases appears to demand something besides the internalist construal of justified belief that the traditional conception holds: it appears to necessitate restricting genuine knowing only to instances where the truth of the agent's belief is "linked" with the causal process that produced it in some reliable way.

Can an agent's belief constitute knowledge if its truth was in fact a matter of luck—if its truth was in fact improbable or merely fortunate, given the process that produced it? In Gettier cases, the agent's justification for her beliefs has come "unglued" from the truth of her belief. In these cases their truth is really a matter of luck, given the process by which the belief was produced. In order to accord with the intuition that the true beliefs in Gettier cases do not amount to knowledge, epistemologists began looking at what went wrong, and at how to strengthen the conditions on knowledge so that truth and justification could not come apart. Where the traditional conception fails, many conclude, is in not demanding of knowledge an objective or external connection between the truth of the agent's belief and the belief-producing cognitive process (BCP) that gave rise to it. Demanding such a truth-connection would be to place an "external" in contrast to an "internal" condition on justification, and theories that place *any* external conditions on justification are classed as externalist theories.[9] An externalist theory that asserts that the production of a belief by a reliable cognitive process is (at least) a necessary condition for it to be justified is called a "process reliabilist" theory of justification.[10]

We return now to the point that Sosa proposed his intellectual virtue-centered epistemology as a means of improving the prospects of a process reliabilist account of epistemic justification. Why did it need improving? While the shift in epistemology toward reliabilism has been widespread, there are also serious objections to reliabilism. Noting the most serious of these, Sosa acknowledges that reliabilism "comes in a great variety of types most of which are clearly unacceptable." We have already seen the first and most incisive revision that Sosa proposed: No previous form of reliabilism explicitly entails the *change in the direction of analysis* described above. Other related revisions or modifications that "virtue-basing" a reliabilist account would suggest are initially indicated by the problem (often seen as a crucial aspect of Gettier-problems) of the "accidental reliability" of a belief-producing cognitive process (hereafter BCP). Can just any reliable BCP provide the kind of justification a true belief needs to in order to constitute knowledge? Can "strange" or "fleeting" processes, for instance, give rise to knowledge? Because virtues, whether ethical or intellectual, are understood as *stable dispositions,* defining epistemic justification in terms of intellectual virtues will respond directly to a serious objection to process reliabilism: that it must, by its very logic, attribute knowledge and justified belief *whenever* reliability is present (and even if the belief has its source in a process that is itself fleeting). To the extent that it can demonstrate a principled way to rule out fleeting, random, and ad hoc processes, the conception of justification-making or justification-conferring BCPs is greatly strengthened

Performing an action due to a demonstrable skill requires a different explanation than success due to mere luck; success due to luck is not reliable or

likely repeatable under normal circumstances. To attribute an action or belief to
the workings of an intellectual virtue is to identify its ground with an attribute of
the agent that is still more stable and less fleeting than is a skill: Sosa and
Goldman each require that justified beliefs be generated by a genuine *power* or
capacity or *competence* of the agent to arrive at truth, and it is such powers of
persons that are identified with intellectual virtue. Sosa identifies five basic
powers and the normal parameters and limits of reliability for each. These five
are the faculties of perception, memory, reason, intuition, and introspection.

While we have used the problem of fleeting processes to indicate an initial
difference between virtue epistemologies and "generic" forms of reliabilism,[11]
the reader will encounter a number of additional problems in the early chapters
of this collection. These help us to understand more fully the revisions that
characterize reliabilist virtue epistemology. Goldman's contribution in chapter 1,
for instance, discusses problem cases of "strange processes," such as that of the
"reliable clairvoyant" (closely associated with what is called the "meta-
incoherence problem"). An agent posited to have such a faculty might be
unaware of it, and unable to connect those beliefs it causes her to have with any
evidential considerations she may possess that would bear upon the rational
acceptability of those beliefs. Is Goldman committed to viewing this reliable
faculty as a virtue, and therefore as justification-conferring? How would the
virtue epistemologist try to square our conceptual understanding of intellectual
virtues with our intuitions regarding such cases?

Two further problems that both Sosa and Goldman address are the
"Generality" and "New Evil Genie" problems, which we might describe here. In
briefest terms, the Generality problem presents reliabilists with the challenge of
describing those cognitive processes that are understood as justification-
conferring, in a way that is neither too broad nor too narrow. Moving beyond the
problems of strange and fleeting processes, the virtue epistemologists will also
need to ask, "How and why do we count certain processes and not others among
the intellectual virtues?" It must not be the case that an account is so specific
that *every* true belief is credited to a virtue or reliable faculty; but neither must it
be the case that the account is so broad that a single faculty is taken to generate
beliefs with widely varying epistemic statuses. The New Evil Genie (or Demon)
problem revolves around cases of systematic deception or wholesale falsehood.
It has been among the most difficult obstacles for reliabilist accounts of
justification, since it highlights strong intuitions about the importance of
subjective justification, intuitions that may be thought to support an internalist
perspective on justification. How are reliabilists to square their method of
attributing intellectual virtues to agents with the consideration that the *degree of
effort* to attain the truth (and the phenomenological *experience* of a victim in the
Genie's world) is by hypothesis indistinguishable from that of the victim's twin,
a reliable agent in the actual world? This problem is posed forcefully by
Lawrence BonJour in our collection, and papers by Goldman, Sosa, and Greco
each suggest different ways of responding to it.

Thus far we have focussed only upon those versions of virtue epistemology that initially developed, as we earlier said, out of concern to improve the prospects of reliabilism. But an alternative "responsibilist" strain of virtue epistemology began to emerge soon after Sosa's initial formulations of his position, as was perhaps first evident in Lorraine Code's *Epistemic Responsibility* (1987).[12] The kinds of virtues responsibilists focus on are akin to those that Richard Paul, Director of the Foundation for Critical Thinking, defines and discusses in chapter 13: the virtues of intellectual humility, courage, empathy, integrity, perseverance, fair-mindedness, and faith in reason. Some of the differences between the reliabilist and responsibilist approaches often seem little more than matters of divergent focus or emphasis. However, in certain respects the differences between "virtue reliabilism" and "virtue responsibilism" are far more substantial and interesting than this. They surface, first and foremost, in the conceptual understanding and identification of the intellectual virtues themselves.

While most forms of virtue epistemology today place a success condition on the ascription of a virtue to an agent, not all share Greco's claim that "the essential aspect of an intellectual virtue is its success component, or in Sosa's and Goldman's terms, its reliability."[13] Responsibilists like Lorraine Code (1987) concede that reliability "maintains a closer connection with truth and warrantability than responsibility can establish." But they do not see reliability as the most important or defining feature of a virtue. Code's book announces a primary interest in the virtues as they relate to *active agency*, and she defines the intellectual virtues more restrictively, as *acquired* intellectual habits and dispositions; only these, she points out, are the proper object of attributions of praise and blame, not the genetically-endowed "faculties" that the reliabilists would include among the intellectual virtues. Justification, responsibilists insist, depends greatly not just on the quantity of evidence an agent has for his or her beliefs, but on the quality of that evidence, and this is most often a function of how well one investigates. Related to this, the reliability of agents may depend crucially on *acts* they perform or *choices* they make in the context of inquiry.

What is important to notice about the responsibilists' list of intellectual virtues is that many of them are analogues of recognized ethical virtues. They are conceived to have their source in acquired habits of character, yet to pertain (not to action but) to thought or belief. To accord with such considerations, responsibilists often seek an account of the intellectual virtues that builds into them the kind of *motivational* constraint that is integral to the Aristotelian conception of the moral virtues. For example, Linda Zagzebski (chapter 9 & 1996) restricts the intellectual virtues to acquired dispositions, and builds into her conception of them an especially strong motivational requirement, as may be required to defend her unique move (chapter 9) "to a virtue epistemology based on virtue in the ethical sense."[14]

This is not to say that most responsibilists do not also acknowledge the importance of a success condition on the attribution of a virtue to an agent. It is indeed very Aristotelian to include both success and motivation conditions (again though, if we base this on how Aristotle understood *moral* virtue, and not on how he himself understood intellectual virtue). "An act is an *act of virtue* A," according to Zagzebski, "just in case it arises from the motivational component of A, is something a person with virtue A would characteristically do in the circumstances, and is successful in bringing about the end of virtue A because of these features of the act."[15] The centrality Zagzebski gives to the motivational component of *acts of virtue* leads us to the important recognition that there is a spectrum of positions from stronger to weaker on the understanding of what constitutes a virtue epistemology. Responsibilists share concerns over issues like proper motivation, rationality, and doxastic responsibility. They appear especially interested in how agency *works*, and in how responsible agents can practically *apply* the virtues of an ideal critical thinker to the context of their inquiry. These issues can be seen as aspects of an account of active epistemic agency, and no dubious voluntarism about belief is suggested by such concerns in and of themselves. But the concerns of responsibilists are enveloped within conceptions of virtue theory that are generally "stronger" than those current among virtue reliabilists.

To a substantial degree, the range or spectrum of views I am alluding to can be understood by referring back to debates within ethics over the past two decades. One rather contentious issue in ethics has been the dividing line between "a theory of virtue" and "a virtue theory." It is very difficult to be clear about the dividing line between the positions these terms represent, and language often confounds. There are those who have a theory of virtue, but would not describe themselves as "virtue theorists," which term they reserve for a thesis concerning the *primacy* of the virtues that they consider "radical"; and as we are now seeing, even among those who describe themselves as virtue theorists, there is significant divergence over the implications of such an approach. What we can say is that the strongest forms of virtue ethics are generally characterized by an additional claim about the conceptual primacy of the virtues: Not only are virtues conceptually prior to specifications of rules, they are also conceptually prior to specification of ends; not only the "right," but also the "end" of the ethical life (the Good or the Good life), is derivative from or at least partly *constituted by* the virtues.[16]

For its proponents such a view is not radical, but simply reflects a return out of modernism to some of the assumptions that were basic to classical thought. For Aristotle it seems, the life according to virtue is not merely a means, but in a complete life is also partly constitutive of *eudaimonia*, or human flourishing. Staying with virtue ethics for the moment will also help to clarify how these concerns express themselves in contemporary philosophical debate. Those who would implicate the entire modernist tradition in ethics—who would characterize it as "act" rather than "agent" centered, or as concerned with "doing" in contrast to "being"—also tend to reject modernist typologies of normative ethical theories. While certainly conceding that consequentialists and deontologists, etc., may incorporate within themselves a theory of virtue, they themselves would likely identify virtue theory as indicating a horse of a different color—an agent-centered perspective in ethics that takes the concept of a virtue as *prior to* or more basic than other central ethical concepts, of which the "Good" and the "Right" are of course also top candidates. Reflecting this *formal difference* in their way of ordering the relationships of priority between ends, rules, and virtues, those described as "strong" virtue theorists typically understand virtue theory to resist subsumption under labels such as consequentialism or deontology.

Certainly not all self-described virtue ethicists hold this strong thesis. But what this shows is that the term "virtue theory" admits of a range of denotations, and is often used to indicate a weaker or stronger thesis from one author to the next. This is a well-recognized aspect of debates within ethics, but I raise it here because it is also helpful for understanding certain key differences both among virtue epistemologists and between them and their critics. It is worth noting in this regard that contemporary textbooks often classify epistemological theories as deontological or consequentialist (or deontological/non-deontological) on analogy with theories in ethics (Steup 1996).[17] It should not be surprising, then, that in reading the works of virtue epistemologists we also encounter a range of positions reflecting weaker and stronger claims about what constitutes virtue theory, and a debate strongly analogous in certain respects to one ongoing in ethics.

III

This collection contains papers expressing a wide and exemplary range of virtue-theoretical perspectives on epistemological topics. Some are previously published papers, and others appear in print here for the first time. Our readings divide into four parts. The selections of part I begin with contributions by Sosa and Goldman wherein each author gives an account of knowledge and justified belief in terms of their source in intellectual virtues. Each tries to show how he can satisfactorily handle some of the familiar problems that process reliabilism faces within a virtue-centered version of the more general reliabilist approach. In chapter 1 Alvin Goldman provides a sketch for such a new understanding of epistemology, one that significantly modifies his own previous views. Goldman's "Epistemic Folkways and Scientific Epistemology" is set in the context of a broader effort that he, Sosa, and Hilary Kornblith have shared, of developing a naturalized epistemology. The author provides a guideline for the fuller development of his non-eliminative naturalistic account of knowledge and justification, by distinguishing two separate but inter-related missions of epistemology. One is the descriptive task of detailing our commonsense or "folk" epistemic concepts, and the other is the evaluative task of critically evaluating and if necessary revising these concepts. Goldman explains how both missions of epistemology integrally depend on empirical studies of the human reasoner in the social and cognitive sciences, and why this leads him to characterize his naturalized account as "scientific epistemology."[18]

In chapters 2, "Reliabilism and Intellectual Virtue," and 3, "Three Forms of Virtue Epistemology," we have papers by Ernest Sosa that provide a sound introduction to his developed accounts of knowledge and justification. Here we see Sosa grappling with those major problems for reliabilist accounts that we have already outlined in section II of the introduction, above. But together with this we see Sosa develop the view he calls "virtue perspectivism," which leads away from a strict causal account in the direction of what can be called a "mixed" or mixed externalist account of justification. Distinguishing between animal and reflective knowledge, and between aptness and justification, Sosa develops both subjective and objective conditions for the justified true beliefs that constitute human reflective knowledge. In chapter 3, Sosa explains the similarities and differences between the latest virtue-epistemic version of Goldman's causal theory of knowing, the "proper functionalism" of Alvin Plantinga, and his own virtue perspectivism. In the conclusion he makes the conciliatory suggestion that the disagreements between the three "seem relatively small, when compared with the large areas of agreement. . . . It seems appropriate to view the three approaches as varieties of a single more fundamental option in epistemology, one which puts the explicative emphasis on truth-conducive intellectual virtues or faculties, and is properly termed 'virtue epistemology'."[19]

In chapter 4, "Ever Since Descartes," Hilary Kornblith argues for a form of reliabilism with the flexibility to accommodate the important intuitions that have long informed internalist conceptions of justification. Kornblith's work has exuded a strong influence in the development of "mixed" accounts of justification, and this characteristic is in turn a reason why virtue epistemologists think that their approach contributes substantially to resolving the dispute between internalism and externalism in epistemology.[20] The author here develops a framework that makes it both historically and theoretically understandable how the reliability constraint on justification is compatible with an "internal" (or inner coherence) constraint, and with an "action-theoretic" (or responsibility/motivational) constraint. The latter, the important focus of responsibilist virtue epistemology, concerns whether the chosen acts by which an agent's belief-forming cognitive processes are influenced were responsibly motivated by a *desire* for true beliefs. In connecting the action-theoretic constraint with the issue of subjective justification, Kornblith's paper also serves to introduce the reader to a range of issues concerning active epistemic agency that receive further direct attention in parts III and IV of the collection.

Part II contains papers that further develop the naturalistic orientation of reliabilist virtue epistemology; these contributions provide a closer focus on a virtue-based account of knowledge and the resources it provides for responding to the challenge of skepticism. In chapter 5, a specially edited selection from *Putting Skeptics in Their Place* (Cambridge, 2000), John Greco develops "agent reliabilism" as an account of knowledge as arising from the cognitive abilities or powers of epistemic agents. Greco argues that agent reliabilism has unique resources for addressing an important kind of skeptical argument, one that trades on the assumption that for agents to have knowledge they must be able to discriminate the truth of their beliefs from alternative possibilities. In the course of explicating a distinction between relevant and irrelevant alternative possibilities and using it to answer the skeptic's charge, Greco develops a sophisticated possible-worlds analysis for abilities, including cognitive abilities.

In chapters 6 and 7, Jonathan Dancy and Lawrence BonJour discuss Sosa's epistemology as presented in the collected essays of *Knowledge in Perspective* (1991). Both authors are concerned with aspects and implications of Sosa's naturalism, especially with his understanding of supervenience. Dancy attempts to drive a wedge between Sosa's "formal foundationalism" and the doctrine of supervenience which he sees supporting it. He also challenges Sosa's conception of what makes a feature a virtue. Dancy here argues for an alternative non-consequentialist conception of virtue, thereby directing our attention to a major issue of debate among virtue epistemologists which will come under closer scrutiny in part III of the collection. BonJour develops a skeptical dilemma for Sosa with respect to the latter's iterative condition on reflective knowledge, the requirement that an agent have "epistemic perspective" on the reliability of his/her own belief-producing cognitive faculties. In his responses to both authors in chapter 8, Sosa details his understanding of the supervenience of evaluative epistemic properties on non-evaluative properties. He also engages BonJour in debate over the problem of skepticism and Dancy in debate over the background assumptions informing his approach to the definition and identification of the intellectual virtues.

In part III, our focus shifts to a debate between those forms of virtue epistemology with a predominantly reliabilist orientation and those with a predominantly responsibilist orientation. This distinction between these two strains of virtue epistemology should not be used to exaggerate differences, since we have already pointed out many shared tenets and common interests among those who describe themselves as working within virtue epistemology. (Indeed I think that certain of the tensions that exist among virtue epistemologists are unnecessary, arising primarily from divergent interests in the complex topic of epistemic agency.)[21] However that may ultimately be seen, these differences are interesting in their own right and at times quite sharply expressed; in part III of the collection we see them laid out and debated in turn. Here we find a broadening range of interests in the intellectual virtues and an account directed specifically towards active, as contrasted with passive, epistemic agency. Corresponding to these interests, we also find that many new and difficult questions arise. To identify but a few: Do all virtues carry a reliability constraint? Do some or all also carry a motivational constraint, such as that which one finds in an Aristotelian moral virtue? What is the relationship between a "motive" and an "end-in-view"? Do responsibilists conform to the naturalistic orientation that characterizes the reliabilist approach? Is a "unifying" account of ethical and epistemic virtue plausible? What theoretical advantages might such an account hold?

Among our contributors, perhaps few differences will appear more marked to the reader than that between John Greco, who argues that any view making justification or knowledge a function of agent reliability constitutes a version of virtue epistemology, and Linda Zagzebski, whose rejection of that view is apparent in her provocative title "From Reliabilism to Virtue Epistemology." Zagzebski (chapter 9) begins part III with a discussion of process reliabilism and the difficulties it faces in adequately explaining what makes "the good of knowledge" greater than "the good of true belief." This problem is crucial, as the author sees it, and it "pushes us first in the direction of three offspring of process reliabilism—faculty reliabilism, proper functionalism, and agent reliabilism, and finally to a virtue epistemology based on virtue in the ethical sense."

Julia Driver (chapter 10) is known to us primarily for her outstanding past work in ethical theory, and her contribution here illustrates the fruitfulness of cross-fertilization between philosophical subdisciplines. The analysis she offers in "Ethical and Epistemic Virtue" illuminates disanalogies as well as analogies between ethical and epistemic evaluation. Her approach to this topic comes out of a consequentialist background aligned with reliabilist views in epistemology. From this perspective she offers a critique of Zagzebski's "pure virtue theory," which she compares with Michael Slote's agent-based form of virtue ethics.

Driver's critique of Zagzebski underlines another issue that is a matter of pointed debate: the plausibility of a unified account of ethical and epistemic virtue. James Montmarquet's paper in chapter 11, "An 'Internalist' Conception of Epistemic Virtue," provides an account of the relationship between the ethical and epistemic virtues that is critical, on the one hand, of Zagzebski's strong "assimilationist position" and, on the other, of the strong "externalist anti-assimilationist position" (which Driver may be thought to exemplify in arguing for "the disunity of virtue").[22] The alternative model Montmarquet develops for the relationship between the virtues is quite unique in that it does not arrange them by content or domain, but rather by the susceptibility of each disposition to direct control. This innovative approach issues in a model reflecting "a three-fold distinction cutting across the moral/epistemic divide."

In chapter 12, "Regulating Inquiry," Christopher Hookway begins with the topic of *reasons for belief.*[23] The intellectual virtues, on Hookway's view, play at least two important roles in respect to believing for reasons, for as he argues, "virtues. . . enable us to respond to reasons: they provide a sensitivity to rational requirements in particular cases, and they are motivating." To understand the first, normative aspect of reasons, Hookway leads us into issues of rationality, while to explore the second, motivational aspect, he asks us to consider cases of the intellectually *akratic* individual. If I accept that I have a sound reason to doubt or believe some proposition, must I be *motivated* to doubt or believe it?

To resolve the problematic nature of views that would affirm this claim unqualifiedly, Hookway presents a pragmatist-inspired account on which motivation may be present, in certain instances (and to the advantage of the agent), not by conscious reflection but by force of unconscious habit.

The discussions of the relationship between ethical and epistemic virtues in part III invite us to explore further, in part IV, certain topics that have been of special interest for virtue ethicists and epistemologists alike. Chapter 13 is "Critical Thinking, Moral Integrity, and Citizenship: Teaching for the Intellectual Virtues," by Richard Paul, a developer of and foremost advocate for a critical thinking curriculum at all levels of public education. Paul critiques pedagogical approaches that presume a sharp separation of the affective and moral from the cognitive dimensions of learning. In response to a model of "compartmentalized domains," Paul explores what he sees as the intimate connections between critical thinking, moral integrity, and responsible citizenship: "The problems of education for fairminded independence of thought, for genuine moral integrity, and for responsible citizenship are not three separate issues but one complex task." The intellectual virtues themselves are interdependent, and one does not develop students' thinking skills "without in some sense simultaneously developing their autonomy, their rationality, and their character."[24] Critical thinking in its richest and most valuable sense is not simply a matter of cognitive skills, any more than moral integrity and responsibility are merely matters of good intention. On Paul's view, "Skills, values, insights, and intellectual traits are mutually and dynamically interrelated. It is the whole person who thinks, not some fragment of the person."

In my own contribution to the collection in chapter 14, "Virtue Theory and the Fact/Value Problem," I attempt both to analyze and to mediate the dispute between "virtue reliabilist" and "virtue responsibilist" epistemologies. The analysis casts the debate over the definition and identification of the virtues in terms of background understandings of the Greek tradition of virtue theory. The debate can be usefully understood in terms of competing interpretations of Aristotle's own approach, or more generally if one prefers, in terms of contrasts between Platonic and Aristotelian conceptions of virtue. The mediating suggestions I make concerning a plausible form of a unified account of ethical and intellectual virtue reflect the unique resources I find in virtue theory and in American pragmatism.

In chapter 15, "Epistemic Vice," Casey Swank turns our attention from an account of epistemic virtue to that of epistemic vice, and challenges what he takes to be the received view of the latter. In sorting out the differences between understanding an epistemic vice as something "bad and epistemic" versus something "epistemically bad," Swank focuses criticism on truth-centered accounts of epistemic virtue and vice, and indicates the direction an alternative, non-truth-linked account would need to take.

In our final selection, Linda Zagzebski's "*Phronesis* and Religious Belief," the author breaks significant new ground by outlining a theory of rationality with integral ties to virtue theory. She discusses why she thinks it is crucial, in debating the rationality of religious belief, to distinguish a weaker principle of rational permissibility for beliefs from a stronger principle of rational praiseworthiness. For the author, the *phronimos* or person of practical intelligence "is the paradigm in relation to which a host of concepts of epistemic evaluation can be defined." Her weaker and stronger principles are therefore articulated in terms of the differences between what the *phronimos* "might" believe, and what she/he "would" and "would *not*" believe, under suitable background and evidential circumstances. In her conclusion, she applies her principles to the appraisal of claims made by Alvin Plantinga on the part of Calvinistic "reformed epistemology." The upshot here is a quite original argument casting doubt on the rational defensibility of Plantinga's model of "properly basic" Christian belief.

IV

As a final word, let me draw attention to the title of our collection. I choose "character" over "virtue" in the title both because I hope that this collection contributes to philosophical discussion of intellectual character and because the term "character" appears to have rather less connection in common language with specifically moral connotations than does "virtue." Yet intellectual character—an idea associated with contemporary virtue epistemology—may appear peculiar in the backdrop of classical philosophy, so that it is important to acknowledge these differences of terminology when they are present. On the surface, the extended sense that the term "character" must take on in order to include intellectual in addition to ethical virtue would seem to commit the speaker to a category error. It appears as a usage out of skew with standard Aristotelian terminology, where "virtue of character" translates *ethike arete* (from *ethos,* character), and are thereby distinguished from *dianoetike arete,* "virtue of thought." Related to this, there are obvious differences between genetically-endowed faculties and those cognitive habits and dispositions that are acquired *either* by habit or teaching. As you will discover in the chapters contained here, there can indeed be serious disagreement among virtue epistemologists concerning the relative degree of control we have over our intellectual and our ethical dispositions. Yet it is one of the primary purposes of this collection to bring those questions about control over, and responsibility for, intellectual dispositions to the forefront for further inquiry.

Some philosophers may prefer to speak simply of intellect or intellectual virtue. But I find little to object to in Lorraine Code's statement that "virtue, either intellectual or moral, is an attribute of character." Like the responsibilist Code, reliabilists also speak of the intellectual virtues as they identify them as part of a person's intellectual character, so that the *presence* of the term in the title seems not itself in contention among virtue epistemologists. We must be careful here, however, because it is nonetheless true that reliabilists and responsibilists are likely to apply different *connotations* to the idea of intellectual character. For reliabilists not all intellectual virtues are acquired traits, and hence not all are traits for which the agent is responsible, as the term "character" suggests when taken in its traditional association *ꙗthos,* related etymologically to *ethos* (habit). For reasons we have already briefly explored, the reliabilist strain of virtue epistemology will resist what they take to be overly restrictive definitions by insisting that the initial, shared sense of intellectual virtue or character be a broad one. From his first proposal for an intellectual virtue-centered epistemology, Sosa has indicated that "the most useful and illuminating notion of intellectual virtue will prove broader than our tradition would suggest and must give due weight not only to the subject and his intrinsic nature but also to his environment and to his epistemic community."[25]

Sosa's proposal for a broad definition of intellectual virtue is obviously motivated by the concerns of philosophic naturalism.[26] But if one cares to consider historical antecedents, one may find the closest match in classical thought in Plato's conception of virtue, with its sense that a thing has virtue (even for instance an eye or other perceptual faculty) that performs its function well.[27] The sense that Sosa suggests seems harder to square with Aristotle's ideas about virtue,[28] but I would point out that "character" is used to translate another term besides *ꙗthos* in Aristotle's vocabulary: *poios.* Terence Irwin writes that since the *phronimos* or person of practical intelligence is to be trained to act according to correct reason, "training in reasoning and deliberation is required too. It is someone's character that makes him the 'sort of' (*poios*) person he is. Hence 'character' often translates *poios.*"[29] This acknowledges a sense in common language of "the sort of person he/she is" or, better, of persons being "of the sort" to do x. This sense of character need not be restricted to ethical traits, and furthermore appears consistent with Aristotle's acknowledgment that ethical and intellectual virtues are both *hexeis,* states that include a tendency to bring about an end under certain circumstances. It leaves it to context, however, to determine whether a particular virtue also involves a decision (*prohairesis*) that is the result of a rational *desire* for some good as an end in itself, and whether there is a level of responsibility for the trait that makes its possessor a potential subject for judgments of praise or blame. Readers of reliabilist persuasion then may choose to take the term "character" in the title to indicate an extended sense closest to how Irwin sometimes translates the Greek *poios.*

For readers more inclined towards responsibilism, however, the term "character" in the title of our collection will take on connotations that go beyond this broad initial sense. It will seem to invite a closer tie to *ꙗthos* in Aristotle's vocabulary, and perhaps even *substantive connections* rather than merely *formal analogies* between ethical and epistemic evaluation. The person of intellectual virtue, as responsibilists understand that person, isn't only one who "gets things right," but one who does so through the development of his or her capacities of judgment. Still, the responsibilist identification of virtues like intellectual humility, courage, trustworthiness, fairmindedness, etc.—and their under-standing of these as *springing* from habit yet *pertaining* to intellect—likely would have confounded Aristotle! The latter appears to have thought of intellectual dispositions as non-ethical dispositions to hit the truth (see also my paper in chapter 14 for a fuller development of these connections with classical virtue theory). But it remains an available option for contemporary virtue theorists to choose to diverge from classical theory in this way, as long as the differences that mark approaches as "neo-Aristotelian" or as "non-Aristotelian" are clearly articulated. For instance, consider the distinction Aristotle draws in the *Nicomachean Ethics* between "habituation" and "teaching" as the respective modes of acquisition for the ethical and intellectual virtues. Perhaps that distinction, as Zagzebski has explicitly urged, is an overgeneralization that contemporary virtue theory can do without, much as it does without certain other features of Aristotle's thought, like his conception of human teleology or his keying of the intellectual virtues to specific "spheres" (*NE* 1139b15).

Those of responsibilist orientation perceive synergistic connections between the human reasoner and the human valuer. Therefore they emphasize not just the *distinction* between intellectual and ethical virtues, but also the intimate *relationships* among the kinds of traits that make for excellence in an integrated, properly attuned individual. They may also perceive the kind of parity that they find desirable in an approach to ethical and epistemic evaluation already present in classical virtue theory, at least potentially. We should distinguish inspiration and substantial support, however, and be clear that it is their own undertaking, and not that of the ancients, should they choose to develop virtue theory in the direction of a unified theory of value across epistemology and ethics. I hope that this adequately explains for the reader of our collection why—the noted problems not withstanding—I place the term "character" in the title, evoking as it must both the commonalities and differences among philosophers working today in the area of virtue epistemology.

Notes

1. Most epistemologists take the epistemic goal as monistic or singular: generally speaking, the goal is truth. Some, though, take the lead of William James in seeing maximizing true beliefs and minimize false ones as separable goals occasionally in conflict; when tension does occur, efforts to realize them may require prioritizing different intellectual virtues, such as intellectual courage or caution.

2. For an extensive bibliography of contemporary virtue epistemology, see my "Recent Work on Virtue Epistemology," *American Philosophical Quarterly* 34, 1, 1997: 410-430.

3. "The Raft and the Pyramid," reprinted in *Knowledge in Perspective: Selected Essays in Epistemology*. Cambridge: Cambridge University Press, 1991, 189.

4. John Greco, "Virtue Epistemology," from the Stanford Encyclopedia of Philosophy; online at http://plato.stanford.edu. Certainly there are varying degrees of

strength in the relationship seen to exist between justification and virtue. Jennifer Battaly, for instance, distinguishes between stronger "conceptual," middling "ontological," and weakest "indicator" views about the dependence of justification and knowledge on intellectual virtue. "What is Virtue Epistemology?," paper presented at the 20th World Congress of Philosophy, Boston, 1998.

5. John Greco, "Agent Reliabilism," in James Tomberlin, ed., *Philosophical Perspectives* 13. Atascadero, Calif.: Ridgeview Pub. Co., forthcoming.

6. Hookway, "Cognitive Virtues and Epistemic Evaluations," *International Journal of Philosophical Studies* 2, 2 1994: 211-227; quotes on 211 & 225.

7. Classifying theories (whether in ethics or epistemology) by the formal relationships of priority they exhibit between virtues, ends, and rules is discussed in depth throughout Linda Zagzebski's *Virtues of the Mind*. She also describes a range of associations of the term "virtue theory" by distinguishing strong and weak theses. She places herself at the strong end, noting substantial parallels between her own approach to virtue epistemology and that of Michael Slote's "radically" agent-based virtue ethics.

8. E. L. Gettier, "Is Justified True Belief Knowledge," *Analysis* 23, 1963: 121-123.

9. Internal conditions are those that an agent has introspective awareness of or access to, and neither the specific, causally-responsible BCP nor its objective reliability are things that the agent always or necessarily *has* such introspective access to. They are matters of objective fact that may stand outside the *evidential* relationships of which the agent is aware when she reflects on her own reasons for holding a belief. The reliabilist says that "epistemizing" justification—the kind that makes true beliefs deserve to be called "knowledge," the term of highest praise—must therefore be a function of more than just such relationships among the agent's beliefs. Given the possibility of bad as well as good epistemic luck, and the kinds of creatures we are, the truth-conduciveness of a human cognitive process can only be determined probabilistically, by its delivering a high ratio of true belief, that is, a preponderance of true over false beliefs. But since internalists understand the conditions on justification as exclusively internal conditions, and externalists are those that reject this exclusivity thesis, such a truth-linked theory will be classed as externalist.

10. Especially early in the development of reliabilism, the claim was often made that the reliability of a BCP is also *sufficient* for justification. This claim has been widely qualified in recent years, and I emphasize below that most virtue epistemologies present "mixed" or "mixed externalist" accounts of justification, which also preserve an important role for subjective justification as part of the sufficient conditions for at least "higher" or human reflective knowledge.

11. Sosa 1993, 65 fn 25. "Generic" is an umbrella term covering reliable process, mechanism, and indicator accounts. See Sosa 1991, 131. Some of the indicated objections are introduced below.

12. Lorraine Code, *Epistemic Responsibility*. Hanover: University Press of New England, 1987.

13. John Greco, "Two Kinds of Intellectual Virtue," in *Philosophy and Phenomenological Research*, forthcoming 2000.

14. Aristotle understood the intellectual virtue of *phronesis* or intelligence (more precisely practical intelligence or practical wisdom) as "yoked together" with ethical virtue: "Besides, intelligence is yoked together with virtue of character, and so is this virtue with intelligence. For the origins of intelligence express the virtues of character; and correctness in virtues of character express intelligence" (*NE*1178a17). Zagzebski

proposes a conception of *phronesis* with this same kind of intimacy, but broad enough to function as a balancer, mediator, and coordinator of the intellectual virtues as well as the moral.

15. Linda Zagzebski, "*Precis* of *Virtues of the Mind*," in a symposium on her book in *Philosophy and Phenomenological Research*, forthcoming 2000.

16. My terminology here differs from the more complex categorization of virtue theories that Linda Zagzebski has given in *Virtues of the Mind* (Cambridge: Cambridge University Press, 1996). There she uses the strong/weak distinction to represent the difference between theories that *define* rightness by what the person of virtue would or might do and those that merely take this as the best *criterion* or way to identify the rightness of an action.

17. Matthias Steup, *An Introduction to Contemporary Epistemology*. Upper Saddle River, N.J.: Prentice Hall, 1996. Steup's distinction is between epistemic deontologism and non-deontologism. It is of course common to order one's classification model by a simple exhaustive dichotomy like this. Even if a scheme of classification is intended to be exhaustive, the choice and understanding of the main term may be called into question if it is found that some theories cut across it in ways that make their classification under it problematic. Steup's distinction would tend to overlook all the assumptions that reliabilist and responsibilist virtue epistemologists share in common, and divide the field of virtue epistemology, placing virtue reliabilists with epistemological non-deontologism and virtue responsibilists with epistemological deontologism.

18. While the excerpted paper provides a suitable outline of this project for a naturalized epistemology, to find this project worked out in depth and detail the reader may want to examine the papers collected in *Liaisons: Philosophy Meets the Cognitive and Social Sciences*. Cambridge, Mass.: MIT Press, 1992.

19. Goldman's substantial agreement with Sosa's irenic conclusion should be obvious from his own selection (chapter 1). Plantinga, however, responds to Sosa's "irenic conclusion" by inverting the suggested relationship between proper functionalism and virtue epistemology. This explicit denial that proper functionalism is a form of virtue epistemology seems sufficiently clear for me to demand a separate classification of proper functional accounts; but John Greco suggests otherwise, saying that even this insistence on proper function rather than intellectual virtue as his foundational concept "reflect(s) disagreements over what is truly of value in virtue theory" (online Stanford Encyclopedia of Philosophy). This claim seems to flow from Greco's own identification of virtue epistemology with all forms of "agent reliabilism," among which proper functionalism would be counted..

20. Virtue epistemologists share a broad range of assumptions that bring them together with interest in both descriptive and evaluative issues regarding epistemic agency. One of the assumptions virtue epistemologists share that I regard as definitive of their unique philosophical approach is the need for a "dual component" conception of justification, sometimes also called a "mixed externalist" account of justification. This is one that integrates constraints on an agent's faculty reliability with constraints on the agent's responsibility in gathering and processing evidence. So to cite but three instances, Ernest Sosa writes that in his virtue perspectivism, a proposition is evident or reflectively known (from the K point of view) to a subject "only if *both* he is rationally justified in believing it *and* is in a position to know (from the K point of view) whether it is true." From "How Do You Know?," in *Knowledge in Perspective*, 28. And Linda Zagzebski, author of *Virtues of the Mind* (1996), defines knowledge and justification through a

"dual-component" account of intellectual virtue, which builds into the conception of the virtues themselves both "a characteristic motivation to produce a certain desired end and reliable success in bringing about that end" (134). Greco also describes his as a "mixed theory": "The main idea is that an adequate account of knowledge ought to contain both a responsibility condition and a reliability condition. Moreover, a virtue account can explain how the two are tied together. In cases of knowledge, objective reliability is grounded in epistemically responsible action." Stanford Online Encyclopedia. See my chapter 14 for more on "mixed accounts" on justification.

21. Hookway underlines this point in saying that "Focusing on the context of inquiry, a kind of activity, encourages the expectation that there might be structural parallels between problems of practical reason and problems of theoretical reason." Indeed, the responsibilists generally take these parallels or analogies to be much stronger than do reliabilists.

22. For an earlier but fuller account by Montmarquet, see his *Epistemic Virtue and Doxastic Responsibility*. Lanham, Md.: Rowman & Littlefield, 1993.

23. See also Christopher Hookway, "Cognitive Virtues and Epistemic Evaluation," *International Journal of Philosophical Studies* 2, 2, 1994: 211-227. For another lucid contemporary pragmatist account of rational acceptance, see D. S. Clarke, Jr., *Rational Acceptance and Purpose*. Lanham, Md.: Rowman & Littlefield, 1989.

24. Richard Paul, "The Contribution of Philosophy to Thinking," from *Critical Thinking*. Sonoma, Calif.: Foundation for Critical Thinking, 1993, 424 & 425.

25. "Raft and the Pyramid," reprinted in Sosa (1991), 190.

26. I do not mean to imply that virtue reliabilists do not see epistemology as a normative discipline. On the contrary, Greco writes that "virtue epistemology begins with the assumption that epistemology is a normative discipline. The main idea of virtue epistemology is to understand the kind of normativity involved on the model of virtue theories in ethics." Stanford Online Encyclopedia. What I mean is that, while justification is a normative concept, the reliabilist approach to defining virtue broadly and consequentially is intended to make it part of the non-evaluative basis from which evaluative concepts like justification derive. On my view it is when virtues are taken to represent shared communal values or norms that the shift is made to their prescriptive sense.

27. We still employ "virtue" to indicate nonmoral goods in many contexts, and though not as common, the Oxford Educated Dictionary employs a broad definition of a virtue as "excellence in respect of nature or of operation; worth or efficacy of any kind."

28. Zagzebski for instance argues that "It is quite obvious that sight, hearing, and memory are faculties, and . . . the Greeks identified virtues, not with faculties themselves, but with the excellences of faculties" (Zagzebski 1996, 10).

29. Terrence Irwin, comments on his translation of Aristotle's *Nicomachean Ethics*. Indianapolis: Hackett Publishing Co., 1985, 389-390.

Part I

Reliability and Intellectual Virtue

1

Epistemic Folkways
and Scientific Epistemology

Alvin Goldman

I

What is the mission of epistemology, and what is its proper methodology? Such meta-epistemological questions have been prominent in recent years, especially with the emergence of various brands of "naturalistic" epistemology. In this paper, I shall reformulate and expand upon my own meta-epistemological conception (most fully articulated in Goldman, 1986), retaining many of its former ingredients while reconfiguring others. The discussion is by no means confined, though, to the meta-epistemological level. New substantive proposals will also be advanced and defended.

Let us begin, however, at the meta-epistemological level, by asking what role should be played in epistemology by our ordinary epistemic concepts and principles. By some philosophers' lights, the sole mission of epistemology is to elucidate commonsense epistemic concepts and principles: concepts like knowledge, justification, and rationality, and principles associated with these concepts. By other philosophers' lights, this is not even part of epistemology's aim. Ordinary concepts and principles, the latter would argue, are fundamentally naive, unsystematic, and uninformed by important bodies of logic and/or mathematics. Ordinary principles and practices, for example, ignore or violate the probability calculus, which ought to be the cornerstone of epistemic rationality. Thus, on the second view, proper epistemology must neither *end* with naive principles of justification or rationality, nor even *begin* there.

My own stance on this issue lies somewhere between these extremes. To facilitate discussion, let us give a label to our commonsense epistemic concepts and norms; let us call them our *epistemic folkways*. In partial agreement with the first view sketched above, I would hold that *one* proper task of epistemology is to elucidate our epistemic folkways. Whatever else epistemology might proceed to do, it should at least have its roots in the concepts and practices of the folk. If these roots are utterly rejected and abandoned, by what rights would the new discipline call itself 'epistemology' at all? It may well be desirable to reform or transcend our epistemic folkways, as the second of the views sketched above recommends. But it is essential to preserve continuity; and continuity can only be recognized if we have a satisfactory characterization of our epistemic folkways. Actually, even if one rejects the plea for continuity, a description of our epistemic folkways is in order. How would one know what to criticize, or what needs to be transcended, in the absence of such a description? So a first mission of epistemology is to describe or characterize our folkways.

Now a suitable description of these folk concepts, I believe, is likely to depend on insights from cognitive science. Indeed, identification of the semantic contours of many (if not all) concepts can profit from theoretical and empirical work in psychology and linguistics. For this reason, the task of describing or elucidating folk epistemology is a *scientific* task, at least a task that should be informed by relevant scientific research.

The second mission of epistemology, as suggested by the second view above, is the formulation of a more adequate, sound, or systematic set of epistemic norms, in some way(s) transcending our naive epistemic repertoire. How and why these folkways might be transcended, or improved upon, remains to be specified. This will partly depend on the contours of the commonsense standards that emerge from the first mission. On my view, epistemic concepts like knowledge and justification crucially invoke psychological faculties or processes. Our folk understanding, however, has a limited and tenuous grasp of the processes available to the cognitive agent. Thus, one important respect in which epistemic folkways should be transcended is by incorporating a more detailed and empirically based depiction of psychological mechanisms. Here too epistemology would seek assistance from cognitive science.

Since both missions of epistemology just delineated lean in important respects on the deliverances of science, specifically cognitive science, let us call our conception of epistemology *scientific epistemology*. Scientific epistemology, we have seen, has two branches: *descriptive* and *normative*. While descriptive scientific epistemology aims to describe our ordinary epistemic assessments, normative scientific epistemology continues the practice of making epistemic judgments, or formulating systematic principles for such judgments.[1] It is prepared to depart from our ordinary epistemic judgments, however, if and when that proves advisable. In the remainder of this paper, I shall sketch and defend the particular forms of descriptive and normative scientific epistemology that I favor.

II

Mainstream epistemology has concentrated much of its attention on two concepts (or terms): knowledge and justified belief. This essay focuses on the latter. We need not mark this concept exclusively by the phrase 'justified belief'. A family of phrases pick out roughly the same concept: 'well-founded belief,' 'reasonable belief,' 'belief based on good grounds,' and so forth. I shall propose an account of this concept that is in the reliabilist tradition, but departs at a crucial juncture from other versions of reliabilism. My account has the same core idea as Ernest Sosa's *intellectual virtues* approach, but incorporates some distinctive features that improve its prospects.[2]

The basic approach is, roughly, to identify the concept of justified belief with the concept of belief obtained through the exercise of intellectual virtues (excellences). Beliefs acquired (or retained) through a chain of "virtuous" psychological processes qualify as justified; those acquired partly by cognitive "vices" are derogated as unjustified. This, as I say, is a *rough* account. To explain it more fully, I need to say things about the psychology of the epistemic evaluator, the possessor and deployer of the concept in question. At this stage in the development of semantical theory (which, in the future, may well be viewed as part of the "dark ages" of the subject), it is difficult to say just what the relationship is between the meaning or "content" of concepts and the form or structure of their mental representation. In the present case, however, I believe that an account of the form of representation can contribute to our understanding of the content, although I am unable to formulate these matters in a theoretically satisfying fashion.

The hypothesis I wish to advance is that the epistemic evaluator has a mentally stored set, or list, of cognitive virtues and vices. When asked to evaluate an actual or hypothetical case of belief, the evaluator considers the processes by which the belief was produced, and matches these against his list of virtues and vices. If the processes match virtues only, the belief is classified as justified. If the processes are matched partly with vices, the belief is categorized as unjustified. If a belief-forming scenario is described that features a process not on the evaluator's list of either virtues or vices, the belief may be categorized as neither justified nor unjustified, but simply *non*-justified. Alternatively (and this alternative plays an important role in my story), the evaluator's judgment may depend on the (judged) *similarity* of the novel process to the stored virtues and vices. In other words, the "matches" in question need not be perfect.

This proposal makes two important points of contact with going theories in the psychology of concepts. First, it has some affinity to the *exemplar* approach to concept representation (cf. Medin and Schaffer, 1978; Smith and Medin, 1981; Hintzman, 1986). According to that approach, a concept is mentally represented by means of representations of its positive instances, or perhaps types of instances. For example, the representation of the concept *pants* might include a representation of a particular pair of faded blue jeans and/or a representation of the type *blue jeans*. Our approach to the concept of justification shares the spirit of this approach insofar as it posits a set of examples of virtues and vices, as opposed to a mere abstract characterization— e.g., a definition—of (intellectual) virtue or vice. A second affinity to the exemplar approach is in the appeal to a similarity, or matching, operation in the classification of new target cases. According to the exemplar approach, targets are categorized as a function of their similarity to the positive exemplars (and dissimilarity to the foils). Of course, similarity is invoked in many other approaches to concept deployment as well (see E. Smith, 1990). This makes our account of justification consonant with the psychological literature generally, whether or not it meshes specifically with the exemplar approach.

Let us now see what this hypothesis predicts for a variety of cases. To apply it, we need to make some assumptions about the lists of virtues and vices that typical evaluators mentally store. I shall assume that the virtues include belief formation based on sight, hearing, memory, reasoning in certain "approved" ways, and so forth. The vices include intellectual processes like forming beliefs by guesswork, wishful thinking, and ignoring contrary evidence. *Why* these items are placed in their respective categories remains to be explained. As indicated, I plan to explain them by reference to reliability. Since the account will therefore be, at bottom, a reliabilist type of account, it is instructive to see how it fares when applied to well-known problem cases for standard versions of reliabilism.

Consider first the demon-world case. In a certain possible world, a Cartesian demon gives people deceptive visual experiences, which systematically lead to false beliefs. Are these vision-based beliefs justified? Intuitively, they are. The demon's victims are presented with the same sorts of visual experiences that we are, and they use the same processes to produce corresponding beliefs. For most epistemic evaluators, this seems sufficient to induce the judgment that the victims' beliefs are justified. Does our account predict this result? Certainly it does. The account predicts that an epistemic evaluator will match the victims' vision-based processes to one (or more) of the items on his list of intellectual virtues, and therefore judge the victims' beliefs to be justified.

Turn next to BonJour's (1985) cases in which hypothetical agents are assumed to possess a perfectly reliable clairvoyant faculty. Although these agents form their beliefs by this reliable faculty, BonJour contends that the beliefs are not justified; and apparently most (philosophical) evaluators agree with that judgment. This result is not predicted by simple forms of reliabilism.[3] What does our present theory predict? Let us consider the four cases in two groups. In the first three cases (Samantha, Casper, and Maud), the agent has contrary evidence that he or she ignores. Samantha has a massive amount of apparently cogent evidence that the President is in Washington, but she nonetheless believes (through clairvoyance) that the President is in New York City. Casper and Maud each have large amounts of ostensibly cogent evidence that he/she has no reliable clairvoyant power, but they rely on such a power nonetheless. Here our theory predicts that the evaluator will match these agent's belief-forming processes to the vice of ignoring contrary evidence. Since the processes include a vice, the beliefs will be judged to be unjustified.

BonJour's fourth case involves Norman, who has a reliable clairvoyant power but no reasons for or against the thesis that he possesses it. When he believes, through clairvoyance, that the President is in New York City, while possessing no (other) relevant evidence, how should this belief be judged? My own assessment is less clear in this case than the other three cases. I am tempted to say that Norman's belief is *non*-justified, not that it is thoroughly *un*justified. (I construe unjustified as "having negative justificational status," and non-justified as "lacking positive justificational status.") This result is also readily predicted by our theory. On the assumption that I (and other evaluators) do not have clairvoyance on my list of virtues, the theory allows the prediction that the belief would be judged neither justified nor unjustified, merely non-justified. For those evaluators who would judge Norman's belief to be *un*justified, there is another possible explanation in terms of the theory. There is a class of putative faculties, including mental telepathy, ESP, telekinesis, and so forth, that are scientifically disreputable. It is plausible that evaluators view any process of basing beliefs on the supposed deliverances of such faculties as vices. It is also plausible that these evaluators judge the process of basing one's belief on clairvoyance to be *similar* to such vices. Thus, the theory would predict that they would view a belief acquired in this way as unjustified.[4]

Finally, consider Plantinga's (1988) examples that feature disease-triggered or mind-malfunctioning processes. These include processes engendered by a brain tumor, radiation-caused processes, and the like. In each case Plantinga imagines that the process is reliable, but reports that we would not judge it to be justification conferring. My diagnosis follows the track outlined in the Norman case. At a minimum, the processes imagined by Plantinga fail to match any virtue on a typical evaluator's list. So the beliefs are at least non-justified. Furthermore, evaluators may have a prior representation of pathological processes as examples of cognitive vices. Plantinga's cases might be judged (relevantly) similar to these vices, so that the beliefs they produce would be declared unjustified.

In some of Plantinga's cases, it is further supposed that the hypothetical agent possesses countervailing evidence against his belief, which he steadfastly ignores. As noted earlier, this added element would strengthen a judgment of unjustifiedness according to our theory, because ignoring contrary evidence is an intellectual vice. Once again, then, our theory's predictions conform with reported judgments.

Let us now turn to the question of how epistemic evaluators acquire their lists of virtues and vices. What is the basis for their classification? As already indicated, my answer invokes the notion of reliability. Belief-forming processes based on vision, hearing, memory, and ("good") reasoning are deemed virtuous because they (are deemed to) produce a high ratio of true beliefs. Processes like guessing, wishful thinking, and ignoring contrary evidence are deemed vicious because they (are deemed to) produce a low ratio of true beliefs.

We need not assume that each epistemic evaluator chooses his or her catalogue of virtues and vices by direct application of the reliability test. Epistemic evaluators may partly inherit their lists of virtues and vices from other speakers in the linguistic community. Nonetheless, the hypothesis is that the selection of virtues and vices rests, ultimately, on assessments of reliability.

It is not assumed, of course, that all speakers have the same lists of intellectual virtues and vices. They may have different opinions about the reliability of processes, and therefore differ in their respective lists.[5] Or they may belong to different sub-cultures in the linguistic community, which may differentially influence their lists. Philosophers sometimes seem to assume great uniformity in epistemic judgments. This assumption may stem from the fact that it is mostly the judgments of philosophers themselves that have been reported, and they are members of a fairly homogeneous sub-culture. A wider pool of "subjects" might reveal a much lower degree of uniformity. That would conform to the present theory, however, which permits individual differences in catalogues of virtues and vices, and hence in judgments of justifiedness.

If virtues and vices are selected on the basis of reliability and unreliability, respectively, why doesn't a hypothetical case introducing a novel reliable process induce an evaluator to add that process to his list of virtues, and declare the resulting belief justified? Why, for example, doesn't he add clairvoyance to his list of virtues, and rule Norman's beliefs to be justified?

I venture the following explanation. First, people seem to have a trait of *categorial conservatism*. They display a preference for "entrenched" categories, in Goodman's (1955) phraseology, and do not lightly supplement or revise their categorial schemes. An isolated single case is not enough. More specifically, merely imaginary cases do not exert much influence on categorial structures. People's cognitive systems are responsive to live cases, not purely fictional ones. Philosophers encounter this when their students or non-philosophers are unimpressed with science fiction-style counterexamples. Philosophers become impatient with this response because they presume that possible cases are on a par (for counterexample purposes) with actual ones. This phenomenon testifies, however, to a psychological propensity to take an invidious attitude toward purely imaginary cases.

To the philosopher, it seems both natural and inevitable to take hypothetical cases seriously, and if necessary to restrict one's conclusions about them to specified "possible worlds." Thus, the philosopher might be inclined to hold: "If reliability is the standard of intellectual virtue, shouldn't we say that clairvoyance is a virtue *in the possible worlds* of BonJour's examples, if not a virtue in general?" This is a natural thing for philosophers to say, given their schooling, but there is no evidence that this is how people naturally think about the matter. There is no evidence that "the folk" are inclined to relativize virtues and vices to this or that possible world.

I suspect that concerted investigation (not undertaken here) would uncover ample evidence of conservatism, specifically in the normative realm. In many traditional cultures, for example, loyalty to family and friends is treated as a cardinal virtue.[6] This view of loyalty tends to persist even through changes in social and organizational climate, which undermine the value of unqualified loyalty. Members of such cultures, I suspect, would continue to view personal loyalty as a virtue even in *hypothetical* cases where the trait has stipulated unfortunate consequences.

In a slightly different vein, it is common for both critics and advocates of reliabilism to call attention to the relativity of reliability to the domain or circumstances in which the process is used. The question is therefore raised: What is the relevant domain for judging the reliability of a process? A critic like Pollock (1986, pp. 118-119), for example, observes that color vision is reliable on earth but unreliable in the universe at large. In determining the reliability of color vision, he asks, which domain should be invoked? Finding no satisfactory reply to this question, Pollock takes this as a serious difficulty for reliabilism. Similarly, Sosa (1988 and forthcoming) notes that an intellectual structure or disposition can be reliable with respect to one field of propositions but unreliable with respect to another; and reliable in one environment but unreliable in another. He does not view this as a difficulty for reliabilism, but concludes that any talk of intellectual virtue must be relativized to field and environment.

Neither of these conclusions seems apt, however, for purposes of *description* of our epistemic folkways. It would be a mistake to suppose that ordinary epistemic evaluators are sensitive to these issues. It is likely—or at least plausible—that our ordinary apprehension of the intellectual virtues is rough, unsystematic, and insensitive to any theoretical desirability of relativization to domain or environment. Thus, as long as we are engaged in the description of our epistemic folkways, it is no criticism of the account that it fails to explain what domain or environment is to be used. Nor is it appropriate for the account to introduce relativization where there is no evidence of relativization on the part of the folk.

Of course, we do need an explanatory story of how the folk arrive at their selected virtues and vices. And this presumably requires some reference to the domain in which reliability is judged. However, there may not be much more to the story than the fact that people determine reliability scores from the cases they personally "observe." Alternatively, they *may* regard the observed cases as a sample from which they infer a truth ratio in some wider class of cases. It is doubtful, however, that they have any precise conception of the wider class. They probably don't address this theoretical issue, and don't do (or think) anything that commits them to any particular resolution of it. It would therefore be wrong to expect descriptive epistemology to be fully specific on this dimension.

A similar point holds for the question of process individuation. It is quite possible that the folk do not have highly principled methods for individuating cognitive processes, for "slicing up" virtues and vices. If that is right, it is a mistake to insist that descriptive epistemology uncover such methods. It is no flaw in reliabilism, considered as descriptive epistemology, that it fails to unearth them. It may well be desirable to develop sharper individuation principles for purposes of normative epistemology (a matter we shall address in section III). But the missions and requirements of descriptive and normative epistemology must be kept distinct.

This discussion has assumed throughout that the folk have lists of intellectual virtues and vices. What is the evidence for this? In the moral sphere ordinary language is rich in virtues terminology. By contrast, there are few

common labels for intellectual virtues, and those that do exist—
'perceptiveness,' 'thoroughness,' 'insightfulness,' and so forth—are of limited
value in the present context. I propose to identify the relevant intellectual virtues
(at least those relevant to *justification*) with the belief-forming capacities,
faculties, or processes that would be accepted as answers to the question "How
does X know?" In answer to this form of question, it is common to reply: "He
saw it," "He heard it," "He remembers it," "He infers it from such-and-such
evidence," and so forth. Thus, basing belief on seeing, hearing, memory, and
(good) inference are in the collection of what the folk regard as intellectual
virtues. Consider, for contrast, how anomalous it is to answer the question "How
does X know?" with "By guesswork," "By wishful thinking," or "By ignoring
contrary evidence." This indicates that *these* modes of belief formation—
guessing, wishful thinking, ignoring contrary evidence—are standardly regarded
as intellectual *vices*. They are not ways of obtaining knowledge, nor ways of
obtaining justified belief.

Why appeal to "knowledge"-talk rather than "justification"-talk to identify
the virtues? Because 'know' has a greater frequency of occurrence than
'justified,' yet the two are closely related. Roughly, justified belief is belief
acquired by means of the same sorts of capacities, faculties, or processes that
yield knowledge in favorable circumstances (i.e., when the resulting belief is
true and there are no Gettier complications, or no relevant alternatives).

To sum up the present theory, let me emphasize that it depicts justificational
evaluation as involving two stages. The first stage features the acquisition by an
evaluator of some set of intellectual virtues and vices. This is where reliability
enters the picture. In the second stage, the evaluator applies his list of virtues
and vices to decide the epistemic status of targeted beliefs. At this stage, there is
no direct consideration of reliability.

There is an obvious analogy here to rule utilitarianism in the moral sphere.
Another analogy worth mentioning is Kripke's (1980) theory of *reference-
fixing*. According to Kripke, we can use one property to fix a reference to a
certain entity, or type of entity; but once this reference has been fixed, that
property may cease to play a role in identifying the entity across various
possible worlds. For example, we can fix a reference to heat as the phenomenon
that causes certain sensations in people. Once heat has been so picked out, this
property is no longer needed, or relied upon, in identifying heat. A phenomenon
can count as heat in another possible world where it doesn't cause those
sensations in people. Similarly, I am proposing, we initially use reliability as a
test for intellectual quality (virtue or vice status). Once the quality of a faculty or
process has been determined, however, it tends to retain that status in our
thinking. At any rate, it isn't reassessed each time we consider a fresh case,
especially a purely imaginary and bizarre case like the demon world. Nor is
quality relativized to each possible world or environment.

The present version of the virtues theory appears to be a successful variant of
reliabilism, capable of accounting for most, if not all, of the most prominent
counterexamples to earlier variants of reliabilism.[7] The present approach also

makes an innovation in naturalistic epistemology. Whereas earlier naturalistic epistemologists have focused exclusively on the psychology of the epistemic agent, the present paper (along with the preceding essay) also highlights the psychology of the epistemic evaluator.

III

Let us turn now to *normative* scientific epistemology. It was argued briefly in section I that normative scientific epistemology should preserve continuity with our epistemic folkways. At a minimum, it should rest on the same types of evaluative criteria as those on which our commonsense epistemic evaluations rest. Recently, however, Stephen Stich (1990) has disputed this sort of claim. Stich contends that our epistemic folkways are quite idiosyncratic, and should not be much heeded in a reformed epistemology. An example he uses to underline his claim of idiosyncracy is the notion of justification as rendered by my "normal worlds" analysis in Goldman (1986). With hindsight, I would agree that that particular analysis makes our ordinary notion of justification look pretty idiosyncratic. But that was the fault of the analysis, not the analysandum. On the present rendering, it looks as if the folk notion of justification is keyed to dispositions to produce a high ratio of true beliefs in the actual world, not in "normal worlds"; and there is nothing idiosyncratic about that. Furthermore, there seem to be straightforward reasons for thinking that true belief is worthy of positive valuation, if only from a pragmatic point of view, which Stich also challenges. The pragmatic utility of true belief is best seen by focusing on a certain sub-class of beliefs, viz., beliefs about one's own *plans of action.* Clearly, true beliefs about which courses of action would accomplish one's ends will help secure these ends better than false beliefs. Let proposition P = "Plan N will accomplish my ends" and proposition P' = "Plan N' will accomplish my ends." If P is true and P' is false, I am best off believing the former and not believing the latter. My belief will guide my choice of a plan, and belief in the true proposition (but not the false one) will lead me to choose a plan that *will* accomplish my ends. Stich has other intriguing arguments that cannot be considered here, but it certainly appears that true belief is a perfectly sensible and stable value, not an idiosyncratic one.[8] Thus, I shall assume that normative scientific epistemology should follow in the footsteps of folk practice and use reliability (and other truth-linked standards) as a basis for epistemic evaluation.

If scientific epistemology retains the fundamental standard(s) of folk epistemic assessment, how might it diverge from our epistemic folkways? One possible divergence emerges from William Alston's (1988) account of justification. Although generally sympathetic with reliabilism, Alston urges a kind of constraint not standardly imposed by reliabilism (at least not process reliabilism). This is the requirement that the processes from which justified beliefs issue must have as their input, or basis, a state *of which the cognizer is aware* (or can easily become aware). Suppose that Alston is right about this as an account of our folk conception of justification. It may well be urged that this ingredient needn't be retained in a scientifically sensitive epistemology. In particular, it may well be claimed that one thing to be learned from cognitive science is that only a small proportion of our cognitive processes operate on consciously accessible inputs. It could therefore be argued that a reformed conception of intellectually virtuous processes should dispense with the "accessibility" requirement.

Alston aside, the point of divergence I wish to examine concerns the psychological units that are chosen as virtues or vices. The lay epistemic evaluator uses casual, unsystematic, and largely introspective methods to carve out the mental faculties and processes responsible for belief formation and revision. Scientific epistemology, by contrast, would utilize the resources of cognitive science to devise a more subtle and sophisticated picture of the mechanisms of belief acquisition. I proceed now to illustrate how this project should be carried out.

An initial phase of the undertaking is to sharpen our conceptualization of the types of cognitive units that should be targets of epistemic evaluation. Lay people are pretty vague about the sorts of entities that qualify as intellectual virtues or vices. In my description of epistemic folkways, I have been deliberately indefinite about these entities, calling them variously "faculties," "processes," "mechanisms," and the like. How should systematic epistemology improve on this score?

A first possibility, enshrined in the practice of historical philosophers, is to take the relevant units to be cognitive *faculties*. This might be translated into modern parlance as *modules*, except that this term has assumed a rather narrow, specialized meaning under Jerry Fodor's (1983) influential treatment of modularity. A better translation might be (cognitive) *systems*, e.g., the visual system, long term memory, and so forth. Such systems, however, are also sub-optimal candidates for units of epistemic analysis. Many beliefs are the outputs of two or more systems working in tandem. For example, a belief consisting in the visual classification of an object ("That is a chair") may involve matching some information in the visual system with a category stored in long-term memory. A preferable unit of analysis, then, might be a *process*, construed as the sort of entity depicted by familiar flow charts of cognitive activity. This sort of diagram depicts a sequence of operations (or sets of parallel operations), ultimately culminating in a belief-like output. Such a sequence may span several cognitive systems. This is the sort of entity I had in mind in previous publications (especially Goldman, 1986) when I spoke of "cognitive processes."

Even this sort of entity, however, is not a fully satisfactory unit of analysis. Visual classification, for example, may occur under a variety of degraded conditions. The stimulus may be viewed from an unusual orientation; it may be partly occluded, so that only certain of its parts are visible; and so forth. Obviously, these factors can make a big difference to the reliability of the classification process. Yet it is one and the same process that analyzes the stimulus data and comes to a perceptual "conclusion." So the same process can have different degrees of reliability depending on a variety of parameter values.

For purposes of epistemic assessment, it would be instructive to identify the parameters and parameter values that are critically relevant to degrees of reliability. The virtues and vices might then be associated not with processes *per se*, but with processes operating *with specified parameter values*. Let me illustrate this idea in connection with visual perception.

Consider Irving Biederman's (1987, 1990) theory of object recognition, Recognition-By-Components (RBC). The core idea of Biederman's theory is that a common concrete object like a chair, a giraffe, or a mushroom is mentally represented as an arrangement of simple primitive volumes called *geons* (*geometrical ions*). These geons, or primitive "components" of objects, are typically symmetrical volumes lacking sharp concavities, such as blocks, cylinders, spheres, and wedges. A set of twenty-four types of geons can be differentiated on the basis of dichotomous or trichotomous contrasts of such attributes as curvature (straight versus curved), size variation (constant versus expanding), and symmetry (symmetrical versus asymmetrical). These twenty-four types of geons can then be combined by means of six relations (e.g., top-of, side-connected, larger-than, etc.) into various possible multiple-geon objects. For example, a cup can be represented as a cylindrical geon that is side-connected to a curved, handle-like geon, whereas a pail can be represented as the same two geons bearing a different relation: the curved, handle-like geon is at the top of the cylindrical geon.

Simplifying a bit, the RBC theory of object recognition posits five stages of processing. (1) In the first stage, low-level vision extracts edge characteristics, such as Ls, Y- vertices, and arrows. (2) On the basis of these edge characteristics, viewpoint-independent attributes are detected, such as curved, straight, size-constant, size-expanding, etc. (3) In the next stage, selected geons and their relations are activated. (4) Geon activation leads to the activation of object models, that is, familiar models of simple types of objects, stored in long-term memory. (5) The perceived entity is then "matched" to one of these models, and thereby identified as an instance of that category or classification. (In this description of the five stages, all processing is assumed to proceed bottom-up; but in fact Biederman also allows for elements of top-down processing.)

Under what circumstances, or what parameter values, will such a sequence of processing stages lead to *correct*, or *accurate*, object identification? Biederman estimates that there are approximately 3,000 common basic-level, or entry-level, names in English for familiar concrete objects. However, people are probably familiar with approximately ten times that number of object models because, among other things, some entry-level terms (such as *lamp* and *chair*) have several readily distinguishable object models. Thus, an estimate of the number of familiar object models would be on the order of 30,000.

Some of these object models are simple, requiring fewer than six components to appear complete; others are complex, requiring six to nine components to appear complete. Nonetheless, Biederman gives theoretical considerations and empirical results suggesting that an arrangement of only *two* or *three* geons almost always suffices to specify a simple object and even most complex ones. Consider the number of possible two-geon and three-geon objects. With twenty-four possible geons, Biederman says, the variations in relations can produce 186,624 possible two-geon objects. A third geon with its possible relations to another geon yields over 1.4 billion possible three-geon objects. Thus, if the 30,000 familiar object models were distributed homogeneously throughout the space of possible object models, Biederman reasons, an arrangement of two or three geons would almost always be sufficient to specify any object. Indeed, Biederman puts forward a *principle of geon recovery*: If an arrangement of two or three geons can be recovered from the image, objects can be quickly recognized even when they are occluded, rotated in depth, novel, extensively degraded, or lacking in customary detail, color, and texture.

The principle of three-geon sufficiency is supported by the following empirical results. An object such as an elephant or an airplane is complex, requiring six or more geons to appear complete. Nonetheless, when only three components were displayed (the others being occluded), subjects still made correct identifications in almost 80 percent of the nine-component objects and more than 90 percent of the six-component objects. Thus, the reliability conferred by just three geons and their relations is quite high. Although Biederman doesn't give data for recovery of just one or two geons of complex objects, presumably the reliability is much lower. Here we presumably have examples of parameter values—(1) number of components in the complete object, and (2) number of recovered components—that make a significant difference to reliability. The same process, understood as an instantiation of one and the same flow diagram, can have different levels of reliability depending on the values of the critical parameters in question. Biederman's work illustrates how research in cognitive science can identify both the relevant flow of activity and the crucial parameters. The quality (or "virtue") of a particular (token) process of belief-acquisition depends not only on the flow diagram that is instantiated, but on the parameter values instantiated in the specific tokening of the diagram.

Until now reliability has been my sole example of epistemic quality. But two other dimensions of epistemic quality—which also invoke truth or accuracy— should be added to our evaluative repertoire. These are *question answering power* and *question answering speed*. (These are certainly reflected in our epistemic folkways, though not well reflected in the concepts of knowledge or justification.) If a person asks himself a question, such as "What kind of object is that?" or "What is the solution to this algebra problem?," there are three possible outcomes: (A) he comes up with *no answer* (at least none that he believes), (B) he forms a belief in an answer that is *correct*, and (C) he forms a belief in an answer that is *incorrect*. Now reliability is the ratio of cases in category (B) to cases in categories (B) and (C), that is, the proportion of true beliefs to beliefs. Question answering *power*, on the other hand, is the ratio of (B) cases to cases in categories (A), (B), and (C). Notice that it is possible for a system to be highly reliable but not very powerful. An object-recognition system that never yields outputs in category (C) is perfectly reliable, but it may not be very powerful, since most of its outputs could fall in (A) and only a few in (B). The human (visual) object-recognition system, by contrast, is very powerful as well as quite reliable. In general, it is power and not just reliability that is an important epistemic desideratum in a cognitive system or process.

Speed introduces another epistemic desideratum beyond reliability and power. This is another dimension on which cognitive science can shed light. It might have been thought, for example, that correct identification of complex objects like an airplane or an elephant requires more time than simple objects such as a flashlight or a cup. In fact, there is no advantage for simple objects, as Biederman's empirical studies indicate. This lack of advantage for simple objects could be explained by the geon theory in terms of parallel activation: geons are activated in parallel rather than through a serial trace of the contours of the object. Whereas more geons would require more processing time under a serial trace, this is not required under parallel activation.

Let us turn now from perception to learning, especially language learning. Learnability theory (Gold, 1967; Osherson, Stob, and Weinstein, 1985) uses a criterion of learning something like our notion of power, viz., the ability or inability of the learning process to arrive at a correct hypothesis after some fixed period of time. This is called *identification in the limit*. In language learning, it is assumed that the child is exposed to some information in the world, e.g., a set of sentences parents utter, and the learning task is to construct a hypothesis that correctly singles out the language being spoken. The child is presumed to have a learning strategy: an algorithm that generates a succession of hypotheses in response to accumulating evidence. What learning strategy might lead to success? *That* children learn their native language is evident to common sense. But *how* they learn it—what algorithm they possess that constitutes the requisite intellectual virtue—is only being revealed through research in cognitive science.

We may distinguish two types of evidence that a child might receive about its language (restricting attention to the language's grammar): positive evidence and negative evidence. Positive evidence refers to information about which strings of words *are* grammatical sentences in the language, and negative evidence refers to information about which strings of words are *not* grammatical sentences. Interestingly, it appears that children do not receive (much) negative evidence. The absence of negative evidence makes the learning task much harder. What algorithm might be in use that produces success in this situation?

An intriguing proposal is advanced by Robert Berwick (1986a; cf. Pinker, 1990). In the absence of negative evidence, the danger for a learning strategy is that it might hypothesize a language that is a superset of the correct language, i.e., one that includes all grammatical sentences of the target language plus some additional sentences as well. Without negative evidence, the child will be unable to learn that the "extra" sentences are incorrect, i.e., don't belong to the target language. A solution is to avoid ever hypothesizing an overly general hypothesis. Hypotheses should be *ordered* in such a way that the child always guesses the narrowest possible hypothesis or language at each step. This is called the *subset principle*. Berwick finds evidence of this principle at work in a number of domains, including concepts, sound systems, and syntax. Here, surely, is a kind of intellectual disposition that is not dreamed of by the "folk."

Notes

1. Normative scientific epistemology corresponds to what I elsewhere call *epistemics* (see Goldman 1986). Although epistemics is not restricted to the assessment of *psychological* processes, that is the topic of the present paper. So we are here dealing with what I call *primary epistemics*.

2. Sosa's approach is spelled out most fully in Sosa 1985, 1988, and 1991.

3. My own previous formulations of reliabilism have not been so simple. Both "What Is Justified Belief?" and *Epistemology and Cognition* (Goldman 1986) had provisions (e.g., the non-undermining provision of *Epistemology and Cognition*) that could help accommodate BonJour's examples. It is not entirely clear, however, how well these qualifications succeeded with the Norman case, described below.

4. Tom Senor presented the following example to his philosophy class at the University of Arkansas. Norman is working at his desk when out of the blue he is hit (via clairvoyance) with a very distinct and vivid impression of the President at the Empire State Building. The image is phenomenally distinct from a regular visual impression but is in some respects similar and of roughly equal force. The experience is so overwhelming that Norman just can't help but form the belief that the President is in New York. About half of Senor's class judged that in this case Norman justifiably believes that the President is in New York. Senor points out, in commenting on this paper, that their judgments are readily explained by the present account, because the description of the clairvoyance process makes it sufficiently similar to vision to be easily "matched" to that virtue.

5. Since some of these opinions may be true and others false, people's lists of virtues and vices may have varying degrees of accuracy. The "real" status of a trait as a virtue or vice is independent of people's opinions about that trait. However, since the enterprise of descriptive epistemology is to describe and explain evaluators' judgments, we need to advert to the traits they *believe* to be virtues or vices (i.e., the ones on their mental lists).

6. Thanks to Holly Smith for this example. She cites Riding 1989, chapter 6 for relevant discussion.

7. It should be noted that this theory of justification is intended to capture what I call, in Essay 7, the *strong* conception of justification. The complementary conception of *weak* justification will receive attention in section IV of this essay (omitted here; see *Liaisons*, chapter 9 for the complete text).

8. For further discussion of Stich, see Goldman 1999.

References

Alston, W. 1988. "An Internalist Externalism." *Synthese* 74, 265-283.

Biederman, I. 1990. "Higher-Level Vision." In D. Osherson, S. M. Kosslyn, and J. M. Hollerbach, eds. *Visual Cognition and Action: An Invitation to Cognitive Science.* Cambridge, Mass.: MIT Press.

———. 1987. "Recognition-By-Components: A Theory of Human Image Understanding." *Psychological Review* 94, 115-147.

Berwick, R. 1986. "Learning From Positive-Only Examples: The Subset Principle and Three Case Studies." In R. S. Michalski, J. G. Carbonell, and T. M. Mitchell, eds. *Machine Learning: An Artificial Intelligence Approach,* Vol. 2. Los Altos, Calif.: Morgan Kaufman.

BonJour, L. 1985. *The Structure of Empirical Knowledge.* Cambridge, Mass.: Harvard University Press.

Fodor, J. 1983. *The Modularity of Mind.* Cambridge, Mass.: MIT Press/A Bradford Book.

Gold, E. M. 1967. "Language Identification in the Limit." *Information and Control* 10, 447-474.

Goldman, A. 1986. *Epistemology and Cognition.* Cambridge, Mass.: Harvard University Press.

———. "Review of S. Stich, The Fragmentation of Reason." *Philosophy and Phenomenological Research,* forthcoming.

Goodman, N. 1955. *Fact, Fiction, and Forecast.* Cambridge, Mass.: Harvard University Press.

Hintzman, D. 1986. "'Schema Abstraction' in a Multiple-Trace Memory Model." *Psychological Review* 93, 411-428.

Kripke, S. 1980. *Naming and Necessity.* Cambridge, Mass.: Harvard University Press.

Medin, D. L., and M. M. Schaffer. 1978. "A Context Theory of Classification Learning." *Psychological Review* 85, 227-238.

Osherson, D., M. Stob, and S. Weinstein. 1985. *Systems That Learn.* Cambridge, Mass.: MIT Press/A Bradford Book.

Pinker, S. 1990. "Language Acquisition." In D. N. Osherson and H. Lasnik, eds., *Language: An Invitation to Cognitive Science.* Cambridge, Mass.: MIT Press/A Bradford Book.

Plantinga, A. 1988. "Positive Epistemic Status and Proper Function." In J. E. Tomberlin, ed., *Philosophical Perspectives* Vol. 2. Atascadero, Calif.: Ridgeview.

Pollock, J. 1986. *Contemporary Theories of Knowledge.* Totowa, N.J.: Rowman & Littlefield.

Smith, E. E. 1990. "Categorization." In D. N. Osherson and E. E. Smith, eds. *Thinking: An Invitation to Cognitive Science.* Cambridge, Mass.: MIT Press/A Bradford Book.

Smith, E. E., and M. Medin. 1981. *Categories and Concepts.* Cambridge, Mass.: Harvard University Press.

Sosa, E. 1985. "Knowledge and Intellectual Virtue." *The Monist* 68, 226-263. [Reprinted in Sosa, 1991].

———. 1988. "Beyond Scepticism, to the Best of our Knowledge." *Mind* 97, 153-188.

———. 1991. "Reliabilism and Intellectual Virtue." In *Knowledge in Perspective.* Cambridge: Cambridge University Press.

Stich, S. 1990. *The Fragmentation of Reason.* Cambridge, Mass.: MIT Press/A Bradford Book.

2

Reliabilism and Intellectual Virtue

Ernest Sosa

Externalism and reliabilism go back at least to the writings of Frank Ramsey early in this century.[1] The generic view has been developed in diverse ways by David Armstrong, Fred Dretske, Alvin Goldman, Robert Nozick, and Marshall Swain.[2]

Generic Reliabilism

Generic reliabilism might be put simply as follows:

> S's belief that p at t is justified if it is the outcome of a process of belief acquisition or retention that is reliable, or leads to a sufficiently high preponderance of true beliefs over false beliefs.

That simple statement of the view is subject to three main problems: the generality problem, the new evil-demon problem, and the meta-incoherence problem (to give it a label). Let us consider these in turn.

The generality problem for such reliabilism is that of how to avoid processes that are too specific or too generic. Thus we must avoid a process with only one output ever, or one artificially selected so that if a belief were the output of such a process it would indeed be true; for every true belief is presumably the outcome of some such too-specific processes, so that if such processes are allowed, then every true belief would result from a reliable process and would be justified. But we must also avoid processes that are too generic, such as perception (period), which surely can produce not only justified beliefs but also unjustified ones, even if perception is on the whole a reliable process of belief acquisition for normally circumstanced humans.[3]

The evil-demon problem for reliabilism is not Descartes's problem, of course, but it is a relative. What if twins of ours in another possible world were given mental lives just like ours down to the most minute detail of experience or thought, etc., though they were also totally in error about the nature of their surroundings, and their perceptual and inferential processes of belief acquisition accomplished very little except to sink them more and more deeply and systematically into error? Shall we say that we are justified in our beliefs while our twins are not? They are quite wrong in their beliefs, of course, but it seems somehow very implausible to suppose that they are unjustified.[4]

The meta-incoherence problem is in a sense a mirror image of the new evil-demon problem, for it postulates not a situation where one is internally justified though externally unreliable, but a situation where one is internally unjustified though externally reliable. More specifically, it supposes that a belief (that the President is in New York) that derives from one's (reliable) clairvoyance is yet not justified if either (a) one has a lot of ordinary evidence against it and none in its favor; or (b) one has a lot of evidence against one's possessing such a power of clairvoyance; or (c) one has good reason to believe that such a power could not be possessed (e.g., it might require the transmission of some influence at a speed greater than that of light); or (d) one has no evidence for or against the general possibility of the power or of one's having it oneself, nor does one even have any evidence either for or against the proposition that one believes as a result of one's power (that the President is in New York).[5]

Goldman's Reliabilisms

How might reliabilism propose to meet the problems specified? We turn first to important work by Goldman, who calls his theory "Historical Reliabilism," and has the following to say about it:

> The theory of justified belief proposed here, then, is an *Historical* or *Genetic* theory. It contrasts with the dominant approach to justified belief, an approach that generates what we may call (borrowing a phrase from Robert Nozick) *Current Time-Slice* theories. A Current Time-Slice theory makes the justificational status of a belief wholly a function of what is true of the cognizer *at the time* of the belief. An Historical theory makes the justificational status of a belief depend on its prior history. Since my Historical theory emphasizes the reliability of the belief-generating processes, it may be called *Historical Reliabilism.*[6]

The insights of externalism are important, and Goldman has been perceptive and persistent in his attempts to formulate an appropriate and detailed theory that does them justice. His proposals have stimulated criticism, however, among them the three problems already indicated.

Having appreciated those problems, Goldman in his book[7] moves beyond Historical Reliabilism to a view we might call rule reliabilism, and, in the light of further problems,[8] has made further revisions in the more recent "Strong and Weak Justification." The earlier theory, however, had certain features designed to solve the new evil-demon problem, features absent in the revised theory. Therefore, some other solution is now required, and we do now find a new proposal.

Under the revised approach, we now distinguish between two sorts of justification:

A belief is *strongly justified* if and only if it is well formed, in the sense of being formed by means of a process that is truth-conducive in the possible world in which it is produced, or the like.

A belief is *weakly justified* if and only if it is blameless though ill-formed, in the sense of being produced by an unreliable cognitive process that the believer does not believe to be unreliable, and whose unreliability the believer has no available way of determining.[9]

Notice, however, that it is at best in a *very* weak sense that a subject with a "weakly justified" belief is thereby "blameless." For it is not even precluded that the subject take that belief to be very ill-formed, so long as he is in error about the cognitive process that produces it. That is to say, S might hold B, and believe B to be an output of P, and hold P to be an epistemically unreliable process, while in fact it is not P but the equally unreliable P′ that produces B. In this case S's belief B would be weakly justified, so long as S did not believe P′ to be unreliable, and had no available means of determining its unreliability. But it seems at best extremely strained to hold S epistemically "blameless" with regard to holding B in such circumstances, where S takes B to derive from a process P so unreliable, let us suppose, as to be epistemically vicious.

The following definition may perhaps give us a closer approach to epistemic blamelessness.

A belief is *weakly justified* (*in the modified sense*) if and only if it is blameless though ill-formed, in the sense of being produced by an unreliable cognitive process while the believer neither takes it to be thus ill-formed nor has any available way of determining it to be ill-formed.

With these concepts, the Historical Reliabilist now has at least the beginnings of an answer both for the evil-demon problem and for the meta-incoherence problem. About the evil demon's victims, those hapless twins of ours, we can now say that though their beliefs are very ill-formed—and are no knowledge even if by luck they, some of them, happen to be true—still there is a sense in which they are justified, as justified as our corresponding beliefs, which are indistinguishable from theirs so far as concerns only the "insides" of our respective subjectivities. For we may now see their beliefs to be weakly justified, in the modified sense defined above.[10]

About the meta-incoherence cases, moreover, we can similarly argue that, in some of them at least, the unjustified protagonist with the wrong (or lacking) perspective on his own well-formed (clairvoyant) belief can be seen to be indeed unjustified, for he can be seen as subjectively unjustified through lack of an appropriate perspective on his belief: either because he positively takes the belief to be ill-formed, or because he "ought" to take it to be ill-formed given his total picture of things, and given the cognitive processes available to him.

Consider now the following definition:

> A belief is *meta-justified* if and only if the believer does place it in appropriate perspective, at least in the minimal sense that the believer neither takes it to be ill-formed nor has any available way of determining it to be ill-formed.

Then any belief that is weakly justified (again, sticking to the unmodified sense) will be meta-justified, but there can be meta-justified beliefs that are not weakly justified. Moreover, no strongly justified belief will be weakly justified, but a strongly justified belief can be meta-justified. Indeed one would wish one's beliefs to be not only strongly justified but also meta-justified. And what one shares with the victim of the evil demon is of course not weak justification. For if, as we suppose, our own beliefs are strongly justified, then our own beliefs are not weakly justified. What one shares with the evil demon's victim is rather meta-justification. The victim's beliefs and our beliefs are equally meta-justified.

Does such meta-justification—embedded thus in weak justification—enable answers both for the new evil-demon problem and for the problem of meta-incoherence? Does the victim of the evil demon share with us meta-justification, unlike the meta-incoherent? The notion of weak justification does seem useful as far as it goes, as is the allied notion of meta-justification, but we need to go a bit deeper,[11] which may be seen as follows.

Going Deeper

Beliefs are states of a subject, which need not be occurrent or conscious, but may be retained even by someone asleep or unconscious, and may also be acquired unconsciously and undeliberately, as are acquired our initial beliefs, presumably, whether innate or not, especially if deliberation takes time. Consider now a normal human with an ordinary set of beliefs normally acquired through sensory experience from ordinary interaction with a surrounding physical world. And suppose a victim in whom evil demons (perhaps infinitely many) implant beliefs in the following way. The demons cast dice, or use some other more complex randomizer, and choose which beliefs to implant at random and in ignorance of what the other demons are doing. Yet, by amazing coincidence, the victim's total set of beliefs is identical to that of our normal human. Now let's suppose that the victim has a beautifully coherent and comprehensive set of beliefs, complete with an epistemic perspective on his object-level beliefs. We may suppose that the victim has meta-justification for his object-level beliefs (e.g., for his belief that there is a fire before him at the moment), at least in the minimal sense defined above: he does not believe such beliefs to derive from unreliable processes, nor has he any available means of determining that they do. Indeed, we may suppose that he has an even stronger form of meta-justification, as follows:

> S has meta-justification, in the stronger sense, for believing that p if (a) S has weaker meta-justification for so believing, and (b) S has meta-beliefs which positively attribute his object beliefs in every case to some faculty or virtue for arriving at such beliefs in such circumstances, and further meta-beliefs that explain how such a faculty or virtue was acquired, and how such a faculty or virtue, thus acquired, is bound to be reliable in the circumstances as he views them at the time.

And the victim might even be supposed to have a similar meta-meta-perspective, and a similar meta-meta-meta-perspective, and so on, for many more levels of ascent than any human would normally climb. So everything would be brilliantly in order as far as such meta-reasoning is concerned, meta-reasoning supposed flawlessly coherent and comprehensive. Would it follow that the victim was internally and subjectively justified in every reasonable sense or respect? Not necessarily, or so I will now try to show.

Suppose the victim has much sensory experience, but that all of this experience is wildly at odds with his beliefs. Thus he believes he has a splitting headache, but he has no headache at all; he believes he has a cubical piece of black coal before him, while his visual experience is as if he had a white and round snowball before him. And so on. Surely there is then something internally and subjectively wrong with this victim, something "epistemically blameworthy." This despite his beliefs being weakly justified, in the sense defined by Goldman, and despite his beliefs being meta-justified in the weaker and stronger senses indicated above.

Cartesians and internalists (broadly speaking) should find our victim to be quite conceivable. More naturalistic philosophers may well have their doubts, however, about the possibility of a subject whose "experience" and "beliefs" would be so radically divergent. For these there is a different parable. Take our victim to be a human, and suppose that the demon damages the victim's nervous system in such a way that the physical inputs to the system have to pass randomizing gates before the energy transmitted is transformed into any belief. Is there not something internally wrong with this victim as well, even though his beliefs may be supposed weakly and meta-justified, as above?

It may be replied that the "internal" here is not internal in the right sense. What is internal in the right sense must remain restricted to the subjectivity of the subject, to that which pertains to the subject's psychology; it must not go outside of that, even to the physiological conditions holding in the subject's body; or at least it must not do so under the aspect of the physiological, even if in the end it is the physiological (or something physical anyhow) that "realizes" everything mental and psychological.

Even if we accept that objection, however, a very similar difficulty yet remains for the conception of the blameless as the weakly justified or meta-justified (in either the weaker or the stronger sense). For it may be that the connections among the experiences and beliefs of the victim are purely random, as in the example above. True, in that example the randomness derives from the randomizing behavior of the demons involved. But there is no reason why the randomizing may not be brought inside. Thus, given a set of experiences or beliefs, there may be many alternative further beliefs that might be added by the subject, and there may be no rational mechanism that selects only one to be added. It may be rather that one of the many alternatives pops in at random: thus it is a radically random matter which alternative further belief is added in any specific case. Our evil demon's victim, though damaged internally in that way, so that his inner mental processes are largely random, may still by amazing coincidence acquire a coherent and comprehensive system of beliefs that makes him weakly justified and even meta-justified, in both the weaker and stronger senses indicated above. Yet is there not something still defective in such a victim, something that would preclude our holding him to be indiscernible from us in all internal respects of epistemic relevance?

Consider again the project of defining a notion of weak justification, however, a notion applicable to evil-demon victims in accordance with our intuitions; or that of defining a notion of meta-justification as above, one applicable equally to the victims and to ourselves in our normal beliefs. These projects may well be thought safe from the fact that a victim might be internally defective in ways that go beyond any matter of weak or meta-justification. Fair enough. But then of course we might have introduced a notion of superweak justification, and provided sufficient conditions for it as follows:

> S is *superweakly justified* in a certain belief if (1) the cognitive process that produces the belief is unreliable, but (2) S has not acquired that belief as a result of a deliberate policy of acquiring false beliefs (a policy adopted perhaps at the behest of a cruel master, or out of a deep need for epistemic self-abasement).

Someone may propose that a similarity between the victim of the evil demon and ourselves is that we all are superweakly justified in our object-level beliefs in fires and the like. This appears correct, but it just does not go far enough. There is much else that is epistemically significant to the comparison between the victim and ourselves, much else that is left out of account by the mere notion of superweak justification. Perhaps part of what is left out is what the notion of weak justification would enable us to capture, and perhaps the notion of meta-justification, especially its stronger variant, would enable us to do even better. Even these stronger notions fall short of what is needed for fuller illumination, however, as I have tried to show above through the victims of randomization, whether demon-derived or internally derived. In order to deal with the new evil-demon problem and with the problem of meta-incoherence we need a stronger notion than either that of the weakly justified or that of the meta-justified, a stronger notion of the internally or subjectively justified.

A Stronger Notion of the "Internally Justified": Intellectual Virtue

Let us define an intellectual virtue or faculty as a competence in virtue of which one would mostly attain the truth and avoid error in a certain field of propositions F, when in certain conditions C. Subject S believes proposition P at time t out of intellectual virtue only if there is a field of propositions F, and there are conditions C, such that: (a) P is in F; (b) S is in C with respect to P; and (c) S would most likely be right if S believed a proposition X in field F when in conditions C with respect to X. Unlike Historical Reliabilism, this view does not require that there be a cognitive process leading to a belief in order for that belief to enjoy the strong justification required for constituting knowledge. Which is all to the good, since requiring such a process makes it hard to explain the justification for that paradigm of knowledge, the Cartesian cogito. There is a truth-conducive "faculty" through which everyone grasps his or her own existence at the moment of grasping. Indeed, what Descartes noticed about this faculty is its infallible reliability. But this requires that the existence that is grasped at a time T be in existence at that very moment T. Grasp of earlier existence, no matter how near to the present, requires not the infallible cogito faculty, but a fallible faculty of memory. If we are to grant the cogito its due measure of justification, and to explain its exceptional epistemic status, we must allow faculties that operate instantaneously in the sense that the outcome belief is about the very moment of believing, and the conditions C are conditions about what obtains at that very moment where we need place no necessary and general requirements about what went before.

By contrast with Historical Reliabilism, let us now work with intellectual virtues or faculties, defining their presence in a subject S by requiring

> that, concerning propositions X in field F, once S were in conditions C with respect to X, S would most likely attain the truth and avoid error.

In fact a faculty or virtue would normally be a fairly stable disposition on the part of a subject *relative to an environment.* Being in conditions C with respect to proposition X would range from just being conscious and entertaining X—as in the case of "I think" or "I am"—to seeing an object O in good light at a favorable angle and distance, and without obstruction, etc.—as in "This before me is white and round." There is no restriction here to processes or to the internal. The conditions C and the field F may have much to do with the environment external to the subject: thus a moment ago we spoke of a C that involved seeing an external object in good light at a certain distance, etc.—all of which involves factors external to the subject.

Normally, we could hope to attain a conception of C and F that at best and at its most explicit will still have to rely heavily on the assumed nature of the subject and the assumed character of the environment. Thus it may appear to you that there is a round and white object before you and you may have reason to think that in conditions C (i.e., for middle-sized objects in daylight, at arm's length) you would likely be right concerning propositions in field F (about their shapes and colors). But of course there are underlying reasons why you would most likely be right about such questions concerning such objects so placed. And these underlying reasons have to do with yourself and your intrinsic properties, largely your eyes and brain and nervous system; and they have to do also with the medium and the environment more generally, and its contents and properties at the time. A fuller, more explicit account of what is involved in having an intellectual virtue or faculty is therefore this:

> Because subject S has a certain inner nature (I) and is placed in a certain environment (E), S would most likely be right on any proposition X in field F relative to which S stood in conditions C. S might be a human; I might involve possession of good eyes and a good nervous system including a brain in good order; E might include the surface of the earth with its relevant properties, within the parameters of variation experienced by humans over the centuries, or anyhow by subject S within his or her lifetime or within a certain more recent stretch of it; F might be a field of propositions specifying the colors or shapes of an object before S up to a certain level of determination and complexity (say greenness and squareness, but not chartreuseness or chiliagonicity); and C might be the conditions of S's seeing such an object in good light at arm's length and without obstructions.

If S believes a proposition X in field F, about the shape of a facing surface before him, and X is false, things might have gone wrong at interestingly different points. Thus the medium might have gone wrong unknown to the subject, and perhaps even unknowably to the subject; or something within the subject might have changed significantly: thus the lenses in the eyes of the subject might have become distorted, or the optic nerve might have become defective in ways important to shape recognition. If what goes wrong lies in the environment, that might prevent the subject from knowing what he believes, even if his belief were true, but there is a sense in which the subject would remain subjectively justified or anyhow virtuous in so believing. It is this sense of internal virtue that seems most significant for dealing with the new evil-demon argument and with the meta-incoherence objection. Weak justification and meta-justification are just two factors that bear on internal value, but there are others surely, as the earlier examples were designed to show examples in which the experience/belief relation goes awry, or in which a randomizer gate intervenes. Can something more positive be said in explication of such internal intellectual virtue?

Intellectual virtue is something that resides in a subject, something relative to an environment though in the limiting case, the environment may be null, as perhaps when one engages in armchair reflection and thus comes to justified belief.

A subject S's intellectual virtue V relative to an "environment" E may be defined as S's disposition to believe correctly propositions in a field F relative to which S stands in conditions C, in "environment" E.

It bears emphasis first of all that to be in a certain "environment" is *not* just a matter of having a certain spatio-temporal location, but is more a matter of having a complex set of properties, only some of which will be spatial or temporal. Secondly, we are interested of course in non-vacuous virtues, virtues that are not possessed simply because the subject would never be in conditions C relative to the propositions in F, or the like, though there may be no harm in allowing vacuous virtues to stand as trivial, uninteresting special cases.

Notice now that, so defined, for S to have a virtue V relative to an environment E at a time t, S does not have to be *in* E at t (i.e., S does not need to have the properties required). Further, suppose that, while outside environment E and while not in conditions C with respect to a proposition X in F, S still retains the virtue involved, *relative* to E, because the following ECF conditional remains true of S:

(ECF) that if in E and in C relative to X in F, then S would most likely be right in his belief or disbelief of X.

If S does so retain that virtue in that way, it can only be due to some components or aspects of S's intrinsic nature I, for it is S's possessing I together with being in E and in C with respect to X in F that fully explains and gives rise to the relevant disposition on the part of S, namely the disposition to believe correctly and avoid error regarding X in F, when so characterized and circumstanced.

We may now distinguish between (a) possession of the virtue (relative to E) in the sense of possession of the disposition, i.e., in the sense that the appropriate complex and general conditional (ECF) indicated above is true of the subject with the virtue, and (b) possession of a certain ground or basis of the virtue, in the sense of possessing an inner nature I from which the truth of the ECF conditional derives in turn. Of course one and the same virtue might have several different alternative possible grounds or bases. Thus the disposition to roll down an incline if free at its top with a certain orientation, in a certain environment (gravity, etc.), may be grounded in the sphericity and rigidity of an object, or alternatively it may be grounded in its cylindricality and rigidity. Either way, the conditional will obtain and the object will have the relevant disposition to roll. Similarly, Earthians and Martians may both be endowed with sight, in the sense of having the ability to tell colors and shapes, etc., though the principles of the operation of Earthian sight may differ widely from the principles that apply to Martians, which would or might presumably derive from a difference in the inner structure of the two species of being.

What now makes a disposition (and the underlying inner structure or nature that grounds it) an intellectual virtue? If we view such a disposition as defined by a C-F pair, then a being might have the disposition to be right with respect to propositions in field F when in conditions C with respect to them, relative to one environment E but not relative to another environment E'. Such virtues, then, i.e., such C-F dispositions, might be virtuous only relative to an environment E and not relative to a different environment E'. And what makes such a disposition a virtue relative to an environment E seems now as obvious as it is that having the truth is an epistemic desideratum, and that being so constituted that one would most likely attain the truth in a certain field in a certain environment, when in certain conditions vis-à-vis propositions in that field, is so far as it goes an epistemic desideratum, an intellectual virtue.

What makes a subject intellectually virtuous? What makes her inner nature meritorious? Surely we can't require that a being have all merit and virtue before it can have any. Consider then a subject who has a minimal virtue of responding, thermometer-like, to environing food, and suppose him to have the minimal complexity and sophistication required for having beliefs at all—so that he is not literally just a thermometer or the like. Yet we suppose him further to have no way of relating what he senses, and his sensing of it, to a wider view of things that will explain it all, that will enable him perhaps to make related predictions and exercise related control. No, this ability is a relatively isolated phenomenon to which the subject yields with infant-like, unselfconscious simplicity. Suppose indeed the subject is just an infant or a higher animal. Can we allow that she knows of the presence of food when she has a correct belief to that effect? Well, the subject may of course have reliable belief that there is something edible there, without having a belief as reliable as that of a normal, well-informed adult, with some knowledge of food composition, basic nutrition, basic perception, etc., and who can at least implicitly interrelate these matters for a relatively much more coherent and complete view of the matter and related matters. Edibility can be a fairly complex matter, and how we have perceptual access to that property can also be rather involved, and the more one knows about the various factors whose interrelation yields the perceptible edibility of something before one, presumably the more reliable one's access to that all-important property.

Here then is one proposal on what makes one's belief that-p a result of enough virtue to make one internally justified in that belief. First of all we need to relativize to an assumed environment, which need not be the environment that the believer actually is in. What is required for a subject S to believe that-p out of sufficient virtue relative to environment E is that the proposition that-p be in a field F and that S be in conditions C with respect to that proposition, such that S would not be in C with respect to a proposition in F while in environment E, without S being most likely to believe correctly with regard to that proposition; and further that by comparison with epistemic group G, S is not grossly defective in ability to detect thus the truth in field F; i.e., it cannot be that S would have, by comparison with G:

(a)   only a relatively very low probability of success,
(b)   in a relatively very restricted class F,
(c)   in a very restricted environment E,
(d)   in conditions C that are relatively infrequent,

where all this relativity holds with respect to fellow members of G and to their normal environment and circumstances. (There is of course some variation from context to context as to what the relevant group might be when one engages in discussion of whether or not some subject knows something or is at least justified in believing it. But normally a certain group will stand out, with humanity being the default value.)

Intellectual Virtue Applied

Consider now again the new evil-demon problem and the problem of meta-incoherence. The crucial question in each case seems to be that of the internal justification of the subject, and this in turn seems not a matter of his superweak or weak or meta justification, so much as a matter of the virtue and total internal justification of that subject relative to an assumed group G and environment E, which absent any sign to the contrary one would take to be the group of humans in a normal human environment for the sort of question under consideration. Given these assumptions, the victim of the evil demon is virtuous and internally justified in every relevant respect, and not just in the respects of enjoying superweak, weak, and meta justification; for the victim is supposed to be just like an arbitrarily selected normal human in all cognitively relevant internal respects. Therefore, the internal structure and goings on in the victim must be at least up to par, in respect of how virtuous all of that internal nature makes the victim, relative to a normal one of us in our usual environment for considering whether we have a fire before us or the like. For those inclined towards mentalism or towards some broadly Cartesian view of the self and her mental life, this means at a minimum that the experience-belief mechanisms must not be random, but must rather be systematically truth-conducive, and that the subject must attain some minimum of coherent perspective on her own situation in the relevant environment, and on her modes of reliable access to information about that environment. Consider next those inclined towards naturalism, who hold the person to be either just a physical organism, or some physical part of an organism, or to be anyhow constituted essentially by some such physical entity; for these it would be required that the relevant physical being identical with or constitutive of the subject, in the situation in question, must not be defective in cognitively relevant internal respects; which would mean, among other things, that the subject would acquire beliefs about the colors or shapes of facing surfaces only under appropriate prompting at the relevant surfaces of the relevant visual organs (and not, e.g., through direct manipulation of the brain by some internal randomizing device).[12]

We have appealed to an intuitive distinction between what is intrinsic or internal to a subject or being, and what is extrinsic or external. Now when a subject receives certain inputs and emits as output a certain belief or a certain choice, that belief or choice can be defective either in virtue of an internal factor or in virtue of an external factor (or, of course, both). That is to say, it may be that everything inner, intrinsic, or internal to the subject operates flawlessly and indeed brilliantly, but that something goes awry—with the belief, which turns out to be false, or with the choice, which turns out to be disastrous—because of some factor that, with respect to that subject, is outer, extrinsic, or external.[13]

In terms of that distinction, the victim of the demon may be seen to be internally justified, just as internally justified as we are, whereas the meta-incoherent are internally unjustified, unlike us.

My proposal is that justification is relative to environment. Relative to our actual environment A, our automatic experience-belief mechanisms count as virtues that yield much truth and justification. Of course relative to the demonic environment D such mechanisms are not virtuous and yield neither truth nor justification. It follows that relative to D the demon's victims are not justified, and yet *relative to A their beliefs are justified*. Thus may we fit our surface intuitions about such victims: that they lack knowledge but not justification.

In fact, a fuller account should distinguish between "justification" and "aptness"[14] as follows:

(a) The "justification" of a belief B requires that B have a basis in its inference or coherence relations to other beliefs in the believer's mind—as in the "justification" of a belief derived from deeper principles, and thus "justified," or the "justification" of a belief adopted through cognizance of its according with the subject's principles, including principles as to what beliefs are permissible in the circumstances as viewed by that subject.

(b) The "aptness" of a belief B relative to an environment E requires that B derive from what relative to E is an intellectual virtue, i.e., a way of arriving at belief that yields an appropriate preponderance of truth over error (in the field of propositions in question, in the sort of context involved).

As far as I can see, however, the basic points would remain within the more complex picture as well. And note that "justification" itself would then amount to a sort of inner coherence, something that the demon's victims can obviously have despite their cognitively hostile environment, but also something that will earn them praise relative to that environment only if it is not just an inner drive for greater and greater explanatory comprehensiveness, a drive that leads nowhere but to a more and more complex tissue of falsehoods. If we believe our world not to be such a world, then we can say that, relative to our actual environment A, "justification" as inner coherence earns its honorific status, and is an intellectual virtue, dear to the scientist, the philosopher, and the detective. Relative to the demon's D, therefore, the victim's belief may be inapt and even unjustified—if "justification" is essentially honorific—or if "justified" simply because coherent then, relative to D, that justification may yet have little or no cognitive worth. Even so, relative to our environment A, the beliefs of the demon's victim may still be both apt and valuably justified through their inner coherence.

The epistemology defended in this volume—virtue perspectivism—is distinguished from generic reliabilism in three main respects [for a further development of these aspects of virtue perspectivism, see "Intellectual Virtue in Perspective," chapter 16 of *KIP*]:

(a) Virtue perspectivism requires not just any reliable mechanism of belief acquisition for belief that can qualify as knowledge; it requires the belief to derive from an intellectual virtue or faculty.

(b) Virtue perspectivism distinguishes between aptness and justification of belief, where a belief is apt if it derives from a faculty or virtue, but is justified only if it fits coherently within the epistemic perspective of the believer—perhaps by being connected to adequate reasons in the mind of the believer in such a way that the believer follows adequate or even impeccable intellectual procedure. This distinction is used as one way to deal with the new evil-demon problem.

(c) Virtue perspectivism distinguishes between animal and reflective knowledge. For animal knowledge one needs only belief that is apt and derives from an intellectual virtue or faculty. By contrast, reflective knowledge always requires belief that not only is apt but also has a kind of justification, since it must be belief that fits coherently within the epistemic perspective of the believer. This distinction is used earlier in this chapter to deal with the meta-incoherence problem, and it also opens the way to a solution for the generality problem.

Notes

1. Frank Ramsey, *The Foundations of Mathematics and Other Logical Essays* (London: Routledge & Kegan Paul, 1931).

2. David Armstrong, *Belief, Truth and Knowledge* (Cambridge University Press, 1973); Fred Dretske, "Conclusive Reasons," *Australasian Journal of Philosophy* 49 (1971): 122; Alvin Goldman, "What Is Justified Belief?" in George Pappas, ed., *Justification and Knowledge* (Dordrecht: D. Reidel, 1979); Robert Nozick, *Philosophical Explanations* (Cambridge, Mass.: Harvard University Press, 1981), chapter 3; Marshall Swain, *Reasons and Knowledge* (Ithaca, N.Y.: Cornell University Press, 1981).

3. This problem is pointed out by Goldman himself (op. cit., p. 12), and is developed

by Richard Feldman in "Reliability and Justification," *The Monist* 68 (1985): 159-74.

4. This problem is presented by Keith Lehrer and Stewart Cohen in "Justification, Truth and Coherence," *Synthese* 55 (1983): 191-207.

5. This sort of problem is developed by Laurence BonJour in "Externalist Theories of Empirical Knowledge," in *Midwest Studies in Philosophy, Vol. 5: Studies in Epistemology*, ed. P. French et al. (Minneapolis: University of Minnesota Press, 1980).

6. See Goldman, "What Is Justified Belief?" pp. 13-14.

7. Alvin Goldman, *Epistemology and Cognition* (Cambridge, Mass.: Harvard University Press, 1986); idem., "Strong and Weak Justification," in *Philosophical Perspectives, Vol. 2: Epistemology* (1988): 51-71.

8. Some of these are pointed out in my "Beyond Scepticism, to the Best of our Knowledge," *Mind* 97 (1988): 153-88.

9. Goldman, "Strong and Weak Justification," p. 56.

10. I will use the modified sense in what follows because it seems clearly better as an approach to blamelessness; but the substance of the critique to follow would apply also to the unmodified sense of weakly justified belief.

11. Though, actually, it is not really clear how these notions will deal with part (d) of the problem of meta-incoherence: cf. Goldman, *Epistemology and Cognition*, pp. 111-12.

12. As for the generality problem, my own proposed solution appears in "Intellectual Virtue in Perspective [Chapter 16, *Knowledge in Perspective* (Cambridge: Cambridge University Press, 1991)].

13. This sort of distinction between the internal virtue of a subject and his or her (favorable or unfavorable) circumstances is drawn in "How Do You Know?" [Chapter 2 in *Knowledge in Perspective*]. There knowledge is relativized to epistemic community, though not in a way that imports any subjectivism or conventionalism, and consequences are drawn for the circumstances within which praise or blame is appropriate (see especially the first part of Section II).

14. For this sort of distinction, see, e.g., "Methodology and Apt Belief" [Chapter 14 of *Knowledge in Perspective*]. The more generic distinction between external and internal justification may be found in "The Analysis of 'Knowledge That P'" [Chapter 1].

3

Three Forms of Virtue Epistemology

Ernest Sosa

Two Alternatives to Proper Functionalism

According to Alvin Plantinga's explicitly developed proper functionalism, my belief B is warranted only if

(1) it has been produced in me by cognitive faculties that are working properly (functioning as they ought to, subject to no cognitive dysfunction in a cognitive environment that is appropriate for my kinds of cognitive faculties), (2) the segment of the design plan governing the production of that belief is aimed at the production of true beliefs, and (3) there is a high statistical probability that a belief produced under those conditions will be true.[1]

In seeking an alternative to proper functionalism, let us try to understand "working properly" without appealing to notions like "design" or "design plan" or "Divine design" or even "evolutionary design." What then might it mean to say that something is "working properly"? According to a very weak and basic notion of "working properly," all that is required for something to work properly relative to goal G in environment E is that it be ϕ'ing where ϕ'ing in E has a sufficient propensity to lead to G. In line with this, the fuller account above might well be replaced by the following simpler account:

(W)   My belief B is warranted only if it is produced in me by a faculty F in a cognitive environment E such that F is working properly relative to the goal of truth acquisition and error avoidance in environment E.

Account W reduces to a form of "reliabilism," in a broad sense,[2] but one that requires one's warranted beliefs to derive from the operation of "faculties."

Against examples like that of the brain lesion, one can now argue that they involve belief-producing processes, but nothing that could properly be called a "faculty." And we can leave for later work the problem of how to define the concept of a "faculty." This is analogous to solving our problems by appeal to "properly working faculties" and leaving it for later reflection to determine the definition of "properly working faculty." What is more, the problems involved in giving an account of what it is to possess a faculty seem rather less forbidding than those that stand in our way to a clear view of what it is to possess a *properly working* faculty.

"True enough," it may be responded, "it is not so hard to get an account of what it is to have a faculty or an intellectual virtue. But once we have the account it is not at all clear why the brain lesion does not give its victim a faculty, a rather restricted and specialized faculty, but nonetheless a faculty." How are we to preclude such "faculties" from providing warrant? Proper functionalism would require the faculty in question to be part of the design plan, whereas the brain lesion "faculty" is said not to be part of the design plan. But this does not solve the problems we have found with proper functionalism. And there is the further problem that it is not really clear that the brain lesion could not be part of the victim's design plan (newly acquired through the accident or whatever it is that causes the lesion). Insofar as it is unclear that the victim's belief B that he has a brain lesion is *not* caused by a faculty that functions properly, therefore, and insofar as that is *not much more clear* than the claim that B is *not* caused by a "faculty" at all, where's the gain in the move from the simpler requirement to the more complex? Why move from simply requiring that a belief must be caused by a reliable faculty if it is to have warrant to requiring more elaborately that the belief must be caused by a faculty that is not only reliable but is functioning properly in some sense that involves design by conscious agent or impersonal process?

That is just a comparative point, however, and the account of warrant in terms of reliable faculties still lacks a convincing explanation of why the belief in the brain lesion does not derive from the operation of a reliable "faculty." It is small consolation to know that an alternative, more elaborate account still faces a similar problem. We may, nevertheless, compatibly with the simpler account, have the resources to solve our problem, and more generally the generality problem, with no need to appeal either to a theological or to an evolutionary account of faculties and their proper working. Let us now explore some ideas towards such a solution.

In a recent paper,[3] Goldman returns to the debate with Plantinga on reliabilism, and he now offers an account of justified belief "that is in the reliabilist tradition, but departs at a crucial juncture from other versions of reliabilism." The main idea of this new account is that of intellectual virtue, and the approach *is* hence a version of what might well be termed "virtue epistemology." Here is how it is used by Goldman in response to Plantinga's brain lesion counterexample and similar examples. About such examples, Goldman now has this to say:

These include processes engendered by a brain tumor, radiation-caused processes, and the like. In each case Plantinga imagines that the process is reliable, but reports that we would not judge it to be justification conferring. My diagnosis [is as follows:]. . . . At a minimum the processes imagined by Plantinga fail to match any virtue on a typical evaluator's list. So the beliefs are at least non-justified. Furthermore, evaluators may have a prior representation of pathological processes as examples of cognitive vices. Plantinga's cases might be judged (relevantly) similar to these vices, so that the beliefs they produce would be declared unjustified.[4]

In some of Plantinga's cases, it is further supposed that the hypothetical agent possesses countervailing evidence against his belief, which he steadfastly ignores. . . . [This] added element would strengthen a judgment of unjustifiedness according to our theory, because ignoring contrary evidence is an intellectual vice.[5]

Goldman's answer to Plantinga rests on four main components, and I quote from Goldman's paper in each case.

Goldman's new approach:

a. "The basic approach is, roughly, to identify the concept of justified belief with the concept of belief acquired through the exercise of intellectual virtues."[6]

b. The "epistemic evaluator has a mentally stored set, or list, of cognitive virtues and vices. When asked to evaluate an actual or hypothetical case of belief, the evaluator considers the processes by which the belief was produced, and matches these *against* his list of virtues and vices."[7]

c. "Belief-forming processes . . . are deemed virtuous because they (are deemed to) produce a high ratio of true beliefs. Processes . . . are deemed vicious because they (are deemed to) produce a low ratio of true beliefs."[8]

d. "To sum up the present theory, . . . it depicts justificational evaluation as involving two stages. The first stage features the acquisition by an evaluator of some set of intellectual virtues and vices. This is where reliability enters the picture. In the second stage, the evaluator applies his list of virtues and vices to decide the epistemic status of targeted beliefs. At this stage there is no direct consideration of reliability."[9]

The proposal might then be formulated briefly as follows (V):

(Va)   X is an *intellectual virtue* $\supset$ X produces a high ratio of true beliefs.

(Vb)   B is a justified belief $\equiv$ B is a belief acquired through the exercise of one or more intellectual virtues.[10]

However, there are at least two main ways to interpret Vb, one of which is this (where W ranges over possible worlds):

J1   ($\forall$w) B is justified in w $\equiv$ B is acquired in w through the exercise of one or more intellectual virtues that are virtuous in w.

The problem with J1, as Goldman well knows, is the "new evil-demon problem," namely the problem that Descartes's evil-demon victim is not deprived of *ordinary* justification, in some straightforward sense; he still derives his beliefs from sources that we all recognize as justification-conferring: namely, sense experience, memory, etc. The environment changes radically, but the victim retains her repertoire of intellectual virtues. True, because the environment of the victim is so radically abnormal and wrong for her normal virtues, her virtues may not qualify as virtuous *relative to that environment.* But, according to Goldman, despite J1 the fact remains that for "most epistemic evaluators . . . the victims' beliefs are justified." And this seems quite right, again in some relevant sense of "justification." So J1 does not provide an adequate explication of Goldman's new approach nor does it promise a full and illuminating enough account of all that is conveyed by ordinary "epistemic justification." Here now is an alternative:

J2   ($\forall$w) B is justified in w $\equiv$ B is acquired in w through the exercise of one or more intellectual virtues that are virtuous in our *actual* world α.

This is not open to the objections lodged above against J1. However, against this Goldman objects that "there is no evidence that 'the folk' are inclined to relativize virtues and vices to this or that possible world." And it is mainly for this reason that Goldman would reject both J1 and J2. His own proposal is much more modest, and has two main parts, as follows.

Goldman's preferred "list" proposal (L):

La   As evaluator one acquires a list of virtues. These are belief-forming processes or mechanisms that one deems reliable or truth-conducive.

Lb   Actual or hypothetical beliefs are then assessed as justified if and only if they derive appropriately from virtues on the list of the evaluator.

Surprisingly, this new account does not reveal what is involved in the notion of epistemic justification itself. One might conceivably think that there is no such notion, and adopt a prescriptivist or noncognitivist stance here, as does Richard Rorty in his recent writings,[11] but this raises problems. How, for example, could we make sense of the following examples?

(Ea) I wish I had only justified beliefs
(Eb) Someone has justified beliefs
(Ec) Anyone who knows that p has a justified true belief that p

The vocabulary of justification functions quite smoothly in contexts—such as

Ea, Eb, and Ec above—where it cannot coherently function in prescriptivist fashion. The prescriptive aspect of that vocabulary cannot be all or nearly all there is to it, therefore, in contrast to vocabulary such as "Hurray"; and we still wonder what is involved in a belief's being epistemically justified. Of course, the "list" proposal, L above, gives us an account of how an evaluator properly goes about evaluating a belief as epistemically justified. And it even includes an account of why an evaluator includes certain virtues or faculties on her preferred list. But it still does not tell us what it is for a virtue or faculty to be virtuous, and what is involved in a belief's being epistemically justified—not just what is *involved in* an evaluator's evaluating it *as justified, n.b., but what would be involved in its actually being epistemically justified.*

Let V1 and V2 be the relativistic principles that combine Va with J1 and J2, respectively. Thus they amount to the following:

V1   ($\forall$w) B is justified$_1$ in w $\equiv$ B derives in w from the exercise of one or more intellectual virtues that in w virtuously produce a high ratio of true beliefs.

V2   ($\forall$w) B, in w, is justified$_2$ $\equiv$ B derives in w from the exercise of one or more intellectual virtues that in our actual world α virtuously produce a high ratio of true beliefs.

It is a virtue of V1 and V2 that they explain and make sense of the content of the "list" proposal.[12] This also enables one to deal with cases Ea–Ec just above, and with other such cases that seem at least initially problematic for account V. So let's have a closer look at the problem that Goldman charges against our V1 and V2 proposed as accounts of respective concepts of epistemic justification.

The problem is supposed to arise when V1 and V2 are regarded as conceptual analyses of epistemic justification. If one thinks of "conceptual analysis" as just a priori reflection leading to certain conclusions, then there are two sorts of such conceptual analysis worth distinguishing. First, meaning analysis, which leads to conclusions that one would reject only if one failed to understand one or another of the constitutive concepts. Secondly, substantive analysis, which leads to conclusions that are a priori and necessary all right, but which are difficult enough that one could certainly make a mistake without that mistake evincing just a failure to understand the words or concepts involved. Meaning analysis might thus lead to a proposition such as: A sister is a female sibling. Substantive analysis, by contrast, might lead to a proposition like: X is a right action iff X is optimific. One can easily reject a result of substantive analysis, while understanding what one rejects and the constitutive concepts; whereas this does not seem possible with regard to the results of meaning analysis. Note also, finally, that either sort of analysis might lead to propositions that are not necessary biconditionals, such as the following: (a) Abortion is wrong. (b) One ought always to treat people as ends. (c) Kp $\rightarrow$ Bp. (d) There are universals, and these exist necessarily.

Presumably V1 and V2 are offered as substantive analyses. We need to keep this in mind when we consider Goldman's claim that there is no evidence that the folk are inclined to relativize virtues and vices. Compare: "X is far from here," as applied to Alpha Centauri; to San Francisco. "She is tall," as applied by a Pygmy; by a Watusi. "It is 5 p.m.," as said in New York; as said in Tokyo. Or take "It is raining." Where do we check for falling water? The point with all these examples is that often enough we relativize necessarily and automatically through contextual features, even if those features are not present to the consciousness of the speaker(s). Might this not be how it is with regard to the relativization proposed by V1 and V2? Might it not be that the folk are relativizing after all, but in the automatic, context-driven way in which we constantly relativize when we use indexicals, as in the examples above? If so, then we can after all accept V1 and V2.

The main point is now that V1 gives us at least a partial account of "justification" (or of something close to warrant, perhaps, or of aptness), one which offers an alternative to proper functionalism, and one secure against the new evil-demon problem.

Actually, my own preferred alternative to proper functionalist epistemology would supplement Goldman's list account (L). I would add not only principles V1 and V2, with their respective senses or sorts of "justification," but also the following reflections on knowledge and its relations to belief, truth, and faculties.

If a faculty operates to give one a belief, and thereby a piece of direct knowledge, one must have some awareness of one's belief and its source, and of the virtue of that source both in general and in the specific instance. Hence it must be that in the circumstances one would (most likely) believe P iff P were the case—i.e., one (at least probabilistically) tracks the truth (which is part of what is involved in the source's operating virtuously in the specific instance). And that must be so, moreover, because P is in a field of propositions F and one is in conditions C with respect to P, such that believing a proposition in field F, while one is in conditions C with respect to it, would make one very likely to be right. And, finally, one must grasp that one's belief non-accidentally reflects the truth of P through the exercise of such a virtue. This account therefore combines requirements of *tracking* and *nonaccidentality*, of *reliable virtues* or *faculties*, and of *epistemic perspective*.

Even if such an account is right for object-level beliefs and direct knowledge, however, more needs to be said about the sort of doxastic ascent apparently required. It would be absurd to require at *every* level that one must ascend to the next higher level in search of justification. Yet it seems no less absurd to allow a meta-level belief B' to help justify or warrant an object level belief B even though B' is itself unjustified or unwarranted. Perhaps we need to require sufficient comprehensive coherence in a body of beliefs for the justification and aptness of its members. Perhaps such a comprehensively coherent body of beliefs would need to include meta-beliefs concerning object-level beliefs and the faculties that give rise to them, and the reliability of these faculties. Nevertheless, we surely would need also to allow that, at some level of ascent, it will suffice for the justification and aptness of a belief that it be non-accidentally true because of its virtuous source, and through its place in an interlocking. comprehensively coherent system of beliefs, *without* needing to be in turn the object of higher-yet beliefs directed upon it. That sketches my preferred alternative to proper functionalism, but this is not the place to lay it out in detail.[13]

Irenic Conclusion

The disagreement among the two Alvins and myself is actually relatively minor when compared with our large areas of agreement. My agreement is especially extensive with Alvin Goldman, as he has also remarked. Indeed, almost all of his recent paper I find acceptable and more. But, for the reasons given, I prefer to interpret it in line with the general account V1 rather than *just* the "list" proposal L. I can even accept the "list" proposal L, and indeed I do. Our disagreement therefore boils down to this: should proposal L be supplemented with accounts V1 and V2, which would give us a general account of two sorts of epistemic justification, enabling us to explain a cognitivist (and not just prescriptivist) "justification," and which, moreover, would also enable us to explain and support Goldman's "list" proposal? The only objection lodged against adopting V1 and V2 is that "there is no evidence that the folk are inclined to relativize virtues and vices." But this is outweighed by the fact that the pertinent relativization may be contextual and implicit.

As for Alvin Plantinga, we agree that "internal" factors are insufficient to give us an account of knowledge or even of warrant; that we must appeal also to the operative faculties; that for knowledge it is required that such faculties be "operating properly" in a way that is truth conducive; that these faculties must not only "operate properly" in general, relative to the pertinent environment of the subject vis-à-vis the sort of proposition involved, but that, further, they must *not* be misfiring or malfunctioning in the specific instance, and giving knowledge only by accident. However, Plantinga and I disagree in our accounts of what is involved in such "proper functioning," since he wishes to explain this in teleological terms, and ultimately (for the "core" cases, anyhow) in theological terms; whereas my own conception of a faculty that functions properly is very weak indeed, and requires only that such a faculty be generally reliable in the environment that is pertinent, and be virtuous in the specific instance as well, ensuring that the subject would (most likely) believe that p, as he does, if and only if it were the case that p.

Since our disagreements seem *relatively* small when compared with the large areas of agreement, it seems appropriate to view the three approaches as varieties of a single more fundamental option in epistemology, one which puts the explicative emphasis on truth-conducive intellectual virtues or faculties, and is properly termed "virtue epistemology."[14]

＊This selection is a retitled excerpt from a book symposium on Alvin Plantinga's *Warrant and Proper Function* (Oxford, 1993). Plantinga's response follows Sosa's paper and can be found in the same volume of *NOUS*. See Acknowledgments section for full reference.

Notes

1. Alvin Plantinga, *Warrant and Proper Function,* Ch. 11 (Oxford: Oxford University Press, 1993).

2. One that does not require the warrant for one's beliefs to be systematically aligned with the reliability of the *causal processes* even the *internal causal processes* that lead to them.

3. Alvin Goldman, "Epistemic Folkways and Scientific Epistemology," in his collection, *Liaisons: Philosophy Meets the Cognitive and Social Sciences* (Cambridge, MA: MIT/Bradford, 1991): 155-175.

4. Goldman 159.

5. Goldman 160.

6. Goldman 157.

7. Goldman 157.

8. Goldman 160.

9. Goldman 163.

10. Note that Goldman's "justified belief" is very close to Plantinga's "warranted belief" and to my own "apt belief." Such Goldmanian "justification" hence goes beyond mere internal "rationality" and the satisfaction of doxastic obligations, etc.

11. "For the pragmatist . . . 'knowledge' is, like 'truth,' simply a compliment paid to the beliefs which we think so well justified that, for the moment, further justification is not needed." From R. Rorty, "Solidarity or Objectivity?" in volume I of his collected papers, *Objectivity, Relativism, and Truth* (Cambridge: Cambridge University Press, 1991), 24.

12. The sense of "justification" captured by V2 (Va plus J2) is that involved in saying that the evil-demon victim retains justification for perceptual beliefs, etc. Nevertheless, there appears also a concept of epistemically justified (or apt) belief that corresponds to V1 (Va and J1). This would be the concept to use in attributing justification to a superior form of life in another possible world, where they flourish epistemically through faculties that would be useless in our earthly habitat.

13. The approach is developed further in my *Knowledge in Perspective* (Cambridge: Cambridge University Press, 1991); especially in Part IV.

14. Though this last must eventually be qualified in Plantinga's case to make room for the role of *design,* and in my own case to make room for the role of *epistemic perspective.* And of course virtue epistemology is itself a type of generic reliabilism. But generic reliabilism comes in a great variety of types most of which are clearly unacceptable.

4

Ever Since Descartes

Hilary Kornblith

Epistemology has changed dramatically since Descartes, but many of the questions epistemologists address today are no different from the questions Descartes addressed. I begin by raising four sets of questions with which Descartes concerned himself, and explain briefly why Descartes regarded these sets of questions as interchangeable. My main purpose, however, is not historical. Rather, I wish to present an outline of a naturalistic approach to these questions. I will not defend naturalistic epistemology. Instead, I hope to explore what a naturalistic approach to some traditional epistemological questions might look like; it is only through a better understanding of the consequences of naturalizing epistemology that we may hope properly to evaluate it. I will argue that questions that Descartes treated as interchangeable will have to be separated by naturalistically minded epistemologists. In the course of evaluating these questions from a naturalistic point of view, I hope to shed some light on the relation between reliability and justification, the dispute between internalist and externalist theories of justification, and the relation between ethics and epistemology.

I

Here then are some questions with which Descartes dealt.

1. (a) How ought we, objectively speaking, to arrive at our beliefs? What processes available to us, if any, are conducive to truth?
   (b) How ought we, subjectively speaking, to arrive at our beliefs? What processes available to us, if any, seem conducive to truth?
2. (a) What actions ought we, objectively speaking, to perform in order to make the processes by which we arrive at our beliefs more conducive to truth? What actions available to us, if any, will bring it about that our beliefs be formed by processes conducive to truth?
   (b) What actions ought we, subjectively speaking, to perform in order to make the processes by which we arrive at our beliefs more

conducive to truth? What actions available to us, if any, would seem to bring it about that our beliefs be formed by processes conducive to truth?

Descartes regards the two questions under 1 (a) as interchangeable because the question about how we ought to arrive at our beliefs is seen as a question about the appropriate means to achieve certain ends. The goal of cognitive activity, according to Descartes, is the recognition of truth and the avoidance of error. If we wish to know what we ought to believe, then we need only inquire as to which ways of acquiring beliefs are conducive to truth.

We may now proceed as follows. The questions under (1) deal with appropriate processes for arriving at beliefs; those under (2), with appropriate actions for an epistemic agent to take. Questions under (a) deal with objectively correct means of achieving certain ends; those under (b), with the subjectively correct means of achieving those same ends. I will argue, first, that Descartes must assimilate the questions under (2) to those under (1); and second, I will argue that the questions under (a) are assimilated to those under (b). Thus, Descartes may treat all of these questions simultaneously without making any distinctions among them.

Descartes runs the questions under (1) together with those under (2) because he believes that belief is subject to direct voluntary control. In responding to an epistemological version of the Problem of Evil in Meditation IV, Descartes suggests that beliefs may only be arrived at as the product of free choice. Thus, an agent with an answer to the questions under (1) need do nothing more than will that he have the appropriate beliefs.

Descartes's a priorism forces him to run the questions under (a) together with those under (b). Because objectively right principles of reasoning are a priori knowable, the principles that seem right from one's present perspective, given sufficiently careful consideration, are objectively right as well. Descartes' a priorism serves two functions here. First, it is a great equalizer, for there can be no relevant differences between the epistemic situations of any two agents when it comes to determining the right principles of reason. Since background beliefs play no role in an agent's attempt to arrive at these principles, my beliefs may be as different from yours as one likes, and yet the same principles of reasoning will seem to be right to each of us. Second, that the objectively right principles of reason are a priori knowable assures not only that you and I will believe the same principles of reason to be right; it assures that the principles we believe to be right will in fact be right.

It is now widely agreed that belief is not subject to direct voluntary control, and I will take this for granted in what follows. This will be sufficient to pry apart questions under (2) from those under (1). Further, in the spirit of naturalistic epistemology, I will assume that there are no a priori knowable truths, or, at any rate, none of any significance for epistemological theorizing. This will force us to separate questions (a) and (b). Where does this leave us now? What bearing do each of these questions have on the others?

II

Question 1 (a), the question of the reliability of various belief-acquisition processes, is a straightforward empirical question. Once Descartes's overly-optimistic view about the transparency of the mind is rejected, we may set about performing various experiments to resolve this issue. Along with Descartes, I assume the goal of cognitive activity to be the recognition of truth and the avoidance of error. It will be obvious how to generalize this approach to accommodate different understandings of cognitive goals.[1]

What then is the epistemological importance of this kind of psychological investigation? Reliabilists,[2] on the one hand, will want to claim that the discovery that a certain process of belief acquisition is reliable just *is* the discovery that the beliefs that issue from that process are justified. According to this view, the properties in virtue of which a belief is deemed justified are wholly external to the agent whose belief it is, in the following sense: the properties that make a belief justified need not be ones that the agent recognizes the belief to have.

This approach faces a number of prima facie difficulties, difficulties which have been made most vivid, to my mind, by Laurence BonJour.[3] First, as BonJour points out, there are cases in which a belief is arrived at by a reliable process, but does not seem to be justified. BonJour gives an example of a person who is in fact clairvoyant, i.e., whose beliefs are formed by a genuinely reliable process, yet who has never had occasion to confirm the accuracy of her clairvoyant deliverances and who has strong reason to believe that clairvoyance is impossible. Such a person, it seems, is not justified in the beliefs that result from her clairvoyant powers, in spite of the fact that they are reliably arrived at. By the same token, it seems, cases may be constructed of beliefs that are justified, though not reliably produced.

Two strategies are available for responding to this kind of challenge to reliabilism. The first is simply to dig in one's heels and insist that while some of the consequences of reliabilism are prima facie counterintuitive, we must simply revise our intuitions.[4] The strength of this strategy is directly proportional to the strength of the underlying motivation for reliabilism, which I believe to be considerable, and inversely proportional to the strength of alternative strategies for rescuing reliabilism or alternatives to reliabilism. Since I hope to motivate an alternative to reliabilism, I shall have nothing more to say about digging in one's heels.

The second strategy to which the reliabilist may resort is based on a version of reliabilism I presented in "Beyond Foundationalism and the Coherence Theory."[5] My strategy there was as follows. Following Goldman, a process is said to be reliable just in case it tends to produce true beliefs in actual and relevant counterfactual situations. Relevant counterfactual situations, however, are in part determined by the agent's background beliefs. For this reason, two agents may have beliefs formed by the very same type of process, and yet, because their background beliefs differ, one of the processes will tend to produce true beliefs in its relevant counterfactual situations, while the other will not. The result of this approach is that one and the same process type—clairvoyance, say—may be justification-conferring in one individual while it is not justification-conferring in another, so long as their background beliefs differ.

My proposal was not fully worked out; in particular, I did not explain how background beliefs determine relevant alternatives. Nevertheless, the formal structure of my proposal suggests that reliabilism may have the flexibility to handle the difficulties raised by BonJour without simply denying BonJour's intuitions.

In what follows, I want to suggest that the motivation behind my earlier proposal confuses two different questions epistemologists should be asking, questions 1 (a) and 1 (b) above; in so doing, I correctly answered neither of these questions. I will approach this point somewhat obliquely, by returning to the issue of the differences between Descartes and naturalistic philosophers on the original three questions.[6]

III

Let us turn then to question 1 (b): How ought we, subjectively speaking, arrive at our beliefs? What processes available to us, if any, seem conducive to truth?

The role an answer to this question is likely to play in a naturalistic epistemology is radically different from the role Descartes believed it would play. According to Descartes, the question about subjectively correct means of acquiring beliefs is the premier question of epistemology.[7] First, answering this question was believed to be a practical prerequisite to arriving at one's beliefs in an objectively correct way.[8] Second, answering this question was nearly sufficient for arriving at one's beliefs in such a way.[9] With an answer to this question in hand, one need only will to have beliefs that are acquired in an objectively correct way, since, according to Descartes, believing is a basic act, and objectively correct means of acquiring beliefs are knowable a priori. Third, the very same processes of belief acquisition will seem to be correct to all individuals. From the point of view of discovering the correct processes of belief acquisition, all individuals are in an equally good position.[10]

All of these points are denied by naturalistic epistemologists. First, objectively correct belief acquisition processes may take place in the absence of any belief about the correctness of these processes. If there are any innate belief acquisition processes which are de facto reliable, these are surely objectively correct means of acquiring beliefs that are not backed by beliefs about their own rightness.[11] Even if there are no innate processes that are sufficiently reliable, the modification of belief acquisition processes is not always mediated by beliefs about which processes are correct. Less than fully reliable processes may thus be fine-tuned in the absence of beliefs about the correct means of belief acquisition. Second, beliefs about the correct means of acquiring beliefs are nowhere near sufficient for objectively correct belief acquisition. Since it is clear that believing is not a basic act, beliefs about the correct means of acquiring beliefs need not easily be acted upon. Even more important, however, is that belief acquisition processes that seem to be correct, no matter how carefully this judgment is reached, need not in fact be correct. Thus, even if one could simply will that one's beliefs be arrived at in the ways one believes to be correct, this would in no way assure that one's beliefs were arrived at in ways that are correct. Third and finally, since the answer to the question about objectively correct belief acquisition processes is not knowable a priori and thus requires reliance on an individual's background beliefs, there may in principle be as many different answers to the question of subjective rightness as there are individuals. In any case, it is clear that there is no single answer to this question that will be reached by all individuals, no matter how carefully the question is considered.

I don't mean to suggest that if epistemology is to be naturalized we must think of each individual agent as going off in his own private epistemic direction. While naturalists cannot appeal to a priority, Descartes's great epistemic equalizer, naturalists have equalizers of their own. There is, of course, the fact that we all inhabit the same world, and it is this world with which we are each trying to come to terms. In addition, there is the social character of cognition. We communicate with one another and we take what others say as prima facie evidence of truth. On a larger scale there are societally recognized experts on various topics. Finally, there is the similarity of our innate cognitive endowment. These factors cannot, of course, perform the job of equalizer as successfully as Descartes believed a priority could, but they do, I think, account for the limitations in epistemic diversity one finds.

On Descartes's view, question 1 (b) is important precisely because in answering it we simultaneously answer question 1 (a), the question about how we ought, objectively speaking, arrive at our beliefs. Naturalistically minded epistemologists do not have this kind of motivation for answering question 1 (b). Why, then, should they attach any importance to it? Why should one care about the processes that merely seem to be truth-conducive in addition to the processes that are truth conducive?

One obvious answer to these questions is that we have no direct access to the objectively correct means of arriving at our beliefs. There is no way to approach question 1 (a) that is independent of question 1 (b). This need not lead us to Descartes's view that the answers to the two questions are identical, nor to the sceptics' view that question 1 (a) cannot be answered and that it is pointless to try to answer it. Recognition that the answers to these two questions not only can be, but frequently are, different provides a motivation for seeking further information, a motivation one would not have if, like the skeptic, one ignored question 1 (a) altogether.[12]

A second reason for taking question 1 (b) seriously even after we recognize that in answering it we have not automatically answered question 1 (a) is that one important kind of evaluation of an agent's beliefs requires that we understand that agent's answer to question 1 (b). This point can be illuminated by an analogy with moral evaluation.[13] One kind of moral evaluation has us ask, "Was

the agent's action one that the correct moral theory would have him perform?"
A second kind of moral evaluation has us ask, "Was the agent's action one that
was morally correct by his own lights?" In the moral realm, we overlook an
important kind of evaluation if we fail to ask either of these questions. If we ask
only the former question, then we have no idea whether the action manifested
moral integrity. If we ask only the latter question, we have no idea whether the
agent acted in a morally acceptable manner. By the same token, if we ask only
whether an agent's beliefs are formed in a reliable manner, we have no idea
whether the belief is appropriately integrated in the agent's cognitive scheme. If
we ask only whether the agent's belief is arrived at in a way that seems right to
him, we have no idea whether the belief is formed in a way that is actually
conducive to the agent's epistemic goals.

Let us return now to my earlier attempt to provide reliabilism with a
response to the difficulties raised by BonJour. BonJour's examples show that a
belief may be reliably produced and yet, by the agent's lights, be unacceptable.
BonJour concludes that reliability has nothing to do with justification. I, on the
other hand, redefined the parameters that determine reliability so that, on my
account of reliability, it was no longer correct to say that the clairvoyant's
beliefs are reliably produced in spite of the fact that they are regularly and non-
accidentally true. If the present account is correct, my earlier account and
BonJour's make a common error, for both attempt to conflate two epistemic
evaluations into one. On the present account, reliabilism finds its appropriate
domain in answer to question 1 (a); since the proper goal of cognitive activity is
to acquire true beliefs, objectively speaking, one ought to arrive at one's beliefs
by reliable processes. We must now attempt to find out which processes are
reliable. BonJour's examples show that processes that are in fact reliable may
fail to seem so from an agent's subjective perspective. These examples do not in
any way impugn the epistemic value of reliable belief acquisition processes;
rather, in the cases described, there is something wrong with the agent's
subjective perspective. Nevertheless, as BonJour is right to point out, there
would be something epistemically blameworthy about a clairvoyant whose
beliefs, however reliably produced, seemed to her to be unreliably produced;
this is the analog of the moral agent whose actions lack moral integrity in spite
of being dictated by a correct moral theory. The notion of epistemic integrity
that BonJour seeks to elucidate has its appropriate domain in answer to question
1 (b). It is a mistake to try to refashion the concept of reliability, as I did, to
answer this question as well.

If I am right, the dispute between internalism and externalism has been
wrongly understood to the extent that these approaches are seen as rivals.
Rather, some kind of externalist theory needs to be developed in answer to
question 1 (a), and some kind of internalist theory must be developed in answer
to question 1 (b).

IV

We may now turn to the questions under (2), the questions about the appropriate actions to take in order to bring it about that the processes by which we arrive at our beliefs are conducive to truth. These questions deserve separate treatment simply because our beliefs and the processes by which we arrive at them are not subject to direct voluntary control. Even with a theory about how our beliefs ought to be arrived at in hand, some account is needed to explain how we may bring it about that our beliefs be formed in the prescribed way.

Once again, this question divides into an objective and a subjective question. As with question (1), the objective question here is a straightforward empirical matter. We must find out the extent to which our belief forming processes are manipulable, and we must determine the most effective ways to shape our processes of belief acquisition so that they become truth conducive. The empirical investigation required to answer question 2 (a) is thus far more extensive than that required to answer question 1 (a). In spite of this, the evaluation of an action as objectively correct cannot be separated from the evaluation of a process of belief acquisition as objectively correct; objectively correct actions just are those that induce reliable belief acquisition. Unfortunately, in rejecting a priorism, we must recognize that the actions which in fact will achieve this result will not always be such that they will seem to achieve this result from every agent's perspective. The gap between the answer to question 2 (a) and question 2 (b) will thus be just as wide as the gap between answers to questions 1 (a) and 1 (b).

The kinds of actions we may freely undertake to influence the beliefs we have may be divided into two kinds. We may perform acts of seeking and gathering evidence; such acts are designed to exploit the processes of belief acquisition that are already in place. Alternatively, we may perform acts designed to modify these already existing processes; such acts will be analogous to acts designed to modify, develop, or reform habits.[14]

Self-conscious attempts to modify one's belief forming processes may be initiated as a result of awareness of a gap between the processes by which, subjectively speaking, one's beliefs ought to be formed and the processes by which they are in fact formed. That belief acquisition is not directly responsive to the will means that attempts to modify these processes will take time; because the modification takes time, one is left judging that one's beliefs are not arrived at as they should be until the process of modification is completed.

An example will help to make this last point clear. Jones is presenting a certain philosophical theory, call it T, in a seminar. Objections are presented to T that, Jones acknowledges, are devastating. By Jones's own lights, he is no longer justified in believing T. Nevertheless, at a number of subsequent points in the semester, Jones defends various views by showing how they follow from T. Each time this is pointed out to him, he admits his mistake. This disturbs Jones, for he realizes, one the basis of his behavior, that he still believes T even though he also believes himself to be unjustified in believing T. If Jones is responsible, he will try to take various steps to rid himself of the belief that T is correct. This retraining will take time, and until it is completed, Jones will have to acknowledge, again, on the basis of his behavior, that he still believes T. Until Jones succeeds in ridding himself of this belief, he will suffer a lack of integration between his beliefs and the beliefs that are justified by his lights.

How one reacts to this kind of lack of integration reveals a good deal about what one might call one's epistemic character. There is Whitman's notorious approach: "I contradict myself; very well, I contradict myself." No less irresponsible than this complacency, however, is action guided by the desire to achieve epistemic integration by whatever means. Just as Jones might seek to re-integrate his first order beliefs with his epistemic beliefs by giving up his belief T, he might as easily undertake the project of forgetting the evidence against T. This latter project, while it achieves epistemic integration, is not epistemically responsible. We must measure the epistemic responsibility of various acts by the extent to which they are regulated by a desire for the truth, not by the extent to which they are regulated by a desire to achieve epistemic integration.[15]

Each agent, to the extent that he is epistemically responsible, will thus act on her desire for true beliefs. Although this will require that each agent seek the truth in light of the features and limitations of his current perspective, this does not require that she constantly be acting on the basis of beliefs about correct means of acquiring beliefs, for the responsible agent may have very few such beliefs. I may know that my current means of acquiring beliefs stand in need of modification, not because I have some beliefs about correct belief acquisition, but merely because I know that I have made mistakes in certain kinds of situations. Steps can be taken to modify one's means of belief acquisition without knowing intrinsic features of the belief acquisition processes one wants eventually to adopt. I may recognize that someone else's methods of belief acquisition are better than mine, again, not by recognizing intrinsic features of those methods, but merely by noting that he achieves better results than I do. This may lead me to put myself under another person's tutelage, not because I understand his reasons for belief, but simply because I recognize that, whatever his reasons come to, they must have something to recommend them, given his results.[16] Surely this is at least part of the reason people take courses in logic, statistics, and the methodology of science. In this way, one may transcend the limitations of one's current epistemic perspective, or, if one is less fortunate in one's choice of tutors, slip rapidly into a state of epistemic depravity.

There is always the possibility, of course, that the actions that are epistemically responsible are not, in fact, ones that will lead to reliable processes of belief acquisition; this is just to say that the answers to questions 2 (a) and 2 (b) come apart. This should not in any way suggest, however, that perhaps we should not be guided by the desire for true beliefs, any more than the fact that we are morally fallible should suggest that we should not be guided by the desire to do right.

V

I have thus suggested that there are two different objects of epistemic evaluation and that these objects may each be evaluated from either of two perspectives. We may evaluate either the processes by which beliefs are acquired or the freely chosen acts by which these processes are influenced, and we may evaluate either of these objects from either the objective or the subjective perspective. Unlike Descartes, we cannot identify the views from these two perspectives, nor can we reduce the one object of evaluation to the other. The result is that there are four distinct kinds of epistemic evaluation. For any particular belief, we may thus ask each of the following four questions: (1) Was the belief arrived at by way of an objectively correct, that is, a reliable, process?; (2) Was the belief arrived at by way of a subjectively correct process?; (3) Were the actions that were performed objectively correct, i.e., did they induce reliable belief acquisition?; (4) Were the actions that were performed subjectively correct, i.e., were they regulated by a desire for the truth? As has already been noted, questions (3) and (1) are not independent of one another; an affirmative answer to the former requires an affirmative answer to the latter. As the examples already discussed make clear, we thus have three independent kinds of evaluation all told. In this final section, I want to suggest that a proper account of knowledge will have to incorporate each of the three independent evaluations. In particular, I want to suggest that knowledge requires: (1) belief that is arrived at in an objectively correct, that is, reliable, manner; (2) belief that is arrived at in a subjectively correct manner; and (3) belief that is the product of epistemically responsible action, that is, action regulated by a desire for true beliefs.[17]

It is difficult to compare this view about knowledge with other available views precisely because, if I am right, the distinctions I am making here are not typically made.[18] On the other hand, many of the arguments that have been offered for the necessity of various conditions for knowledge, conditions previously thought to be rivals, are ones I simply wish to endorse. Goldman's argument for a reliability constraint, BonJour's argument for an internal constraint,[19] and my own argument for an action-theoretic constraint[20] should all be seen as compatible. When these arguments are conjoined with the distinctions made in this paper, I believe they make a strong case for the account of knowledge I am suggesting here.

Once again, an analogy with ethics is useful, and in particular, an analogy with Aristotle's ethical theory. According to Aristotle, the good individual is one who has appropriate character traits, one who is virtuous. Responsible individuals will attempt to achieve these traits, and they will do so in light of their subjective judgments about which traits are virtues. They will be aided, or hindered, by their upbringing. According to the view of epistemology I am proposing, the ideal epistemic agent is one who has certain intellectual virtues.[21] She is properly attuned to the environment;[22] her beliefs are formed by reliable processes. Epistemically responsible agents will seek to achieve these virtues, and they will do so in light of their subjective judgments about the reliability of their processes of belief acquisition. They will be aided, or hindered, in this project by their innate intellectual endowment.

If this approach is correct, there is a wide range of empirical questions that bears on epistemological issues. What does our innate intellectual endowment look like and to what extent is it conducive to the acquisition of true beliefs? To what extent are our belief acquisition processes modifiable? How may we go about modifying these processes to make them more nearly reliable? These are questions naturalistic epistemologists will need to answer if some of the traditional epistemological questions are to be answered within this new framework.[23]

Notes

1. Since the question about objectively correct means of acquiring beliefs is a question about the appropriate means to achieve the goals of cognition, different accounts of these goals will give rise to different accounts of objectively correct processes. For example, if, along with Daniel Dennett [*Brainstorms* (Montgomery, VT: Bradford Books, 1978), 3-22] and William Lycan [" 'Is' and 'Ought' in Cognitive Science," *Behavioral and Brain Sciences*, 4 (1981): 344-45], we take survival to be the goal of cognition, then objectively correct belief acquisition processes will be those that are conducive to survival. If, along with Hartry Field ["Realism and Relativism," *Journal of Philosophy*, 79 (1982): 553-671], we take these goals to include both reliability and power, the result will be the kind of epistemological relativism that Field favors: favored processes will involve some trade-off between reliability and power, but there will be no fact of the matter as to how this trade-off should be made.

2. The locus classicus here is Alvin Goldman's "What Is Justified Belief?," in G. Pappas, ed., *Justification and Knowledge* (Dordrecht: Reidel, 1978), 1-23.

3. "Externalist Theories of Empirical Knowledge," *Midwest Studies in Philosophy*, V (1980): 53-73.

4. Goldman seems to endorse this approach in discussing a similar problem. See "The Internalist Conception of Justification," *Midwest Studies in Philosophy*, V (1980): 27-51, n11.

5. *Journal of Philosophy*, 77 (1980): 597-612, section VII.

6. I have been influenced here by Fred Schmitt's criticism in his "Reliability, Objectivity and the Background of Justification," *Australasian Journal of Philosophy*, 62 (1984): 1-15.

7. See, for example, Haldane and Ross, *The Philosophical Works of Descartes* (Cambridge: Cambridge University Press, 1931), [hereafter, HR], vol. 1, 86: "That is why, as soon as age permitted me to emerge from the control of my tutors, I entirely quitted the study of letters. And resolving to seek no other science than that which could be found in myself." Also HR I, 98: "For since God has given to each of us some light with which to distinguish truth from error, I could not believe that I ought for a single moment to content myself with the opinions held by others unless I had in view the employment of my own judgment in examining them at the proper time."

8. See, e.g., HR I, 144: I was convinced that I must once for all seriously undertake to rid myself of all the opinions which I had formerly accepted, and commence to build anew from the foundation, if I wanted to establish any firm and permanent structure in the sciences."

9. This does not, I believe, present any difficulty in accounting for Descartes's at-

tempt to answer sceptical doubts. Indeed, I take it that insofar as Descartes believed himself to be successful (in Meditation III) in responding to those doubts, he took himself to have established that subjectively correct means of acquiring beliefs are objectively correct.

10. "For as to reason or sense . . . I would fain believe that it is to be found complete in each individual." HR I, 82. In an earlier passage, Descartes also suggests that there is evidence that "the power of forming a good judgment and of distinguishing the true from the false . . . is by nature equal in all men." HR I, 81.

11. This is not to say that we cannot come to have beliefs about the reliability of innate belief acquisition processes, but only that these beliefs are not themselves innate.

12. A similar point is made in Stephen Darwall, *Impartial Reason* (Ithaca, NY: Cornell University Press, 1983), 44.

13. The analogy with moral evaluation here has also been pointed out in John Pollock's "A Plethora of Epistemological Theories," in G. Pappas, ed. (cited in n2, above), 93-113. It will be clear that I am heavily indebted to Pollock, although the positive claims I defend are dramatically different from his.

14. See also my "Justified Belief and Epistemically Responsible Action," *Philosophical Review*, 102 (1983): 33-49, and John Heil, "Doxastic Agency," *Philosophical Studies*, 43 (1983), 355-64.

15. It is interesting to approach Leon Festinger's work on cognitive dissonance with this kind of evaluation in mind. See A *Theory of Cognitive Dissonance* (Stanford, CA: Stanford University Press, 1957).

16. The extent to which this common practice fails to conform to standard epistemological accounts is noted in Thomas Kuhn, *The Structure of Scientific Revolutions* (Chicago: University of Chicago Press, 1970), passim.

17. This last condition should not be read as requiring that actions with epistemological motivation be found in the causal ancestry of every item of knowledge. Just as moralists have often spoken of the ideal of action regulated by a desire to do right without thereby committing themselves to the suggestion that agents should always be thinking about morality, the requirements of epistemic responsibility do not necessitate that agents should always be thinking about the truth. The point about the moral ideal is convincingly presented by Marcia Baron in "The Alleged Moral Repugnance of Acting From Duty," *Journal of Philosophy*, 81 (1984):197-220.

18. But see Pollock (in work cited in n2, above), and some of the remarks in Thomas Nagel's "Moral Luck" and "Subjective and Objective," in his *Mortal Questions* (Cambridge: Cambridge University Press, 1979).

19. I do not mean to be endorsing BonJour's account of how the internal constraint is to be met, merely his insistence that there is such a constraint to meet.

20. In "Justified Belief and Epistemically Responsible Action," cited in n14, above.

21. That a proper theory of knowledge must be cast in terms of intellectual virtues has also been suggested by Ernest Sosa, "The Raft and the Pyramid," *Midwest Studies in Philosophy*, V (1980): 3-25, and John Heil, "Believing What One Ought," *Journal of Philosophy*, 80 (1983): 752-65.

22. This corresponds nicely with a theme in Aristotle's ethics stressed recently by L. A. Kosman, that the virtuous agent not only performs the correct actions, but is also properly affected by his environment. See "Being Properly Affected: Virtues and Feelings in Aristotle's Ethics," in A. Rorty, ed., *Essays on Aristotle's Ethics* (Berkeley, CA: University of California Press, 1980), 103-16.

23. I have received helpful comments from Alvin Goldman, John Heil, David Shatz,

George Sher, Fred Schmitt, and especially William Alston and David Velleman. After this paper was written, John Pollock sent me a copy of his "Epistemic Norms"; Pollock and I reached many of the same conclusions independently. Work on this paper was in part supported by a University of Vermont Summer Research Grant.

Part II

Knowledge and Skepticism

5

Virtue, Skepticism, and Context

John Greco

I. Agent Reliabilism

Taking skeptical arguments seriously pushes us in a particular direction in epistemology. Specifically, it pushes us toward externalism and reliabilism. There are serious problems with generic reliabilism, however; serious enough to cause some philosophers to reject the position out of hand. One problem is that beliefs can be reliably formed by accident, for example by arbitrarily adopting a method that, unknown to the believer, happens to be reliable. This would seem to violate a "no accident" condition on knowledge. A second problem is that beliefs can be reliably formed and yet subjectively inappropriate. This seemingly violates a "subjective justification" condition on knowledge, and reliabilism has been widely criticized on this point.

Agent reliabilism addresses both problems by drawing on the resources of virtue theory. The main idea is to define knowledge in terms of virtuous cognitive character, and to define virtuous character in terms of proper motivation and reliable success. This takes care of the "no accident" condition on knowledge, in that true belief that is formed through an agent's reliable character is not an accident in any relevant sense. It takes care of the "subjective justification" condition as well, since there is proper motivation, and as Aristotle would say, "the moving principle is within the agent." Roughly, a belief is both subjectively and objectively justified, in the sense required for knowledge, when it is produced by a properly motivated, reliable cognitive character. Agent reliabilism is therefore a kind of virtue epistemology, in the sense that it makes cognitive or intellectual virtue central in the analysis of important epistemic concepts. As such, it is an improvement over previous versions of reliabilism, including process reliabilism, method reliabilism, and evidence reliabilism. All of these fall to one or both of the two problems reviewed above, precisely because they fail to ground knowledge in the virtuous character of the knower.[1]

Agent reliabilism also has the resources to address an important kind of skeptical argument, one that trades on the assumption that knowledge must discriminate truth from alternative possibilities. For example, it is claimed that we cannot know that we are sitting by the fire if we cannot discriminate this state of affairs from the possibility that we are disembodied spirits deceived by an evil demon. A promising strategy in response to this kind of skeptical reasoning is to distinguish between relevant and irrelevant alternative possibilities, and to claim that knowledge requires only that we discriminate among the relevant ones. The problem, then, is to give a theoretical account of what makes an alternative possibility relevant or irrelevant. Agent reliabilism can do just this.

The main idea is that virtues in general are abilities to achieve some result, and abilities in general are functions of success in relevantly close possible worlds. In other words, to say that someone has an ability to achieve X is to say that she would be successful in achieving X in a range of situations relevantly similar to those in which she typically finds herself. But then possibilities that do not occur in typical situations are irrelevant for determining whether a person has some ability in question. For example, it does not count against Babe Ruth's ability to hit baseballs that he cannot hit them in the dark. Likewise, it does not count against our perceptual abilities that we cannot discriminate real tables and fires from demon-induced hallucinations. But then our inability to rule out hypothetical demon scenarios is irrelevant to whether we have knowledge, and the skeptical scenario is not a relevant possibility in that sense. Below I will expand on this main idea. In the course of the discussion we will consider the role of context in knowledge and knowledge attributions.

II. The Skeptical Problem

Consider Descartes's belief that he is sitting by the fire in a dressing gown. Presumably he has this belief because this is how things are presented to him by his senses. However, Descartes reasons, things could appear to him just as they do even if he were in fact not sitting by the fire, but was instead sleeping, or mad, or the victim of an evil deceiver. The point is not that these other things might well be true, or that they ought to be taken seriously as real possibilities. Rather, it is that Descartes's evidence does not rule these possibilities out. And if it does not rule them out, then it cannot be very good evidence for his belief that he is sitting by the fire. Descartes's reasoning follows from a seemingly obvious principle about adequate evidence. Namely, a body of evidence does not adequately support a conclusion unless that evidence effectively rules out other possibilities that are inconsistent with that conclusion. What Descartes notices is that this general principle has skeptical consequences when applied consistently to our perceptual beliefs about objects in the world. Our evidence in such cases is sensory experience, but that experience fails to rule out a host of alternative possibilities.

We get different versions of Descartes's argument according to how we understand the idea of evidence "ruling out" an alternative possibility. Perhaps the most common way to understand the idea is epistemically, so that to rule out a possibility is to know that it is false, or to have good reason for believing that it is false, or to be certain that it is false, etc. But this way of understanding the phrase robs the skeptical argument of its force, for on this understanding it seems wrong that I cannot rule out alternative possibilities. Don't I know, for example, that I am not dreaming? Most of us have the strong intuition that we do know that we are not dreaming in the typical case, and so no skeptical argument will have force if it begins from the assumption that we do not know this.

Someone wishing to defend the skeptic might challenge the claim that we have similar intuitions regarding philosophical dreams. Do I know that my whole life is not a dream, as it would be if I were the victim of an evil deceiver? Or consider the possibility that I am the victim of a psychology experiment in the year 3000. How do I know that I am in fact sitting at a table writing on a computer? Perhaps I am a disembodied brain hooked up to a computer a thousand times more powerful, and programmed to stimulate my severed nerve endings so as to create exactly the experiences I am having now. If we think of the dream possibility in either of these more radical ways, the argument goes, then it no longer seems obvious to us that we know that we are not dreaming. But doesn't it? Don't I know that both these radical dream scenarios are false because I know that I am sitting at my desk writing on my computer? I must confess, I think it *is* obvious that I do know these things. But even if some would disagree, it surely is not obvious that I do *not* know that these dream scenarios are false. And so interpreted this way, the skeptical argument still depends on a premise that does not seem obvious or compelling.[2]

There is at least one other interpretation of "ruling out" available, and I think that it generates a powerful skeptical argument. Suppose that we think of evidence ruling out alternatives in terms of discriminating those alternatives from the state of affairs that is believed to hold.[3] For example, often my evidence for the belief that my wife has come home from work is that I hear her voice announcing her arrival. This auditory experience discriminates her being home from my neighbor's yelling for his children and from my cat's whining for her dinner. It also discriminates that state of affairs from the television set's being on, but not from my wife having set up a tape recorder so as to fool me into thinking she has come home. The current idea is that this is how we should understand the skeptical argument from Descartes. A set of evidence gives me knowledge only if it discriminates the state of affairs I believe to hold from others that are inconsistent with it.

More exactly, the current proposal is this.

> Df. 1   A set of evidence E rules out alternatives to a belief p for a person S if and only if E discriminates p's being true from possibilities that are inconsistent with p's being true.

And,

> Df. 2   E discriminates p's being true from possibilities $q1 \ldots qn$ for S if and only if E would cause S to believe that p is true when p is

true, and E would not cause S to believe that p is true when any of q1. . . .qn is true.

We then have the following interpretation of key premises in Descartes's argument.

(D3)   1. S can know that p is true on the basis of evidence E only if E discriminates p's being true from possibilities that are inconsistent with p's being true.
        2. My evidence for my belief that I am sitting by the fire is my sensory experience.
        3. It is a possibility that I am not sitting by the fire but only dreaming that I am.
        4. Therefore, I can know that I am sitting by the fire only if my sensory experience discriminates my sitting by the fire from my only dreaming that I am. (1,2,3)
        5. But my sensory experience does not discriminate these possibilities for me.
        6. Therefore, I do not know that I am sitting by the fire. (4,5)

At this point the argument is starting to look good. One might deny premise (1), and I think that ultimately this is the right move to make. But no one should think that (1) jumps out as obviously false, or that denying (1) should be considered uncontroversial. Consider that (1) is equivalent to the following claim: that one's evidence can give rise to knowledge only if it discriminates situations where one's belief is true from situations where it is not. That is not implausible, and many would consider it to be obviously true. Especially when considered outside the context of the skeptical argument, the proposition might pass as a platitude.

But in fact premise (1) of (D3) is false, or so I will argue. This diagnosis of the argument presents itself when we consider that (1) treats all alternative possibilities the same way. In other words, (1) requires that our evidence discriminate the truth of our belief from every alternative possibility whatsoever. But it is questionable whether our ordinary concept of knowledge in fact requires that our evidence do this. Knowing that my wife is home from work requires that I have evidence that discriminates this situation from the one in which only my cat is home and is whining loudly for her dinner. But it does not require, or so I would think, that I can discriminate my wife's being home from her being abducted by aliens and replaced with a convincing look-a-like. It had better not require that, for by hypothesis the imposter is convincing, and so my evidence could not discriminate this possibility from the one in which my wife is home. This possibility, like the evil genius and brain in a vat possibilities, is designed so that my evidence cannot discriminate between it and the usual things that I believe on the basis of that evidence.

These last considerations suggest that not all alternative possibilities to a knowledge claim carry the same epistemic weight. To know that someone has committed murder we need to rule out suicide. And to know that my wife is home I must rule out the possibility that it is only my cat or a neighbor that is making some noise. I do not need to rule out other things that are nevertheless clearly possibilities in some broad sense. Some possibilities seem to be *relevant*, in the sense that they do need to be ruled out in order to have knowledge, whereas other possibilities seem not to be relevant in that sense.

This suggests that we revise premise (1) of (D3) as follows, requiring an analogous revision in premise (3) to keep the argument valid.

(D4)   1. S can know that p is true on the basis of evidence E only if E discriminates p's being true from all *relevant* possibilities that are inconsistent with p's being true.
2. My evidence for my belief that I am sitting by the fire is my sensory experience.
3. It is a relevant possibility that I am not sitting by the fire but only dreaming that I am.
4. Therefore, I can know that I am sitting by the fire only if my sensory experience discriminates my sitting by the fire from my only dreaming that I am. (1,2,3)
5. But my sensory experience does not discriminate these possibilities for me.
6. Therefore, I do not know that I am sitting by the fire. (4,5)

On this interpretation premise (1) now seems true. But now a different diagnosis of the argument suggests itself. First, we can make a distinction between normal dreams that occur in sleep, and "philosophical" dreams such as those caused by evil demons and supercomputers in futuristic psychology experiments. We can then say that the possibility that I am fooled by a normal dream is relevant in some cases, but my sensory experience can usually rule it out. In other words, my sensory experience can usually discriminate waking life from a normal dream. Philosophical dreams cannot be so discriminated, but they are not relevant possibilities. So if by dreams we mean normal dreams, then premise (5) of (D4) is false. But if by dreams we mean philosophical dreams, then premise (3) of (D4) is false. Either way, the skeptical argument is unsound.

III. Two Tasks for Working Out This Approach

The relevant possibilities approach has been a popular one, but it needs to be worked out further. First, we want an account of what makes a possibility relevant and why the skeptical hypotheses do not constitute relevant possibilities. In other words, we need an account of "relevant possibility" that a) accords with our pre-theoretical intuitions about which possibilities need to be ruled out and which do not in ordinary cases of knowledge, and b) rules that the skeptical possibilities do not need to be ruled out. Secondly, we do not want our account to be ad hoc. What we would like is an account of knowledge that explains why our account of relevant possibility has the content that it does.

Providing an account of "relevant possibility"

It has been popular to attempt an account of relevant possibility in terms of objective probability.[4] The problem with this solution is that we lack an adequate account of 'objectively probable.' The most natural way to understand that notion is in terms of percentage of a reference class. However, it is hard to see how a reference class could be specified in the present case, or even what a reference class would begin to look like here. For this reason attempts to define relevant possibility along these lines have failed.[5]

I propose that we understand relevant possibility in a different way, making use of the possible world semantics of modal logic. The idea is that it is a *logical* possibility that I am a brain in a vat hooked up to a supercomputer programmed to deceive me. In other words, there are possible worlds in which this is the case. But such possible worlds are 'far away' from the actual world. There are no close possible worlds in which I am a brain in a vat, where 'closeness' is to be understood, roughly, in terms of overall world similarity. The current proposal is then this: a possibility is relevant if it is true in some close possible world, irrelevant if not. This proposal explains many of our pre-theoretical intuitions about which possibilities need be ruled out and which do not in order to know, and it explains why the skeptical possibilities do not need to be ruled out.

More work needs to be done, of course. Most importantly, the proposed account of relevant possibility is too weak as it stands—more possibilities are epistemically relevant than those that are true in close possible worlds. Also, we will have to say more about what constitutes world closeness in order to make the account more informative. But this is the main idea for completing the first task. The details presented below will fix up the account by making it stronger in the required way and by making the notion of world closeness more informative.

Providing an account of knowledge to support our account of relevant possibility

I have already said that agent reliabilism can provide a theoretical understanding of what makes a possibility relevant. In other words, the theory can explain why some possibilities need to be ruled out to have knowledge and why others do not. The main idea was as follows. Cognitive virtues are a kind of power or ability. Abilities in general are stable and successful dispositions to achieve certain results under certain conditions. But abilities can not be defined in terms of actual conditions only. Rather, when we say that someone has an ability we mean that she would be likely to achieve the relevant results in a variety of conditions similar to those that actually obtain. In the language of possible worlds, someone has an ability to achieve some result under relevant conditions only if the person is very likely to achieve that result across close possible worlds. But if knowledge essentially involves having cognitive abilities, and if abilities are dispositions to achieve results across close possible worlds, then this explains why possibilities are relevant only when they are true in some close possible world. Specifically, only such possibilities as these can undermine one's cognitive abilities. In an environment where deception by demons is actual or probable, I lack the ability to reliably form true beliefs and avoid false beliefs. But if no such demons exist in this world or similar ones, they do not affect my cognitive faculties and habits.

In section IV I present and defend a more detailed account of relevant possibility. In section V I further explore the idea of a cognitive virtue by offering a possible worlds analysis for abilities in general and cognitive abilities in particular. In section VI I show how agent reliabilism explains the account of relevant possibility presented in section IV. Finally, section VII further considers the role of context in knowledge and knowledge attributions.

IV. The Relevant Sense of 'Relevant Possibility'

Our first task is to provide an account of relevant possibility such that a) knowledge requires only that our evidence rule out (discriminate) that kind of possibility, and b) the skeptical possibilities involving brains in vats and evil demons turn out not to be relevant possibilities. As a first try consider the following account of relevant possibility, which I believe comes close to meeting our two criteria above. Let us say that a possible world W is close to a possible world W' if and only if, roughly, W is very similar to W'. Then,

> q is a relevant possibility with respect to S's knowing that p is true =
>   i. if q is true, then S does not know that p is true, and
>   ii. in some close possible world, q is true.

What is important to notice is that the above account effectively disallows that evil demons and brains in vats are relevant possibilities. So long as the actual world is anything like we think it is, there are no close worlds in which we are disembodied spirits or brains in vats. And therefore the current account has important consequences for the force of (D4). Premise (3) of that argument implies that the skeptical scenarios are relevant possibilities. On the current account this amounts to saying that the skeptical possibilities are true in some close possible world. But of course there is no reason whatsoever to accept that claim. Presumably such scenarios are logically possible, so that each is true in some far off possible world. But we have no reason to believe that either is true in any close possible world.

Therefore, if the above account of relevant possibility is correct, then it seriously undermines the force of the skeptical argument. The claim that the account is correct is supported by reflection on two further examples. First, imagine that you see Tom Grabit take a book from the library shelf and put it into his bag.[6] On the basis of this evidence you form the belief that Tom Grabit took a library book. Unknown to you, however, Tom has a twin brother Jack, who was also in the library at the time you saw Tom take the book. Intuitively, you do not know that it was Tom who took the book, since if Jack had taken the book you would have been fooled into thinking that Jack was Tom. In order for you to know that Tom took the book you must be able to rule out the possibility that it was Jack who took the book. But consider the case where Tom does not have a twin brother. Must you still be able to rule out the possibility that it was his twin brother who took the book, in order to know that Tom took the book? Intuitively the answer is no. In the case where there is no twin brother it is enough that you saw Tom take the book.

As a second example consider the case of the barn façades. You are driving through a part of the country where, unknown to you, the local residents have constructed sides of barns in order to fool passers-by into thinking that the community is wealthier than it actually is. You drive by a real barn and form the belief that there is a barn ahead. In this case the proposition that you see a barn façade rather than a barn is a relevant possibility. You do not know the latter if you cannot rule out the former. But must you *always* be able to rule out the possibility of a barn façade before you can know that you see a barn from the highway? Intuitively the answer is no, and this is in fact how the account rules.[7]

The proposed account of relevant possibility handles the above cases well. However, it is not quite right and some revisions are necessary. This is because there are possibilities that are not true in any close possible world, but which nevertheless need to be ruled out in order for someone to have knowledge. Consider a revised version of the Tom Grabit example. Everything is as before except that Tom Grabit has no twin brother. However, S believes that Tom does have a twin brother. It seems to me that S's evidence must rule out the possibility that Tom's twin brother took the book, even though the possibility is not true in any close possible world (since Tom in fact has no twin brother). Another version of the Tom Grabit example raises a different problem. Suppose that Tom does not have a twin brother and S does not believe that Tom has a twin brother, but S ought to believe that Tom has a twin brother—S has good reason for believing that Tom has a twin brother. Again, it seems to me that in such a case the possibility that Tom's twin took the book must be ruled out by S's evidence. In these cases the problem is not that the possibility is true in some close possible world, but that S believes, or ought to believe, that the possibility is likely to be true. Fortunately the account can be easily revised to accommodate both of the above cases. Thus we have,

> (RP) q is a relevant possibility with respect to S's knowing that p is true =
>   i. if q is true, then S does not know that p is true; and
>   ii. either   a) in some close possible world q is true, or
>   b) S believes that q is likely to be true, or
>   c) S ought to believe that q is likely to be true.

I believe that (RP) covers all and only those possibilities that must be ruled out in cases of knowledge. Secondly, (RP) continues to exclude the skeptical scenarios as relevant possibilities, assuming that there are no brains in vats or victims of evil demons in our environment, and assuming that we neither believe nor ought to believe that there are.

Before moving on we should address a possible misconception. Namely, one might think that the present strategy against (D4) merely ends in a stalemate with the skeptic. This is because the skeptic will insist that, for all we know, some skeptical hypothesis is true in some close possible world, perhaps because it is true in the actual world. But this kind of objection is misguided. We deemed Descartes's original argument to have force precisely because it claimed only that the skeptical scenarios were in some sense possibilities, and it does seem that we have to allow that assumption. But we have now pushed the argument so that premise (3) of (D4) claims that the scenarios are *relevant* possibilities, and on the present interpretation this amounts to the claim that in some close possible world I *am* a brain in a vat or the victim of an evil deceiver. But now the argument is flawed if it depends on that premise. We will have found an assumption that we need not accept, and that in fact there is no reason whatsoever to accept.

In effect this shows that there is only one way to challenge the present strategy against (D4). Namely, one must challenge the account of relevant possibility in (RP). For if that account is right, clearly the claim that the skeptical scenarios are relevant is implausible. I will now go in the other direction, however. That is, I will now defend the account in (RP) by showing how it is explained by agent reliabilism.

V. A Theory of Virtues and a Virtue Theory of Knowledge

The central idea of agent reliabilism is that knowledge arises from cognitive abilities or powers. An ability in turn is a stable and successful disposition for achieving some result under appropriate conditions. What we need now is a more detailed account of what this amounts to. I will proceed by offering an account of abilities in general, and then an account of cognitive abilities in particular. After that it will be relatively easy to see how the resulting theory explains the proposed account of relevant possibility in (RP).

What is an ability?

Roughly, an ability in general is a stable disposition to achieve some result under appropriate conditions. For example, we say that Don Mattingly has the ability to hit baseballs. By this we mean that Mattingly has a disposition to hit baseballs under normal conditions for playing baseball. Notice that we do not require that Mattingly have perfect success, nor do we require that he have a disposition for hitting baseballs under just any conditions. In general, how high a success rate is required will depend on the kind of ability in question. Likewise, what conditions are appropriate will depend on the kind of ability in question, as well as on other contextual matters.

The above remarks might suggest the following account of having an ability to achieve a result.

A1.   S has an ability to achieve result R in conditions C = S has a high rate of success achieving R when S is in C in actual cases.

The current proposal, however, is both too weak and too strong. First, A1 does not distinguish between having an ability to achieve R and having success achieving R due to good luck. Thus it is possible that in all actual cases of swinging at baseballs, I hit the ball due to amazingly good luck. My bat just happens to be where it ought to on every pitch. In that case I would have great success hitting baseballs in actual cases, but it would be false that I have an ability to hit baseballs. Or consider the case of Mr. Magoo. Magoo in fact is highly successful in avoiding harm, meaning that in the actual world Magoo rarely comes to harm. But we would not say that Magoo has an ability to avoid harm, since he avoids harm only by amazingly good luck. (An inch to the left and that anvil lands on his head!)

For a similar reason the current proposal is too strong. For it might be that S does have an ability to achieve R, but fails in nearly all actual cases due to amazingly bad luck. Just as it is possible to have an ability to achieve R and yet fail in some actual case, it is possible (even if improbable) to have the ability and yet fail in nearly all actual cases. Finally, it makes sense to say that S has an ability to achieve R even if S never achieves R because S never comes under the appropriate conditions. Thus it makes perfect sense to say that you have the ability to count by fives to a thousand, even if you never do so because no actual situation ever calls for it.

These last considerations suggest that having an ability is not a function of what S does in actual cases, but of what S would do in possible cases. And this suggests the following subjunctive account of having an ability.

A2.   S has an ability to achieve result R in conditions C = if S were in C then S would achieve R with a high rate of success.

But this account is also both too weak and too strong, and for somewhat similar reasons as with A1. First, consider the case where S is often in C and has success achieving R in actual cases due to good luck. Then the subjunctive conditional in A2 is true but S does not have an ability to achieve R. Second, consider the case where S is often in C but fails to achieve R in actual cases due to bad luck. Then the subjunctive conditional in A2 is false, but it is possible that S does have an ability to achieve R. I suggest that the following account will avoid all of the problems that we have raised for A1 and A2.

A3.   S has an ability to achieve result R in conditions C = across the range of close possible worlds where S is in C, S achieves R in C with a high rate of success.

Two examples will help to explain the motivation for A3. First, consider that in some close possible world a fair coin will come up heads one hundred times in one hundred tosses. However, across a range of close possible worlds the coin will come up heads fifty percent of the time, since improbable strings of heads will be offset by improbable strings of tails. Now let us consider an example of an ability. There is a close possible world where Mattingly hits .000 for the month of April, due to an improbable string of bad luck. But across the range of close possible worlds Mattingly presumably hits near .300, since strings of bad luck are offset by strings of good luck. The current proposal is that this is why Mattingly has the ability to hit baseballs; he in fact hits near .300 in the actual world, but more importantly he hits near .300 across the range of close possible worlds.

Of course A3 is vague in many ways. It does not say how high the rate of success across close possible worlds must be, or which conditions are the relevant ones. But this is as it should be. First, which conditions are relevant will depend on the ability in question, as well as on context. For example, when we say that Mattingly can hit baseballs we obviously do not mean at night and without lights, but this is well understood in the context of a conversation about baseball. Similarly, contextual features set different boundaries when we say that Mattingly has the ability to hit baseballs and when we say that a little leaguer has the ability to hit baseballs.

Context does not eliminate vagueness completely, but this too is as it should be. This is because the concept of an ability is vague even within contexts. For example, when I claim that a rookie has the ability to hit baseballs do I mean that he can hit in pressure situations? Do I mean that he can hit against the very best pitchers in the league? Normally my claim will be at least somewhat vague in these respects. Sometimes closer attention to context or further stipulation will eliminate such vagueness and sometimes they will not.

Other kinds of vagueness are associated with the concept of world closeness, and these might seem more problematic. We said that closeness is a function of overall world similarity, but what kinds of similarity count and what degree of similarity is important? Again, this will depend on the kind of ability in question, and it will depend on contextual features as well. But also again, fixing kind of ability and contextual features will not eliminate all the vagueness involved.

Having said all this, we can nevertheless give our concept of world closeness a substantial degree of content. First, what counts for world closeness is partly determined by our account as it stands. Specifically, since A3 relativizes abilities to a range of relevant conditions, only worlds in which S is in such conditions will be relevant for consideration. Second, it seems clear that when we say that S has an ability, we mean that S has the ability as S is actually constituted. For example, when we say that Mattingly can hit baseballs, this does not become false because in some possible worlds Mattingly is injured or drugged or out of shape and therefore can no longer hit baseballs. For similar reasons it is clear that only worlds with the same laws of nature as hold in the actual world will count as close.

The issue can be pressed, however. Which aspects of S's constitution are relevant for determining world closeness, where the issue is whether S has the ability to achieve result R in conditions C? The answer seems to be that it is those aspects of S's constitution which, given the actual laws of nature and given conditions C, are relevant to whether S's actions in C result in producing R. In other words, we will want to keep constant any characteristics of S that, given the laws of nature and the relevant conditions, figure into whether the relevant results occur.

For example, we say that Mattingly has the ability to hit baseballs because, given Mattingly's actual constitution, the normal conditions for hitting baseballs, and the laws of nature that actually hold, Mattingly's actions result in a high ratio of hit baseballs. This occurs in the actual world but it would also occur if the world were a little different—if the pitch came in a bit lower, Mattingly would still hit the baseball. On the other hand, it makes no sense to say that Mattingly lacks an ability to hit baseballs because in some possible worlds he is near-sighted. This is because the constitution of Mattingly's eyes figures importantly into the laws of nature that govern the occurrence of the result in question.

We can now make the notion of world closeness more informative. Let us define S's R-constitution as those characteristics of S that, given the actual laws of nature, are relevant to whether S's actions result in producing R when S is in conditions C. Then we may say that a world W is close to the actual world (in the sense relevant to whether S has the ability to produce R in C), only if S has the same R-constitution in W as in the actual world, and only if the laws of nature that hold in W are the same as those that hold in the actual world. A3 should be read with this characterization of world closeness in mind.

According to the above suggestion, the conditions for S's having an ability involve four dimensions, three of which are kept constant and one of which is allowed to vary. To determine whether S has an ability in question we keep constant the actual laws of nature, the set of conditions associated with the ability, and S's R-constitution associated with the ability. We then vary the other conditions of the environment, and we look at S's success rates in the worlds where such variations are kept relatively minor. What kind of environmental variations are important and what makes a variation relatively minor? This is left vague in A3, but context will serve to eliminate much of that vagueness.

What is a cognitive ability?

A cognitive ability has the form of an ability in general, but with the cognitive end of arriving at true beliefs and avoiding false beliefs. Therefore a cognitive ability, in the sense intended, is an ability to arrive at truths in a particular field and to avoid believing falsehoods in that field, when under relevant conditions.

More formally,

(CA)   S has a cognitive ability A(C,F) with respect to proposition p =
         there is a field of propositions F and a set of conditions C such that
                    i. p is in F, and
                    ii. across the range of close possible worlds where S is in C,
                        S has a high rate of success with respect to believing
                        correctly about propositions in F.[8]

The above account successfully distinguishes cognitive abilities such as vision, memory, and reliable reasoning from non-abilities such as dreaming, wishful thinking, and hasty generalization. Thus under normal conditions vision is a cognitive ability with respect to determining color properties of middle-size objects. This is because in the actual world and across close possible worlds we have a propensity to believe correctly about such propositions when in normal conditions. In other words, across these worlds we have a high rate of success. However, we have no such propensity with respect to beliefs caused by dreaming. Even if by coincidence someone were to enjoy actual success in forming true beliefs through dreaming, there would be no high rate of success across close possible worlds and so the lucky dreamer would not count as having a cognitive ability on the above account.

Similarly, (CA) correctly distinguishes between the two Tom Grabit cases and between the two barn façade cases. Thus in the case where Tom has no twin brother, S will very likely be correct about Tom taking the book in the relevant worlds. But in the case where Tom has an indistinguishable twin brother, S's rate of success will drop significantly in close worlds. Likewise, in the case where there are no barn façades in the environment, S will have a propensity to believe correctly about the existence of barns in the relevant worlds. But in the case where there are barn façades in the environment, S's rate of success will drop dramatically across close worlds.

With the present account of cognitive abilities in place we may now look at how agent reliabilism explains the account of relevant possibility in section IV.

VI. Agent Reliabilism and Relevant Possibilities

The way in which agent reliabilism explains clause (iia) of (RP) is straightforward. According to agent reliabilism, knowledge is true belief grounded in cognitive abilities. And according to our account of abilities, they are a function of S's rates of success across close possible worlds. But then possibilities that are true only in far-off worlds do not affect S's abilities in the actual world. If I were a brain in a vat in the actual world, then across close possible worlds I would lack a high rate of success with respect to forming true beliefs about my environment. But so long as I am not a brain in a vat, this mere possibility does not affect my success rate in the actual world and in close possible worlds. Therefore, the mere possibility that I am a brain in a vat is irrelevant to whether I know.

The above result is obvious even when we grant that the concept of world similarity is vague and that this vagueness infects our account of knowledge. This is because it is clear that the world in which I am a brain in a vat is a very far world from the actual world, given that the actual world is anything like we think it is. For although our concept of world similarity is vague, it is not vague in all ways. One stipulation that was made on world closeness was that a world W is close to the actual world only if S has a similar constitution in W as in the actual world. This stipulation was well motivated in our account of what it is to have an ability in section V, and the same stipulation serves nicely here as well. For similar reasons no skeptical scenarios that entail a change in the laws of nature will turn out to be relevant. Even if such scenarios count as logical possibilities they do not count as relevant possibilities, and so do not undermine our capacities for knowledge.

What about clauses (iib) and (iic) of (RP)? These clauses resulted from our intuitions that knowledge should be subjectively justified as well as objectively reliable. Agent reliabilism recognizes these intuitions and can therefore explain these additional clauses of (RP). Because our cognitive abilities include ones governing the evaluation of counter-evidence, a virtuous believer will discriminate among alternative possibilities that she believes might be true. Moreover, she will discriminate possibilities that she ought to think might be true. Let us take a moment to elaborate on this idea.

We are presently working with the following account of knowledge.

> (AR)   S knows p only if
>   (i)   p is true
>   (ii)   S's believing p is the result of dispositions that S manifests when S is thinking conscientiously.
>   (iii)   Such dispositions make S reliable in the present conditions, with respect to p.

The first point is that the dispositions referred to in (AR) will include ones that make S sensitive to counter-evidence to what seems to be the case. So for example, my perceptual faculties will involve forming material object beliefs on the basis of sensory appearances, but also a process of checking those beliefs against background beliefs that I have. This process need not be a conscious one. What is required is that appropriate revisions in my belief system are made as new evidence comes in; either the new evidence will issue in new beliefs and cause conflicting ones to be revised, or it will be resisted and previous beliefs will be maintained. This grounds clause (iib), which says that an alternative possibility is relevant if S believes that it might be true.

The second point is that in particular cases of knowledge a person must manifest the cognitive dispositions that make her reliable in general. Put another way, she must manifest the dispositions that she does when thinking conscientiously. But this grounds clause (iic), which says that a possibility is relevant if S ought to think that it might be true. In other words, if a possibility is such that S would believe that it is likely if S were thinking conscientiously, then S's evidence must rule it out for S to have knowledge. Only then would S be appropriately reliable in the particular case. Accordingly, the nature of our cognition together with the requirements of subjective justification and reliability explain the various clauses in (RP).

Finally, it is the nature of *our* cognition that explains the clauses—it is not an abstract truth about knowledge that (RP) has the content that it does. It is possible, for example, that some beings have perfectly reliable perception without any process for checking counter-evidence. But that is not how human cognition works, and so the need for clauses (iib) and (iic) in an account of what makes a possibility relevant for us.

VII. Knowledge and Context

Recent authors have argued that knowledge (or knowledge attribution) is sensitive to context.[9] Specifically, it has been argued that the *standards* for knowledge depend on context, and so whether a knowledge claim is true is relative to the context in which the claim is made. It follows from this sort of position that a sentence of the form "S knows p" can be true when uttered by one person in her context, and at the same time false when uttered by a different person in a different context. For example, suppose that I make the claim that traffic is light on the parkway right now. In a context where it is not very important that I am right, the standards for knowledge are low. Accordingly, you might truthfully say that I know what I claim about the traffic. But suppose that another person is trying to decide what route to take to the hospital, and that it is very important that she take the best one. In this context the standards for knowledge are raised, and the person might truthfully judge that I do not know what I claim.

Agent reliabilism is at least consistent with this sort of position. One way to accommodate it is to say that the *degree* of reliability required for knowledge changes with context. But another way is to say that the *range* of reliability required for knowledge changes. It will be remembered that we defined a cognitive ability in terms of success across close possible worlds. As we saw above, it is plausible that context affects how far out into relevant possible worlds one's reliability must extend.[10]

This sort of consideration has been put forward as an answer to skepticism. We noted above that the skeptical argument from Descartes could be interpreted in the following way.

(D6)   1. A person can know that p is true only if she knows that every possibility inconsistent with p is false.

2. The skeptical dream hypotheses are inconsistent with my beliefs

about the world, and I do not know that the skeptical dream hypotheses are false.

3. Therefore, I do not know anything about the world.

I said above that interpreting Descartes's argument this way made it implausible. More specifically, I said that premise (2) of the argument was implausible, because it seems that I do know that I am not a brain in a vat, for example. But for those who do find (2) plausible, the contextualist has an answer. Namely, premise (2) is *true* in contexts where the skeptical argument is being considered, and argument (D6) is therefore sound. This is because that context drives the standards of knowledge high. For example, the context requires that our cognitive abilities extend all the way out to far off worlds, where the skeptical hypotheses are true. But in non-philosophical contexts where knowledge claims are usually made, the standards for knowledge are nowhere near as high. The result is that we do know many things about the world in those contexts, and even if it is also true that in "philosophical" contexts we do not.

Therefore, we may conclude that agent reliabilism is at least consistent with various versions of contextualism, and with a contextualist response to skeptical arguments along the lines of (D6).

Notes

1. Agent reliabilism has its historical roots in Aristotle, Aquinas, and Reid, among others. More recently, versions of the position have been defended by Ernest Sosa, *Knowledge in Perspective* (Cambridge: Cambridge University Press, 1991); Alvin Goldman, *Liaisons: Philosophy Meets the Cognitive and Social Sciences* (Cambridge, Mass.: MIT Press, 1992), and Alvin Plantinga, *Warrant and Proper Function* (Oxford: Oxford University Press, 1993).

2. A number of philosophers have thought that Descartes's argument is intuitively plausible on the present reading, but it seems to me that their intuitions have been tutored here. Most non-philosophers, I would think, find it implausible that they do not know they are brains in vats or victims of evil demons. For the contrary view see Keith DeRose, "Solving the Skeptical Problem," *The Philosophical Review* 104, no. 1 (January 1995): 1-52. See also Stewart Cohen, "How to be a Fallibilist," *Philosophical Perspectives* 2 (1988): 91-123; and Robert Nozick, *Philosophical Explanations* (Cambridge, Mass.: Harvard University Press, 1981).

3. For a similar understanding of the concept see Alvin Goldman, "Discrimination and Perceptual Knowledge," *Journal of Philosophy* 73 (1976): 771-791, reprinted in Alvin Goldman, *Liaisons: Philosophy Meets the Cognitive and Social Sciences.*

4. For example see Fred Dretske, "Epistemic Operators," *Journal of Philosophy* 67 (1970): 1007-1023; Alvin Goldman, "Discrimination and Perceptual Knowledge"; and Marshall Swain, "Revisions of 'Knowledge, Causality, and Justification'," in George Pappas and Marshall Swain, eds., *Essays on Knowledge and Justification* (Ithaca: Cornell University Press, 1978). For objections to these views see Ernest Sosa, "Knowledge in Context, Skepticism in Doubt," in James Tomberlin, ed., *Philosophical Perspectives, 2, Epistemology* (Atacadero, Calif.: Ridgeview Publishing Co., 1988). The account I offer

below avoids Sosa's objections by making the notion of objective likelihood more informative, and by adding subjective conditions to the account of "relevant possibility."

5. Ernest Sosa makes this point in "Knowledge in Context, Skepticism in Doubt."

6. Tom Grabit cases were first introduced by Lehrer and Paxson. See Keith Lehrer and Thomas Paxson, "Knowledge: Undefeated Justified True Belief," *The Journal of Philosophy* 66 (1969): 225-237. Reprinted in Pappas and Swain.

7. The example is due to Goldman. See Alvin Goldman, "Discrimination and Perceptual Knowledge."

8. Compare Sosa, *Knowledge in Perspective*, chapter 16.

9. For example, Cohen, "How to be a Fallibilist"; and DeRose, "Solving the Skeptical Problem." My discussion of contextualism below is indebted to both of these authors.

10. A somewhat similar idea is put forward by DeRose in "Solving the Skeptical Problem."

6

Supervenience, Virtues, and Consequences

Jonathan Dancy

It has been very rewarding to be able to spend time on seeing how the various strands of Ernest Sosa's subtle and complex epistemology combine to form an impressive and coherent whole, in which the reader feels that Sosa has avoided the enthusiasm inherent in the adoption of any one of the classic positions, without going to the holistic extreme of supposing that if one avoids the bad parts of a theory one is unable to profit from the good ones. Reading the different papers in *Knowledge in Perspective* (1991) has had several salutory effects on me for which I hope I am suitably grateful, of which perhaps the most noticeable has been that I have had to rethink entirely my reasons for rejecting foundationalism.

On the present occasion[1] I am going to raise two questions about the underlying structure of Sosa's position. As I understand it, virtue perspectivism offers, among other things, a general picture of what one might call the metaphysics of epistemic justification. This is that justification emerges from the operation of the epistemic virtues. A belief is justified if it is the product of a reputable epistemic faculty (intuition, memory, perception, reason, introspection). There are at least these five channels, as it were, for the emergence of justification; though there may in fact be more than five— epistemic theory as such does not pronounce on the actual number of virtues. The list of channels is not just a list, however. It is unified by a feature common to all the faculties that are virtues (i.e., capable of generating justified beliefs), namely their tendency to produce truth. The common presence of this feature systematizes the list, and means that what we have produced is a *theory*, not just a description of how things are.

The theory so produced instantiates what Sosa calls the highest grade of formal foundationalism. There are three grades of formal foundationalism: "first, the supervenience of epistemic justification; second, its explicable supervenience; and, third, its supervenience explicable by means of a simple theory."[2] This is the first matter I want to try to understand better. The first thing to get clear is the relation between formal foundationalism of the lowest grade and some doctrine of the supervenience of justification. Sosa does not always give quite the same account of what the doctrine of supervenience is supposed to be. Here are two versions:

> The *doctrine of supervenience* for an evaluative property Ø is simply that, for every x, if x has Ø then there is a non-evaluative property (perhaps a relational property) Y such that (i) x has Y, and (ii) necessarily, whatever has Y has Ø.[3]
> . . . the supervenience of Ø [is] simply the idea that whenever something has Ø its having it is founded on certain others of its properties which fall into certain restricted sorts.[4]

Are these the same or are they not? I suspect that they are not, and that the confusion between them is partly responsible for Sosa's identification of formal foundationalism of the lowest grade with some doctrine of supervenience.

What I want to suggest is that Sosa has a picture of the metaphysics of epistemic justification, and that he thinks that this picture can be held in place by appeal to the concept of supervenience—but that he is wrong about this. The picture is that justification is a high-level property (for present purposes it counts as a top-level property) and that there are just different ways of getting that property. This remark (which is perhaps all that the lowest grade of formal foundationalism amounts to) might easily be thought of as absolutely trivial, and so perhaps it is. But my present question is what, if anything, it has to do with supervenience.

We do of course want our supervenience doctrine to be true. With that in mind, let us consider the first characterization of supervenience above. For this doctrine to be true, we need to be able to find non-evaluative properties Y such that necessarily whatever has them has Ø. Now surely no ordinary properties Y will be of this sort. For suppose that we start from a case of an object b which has Y and Ø, and which has Ø because it has Y, in the sense that having Y makes it have Ø. Are we to suppose that necessarily whatever has Y has Ø? I don't think so. There may be a second object c which has Y, but only together with some further property Z that prevents Y from making c Ø; we could call Z a defeater. If so, we have a property Y that makes b Ø and does not make c Ø. What this shows us, however, is only that the doctrine of supervenience we are considering is not concerned with thoughts about non-evaluative properties Y, Z, etc. *making* objects Ø. It is just concerned with finding properties or sets of properties such that necessarily whatever has them has Ø. This is important, because though the absence of Z in the first case is not likely to be one of the properties that *make* b Ø, it will still be one of the properties present in a *group* of properties Y, on which b's having Ø supervenes in the present sense.

What this tells us is that Y, in the first definition of supervenience, will have to be a large and complex group of properties, for it will have to include every aspect that can affect, by its presence or absence, the question of whether an object has Ø. For unless we take care to include in Y every respect in which, by differing from b, c might fail to have Ø, we lay ourselves open to a counterexample. In fact, at least where we concern ourselves with the supervenience of high-level evaluative properties such as justification, it is not clear that we can exclude from what we might call the supervenience base any possible properties of beliefs at all. This will mean that in order to keep this doctrine of supervenience true, we have to think of Y simply as the class of non-evaluative properties of beliefs. This gives us the more or less useless truth that if one belief is justified, any other belief that differs from it not at all (so far as the non-evaluative goes) will also be justified. But it will also mean that there is a different Y for each justified belief.

Let us now turn to the second account of supervenience. Here we meet quite new concepts, those of Ø being "founded on" other properties, and the idea that those properties fall into "certain restricted sorts." What I think we see here is a quite different sort of picture, one that focuses on the idea of a property or set of properties *making* a belief justified. First, let us notice that in order to keep the first doctrine true we were forced away from any suggestion that the properties Y were "of restricted sorts," since they needed to be restricted neither in number nor in size; by the end, Y had expanded to include *all* the non-evaluative properties of the relevant belief. This conception of the subvenient is quite different from one that focuses on the properties on which Ø is "founded." I assume here that talk of the justification of a belief being founded on the fact that it is perceptual is equivalent to the more normal talk of the perceptual nature of the belief making it justified. And if so, the differences between the two conceptions are easy to establish. First, we do now have a genuine sense in which the properties that make a belief justified may indeed be restricted in number. These "founding" properties will however be different in conception from the relevant Y, since Y will include properties that count against the justification of the relevant belief, as well as those that, counting in favor, succeed in making it justified. No property that counts against the justification of a belief can be said to be one that makes it justified. Second, if it is indeed true that we should expect to find that only a limited number of a belief's properties contribute in this way to making it justified, the rest playing some supporting or undermining role, or being simply indifferent, there is now much more chance that we should hope to see some pattern emerging case by case. Perhaps there are only five *sorts of ways* in which beliefs are made justified. Only experience can tell, one would suppose.

Let us use the term 'supervenience' to refer to the relations described in Sosa's first account (as I think fits standard practice) and introduce the term 'resultance' for the relation described in the second account.[5] Which relation, if either, is the one to be identified with the core element of formal foundationalism? We should remember that, whichever one it is, its holding should be capable of explanation at the second level of formal foundationalism. Now I think that what Sosa expects to be explaining at that level is the existence of some sort of pattern in what is visible at the first level. And what I am trying to insist on is that the question of whether any such pattern will emerge is not determined in advance by the fact that the evaluative supervenes (in either sense). Let us think in terms of supervenience (proper) first. Here it seems to me that there is nothing that we could look to explain at all, or at least nothing that the various versions of the highest grade of formal foundationalism (coherentism, substantive foundationalism, virtue perspectivism) look much like explanations of. Things look no more promising when we turn to resultance. The 'resultance base' for justification is typically fairly narrow, and there is no reason *in advance* to expect that the same properties will crop up over and over again. So if Sosa's talk of "certain restricted sorts" is supposed to allude to that expectation, it is illegitimate. Resultance itself, as the relation between the higher-level property and the lower-level ones on which here it is founded, has no such consequence. If, on the other hand, that phrase merely means that the resultance base for Ø in a given case is typically fairly limited in size, then this might indeed be thought of as uncontentious or necessarily true. But it hardly gives us anything that, at the second or third levels of formal foundationalism, we might look to explain.

A third thing that might be meant by the phrase "certain restricted sorts" is that for any given evaluative property Ø, the relevant property Y will be metaphysically limited in kind. There is one place where Sosa may be alluding to such an idea. He writes of:

> . . . the very plausible idea that epistemic justification is subject to the supervenience that characterizes normative and evaluative properties generally. Thus, if a car is a good car, then any physical replica of the car must be just as good.[6]

This is just an instance of the old suggestion that any painting physically indistinguishable from a good painting must also be good. Here the restriction is to the physical. Sosa continues:

> If it is a good car in virtue of such properties as being economical, little prone to break down, etc., then surely any exact replica would share all such properties and would thus be equally good. Similarly, if a belief is epistemically justified, it is presumably so in virtue of its character and its basis in perception, memory and inference (if any). Thus any belief exactly like it in its character and its basis must be equally well justified.[7]

Here the intuitive restriction of the supervenience base of evaluation of cars to the physical is echoed by a similar restriction, in the case of epistemic evaluation to "character and basis." But we might wonder whether the restriction has any bite in this case. Is there any property of a belief that is excluded by it? Not obviously. What is more, these restrictions are no part of any doctrine of supervenience. They come from elsewhere

To sum up, then, what I think is happening is that Sosa has a picture of the following sort. Supervenience establishes that there is a limited number of routes to justification. This fact may or may not be explicable. If it is explicable, we achieve a formal foundationalism of the second grade. If it can be explained within a simple theory, we achieve the third grade. His own theory is of the third grade, as are all its most illustrious rivals. The complaint I am making about all this is about the first move. According to me, on neither of the two accounts he offers does supervenience establish any such thing. There is no antecedent reason whatever to be anything other than what Sosa calls a pessimist, namely someone who, denying formal foundationalism, holds that there is no prospect of any general specification of the conditions under which an evaluative property Ø applies.[8] Formal foundationalism of this sort is not uncontentious, and is not identical with any recognizable doctrine of supervenience. Nor is it identical with any doctrine of resultance. Both of these doctrines are compatible with any degree of messiness you like.

The reason for going on about this is to make sure that no feature of Sosa's position is invalidly established by appeal to supervenience. In my view, formal foundationalism, understood as the claim referred to just above, that "the conditions under which an evaluative property would apply can be specified in general, perhaps recursively,"[9] is not identical with and borrows no plausibility from any recognizable doctrine of supervenience. Even if it is true, we have as yet seen no reason to expect it to be.

What we have so far, then, is that there is no antecedent reason to accept any degree of formal foundationalism. But there may be a subsequent reason, namely the discovery that as a matter of fact there is a certain pattern to the ways in which justification results case by case, and that there can be an explanation of this fact. (If the explanation is simple, we achieve the highest grade of formal foundationalism.) And Sosa suggests that this is how things in fact are. There does turn out to be a limited number of ways in which beliefs get justified. A belief is justified if it is the product of a reliable faculty, and there is only a limited number of these. So we do turn out to have the picture that has justification at the top and a certain number of routes to it. And it is at this stage that the notion of an epistemic virtue comes into play, to take us from the lowest grade of formal foundationalism to the highest.

Suppose we establish a certain number of epistemic principles, and list them. Our situation is unattractively unsystematic. To turn it into a theory we need to find some way of systematizing the list. Similarly, if we just have a list of the different sorts of ways in which beliefs become justified, we have as yet no theory. It is the notion of an epistemic virtue that systematizes our list and turns it into a theory. It does this in two stages. First, we establish that all the reliable faculties are epistemic virtues; this moves us up to the second grade of formal foundationalism. Second, we offer an account of why these faculties have the status of virtues. A successful account will systematize our talk of the virtues, i.e., render it unified and simple.

This program seems to me very appealing, and it becomes more so when we ask what the unifying feature is. It is a common relation to the truth. Each virtue is a virtue because it has a tendency to promote true belief.

As far as this goes, however, there was little need to reach the unifying conclusion by travelling through the idea of a virtue. We could have asked directly what unified the various faculties whose operation generates justified belief, and got the answer that these faculties are reliable. The notion of a virtue was not absolutely essential to our intellectual passage here. But by using it we key our talk of justification into talk of epistemic praise and blame. Sosa often wants to describe certain benighted people as blameless, at least so far as their internal workings are concerned. He even goes so far as to speak of having or not having a "flawed epistemic character,"[10] and of "intellectually virtuous nature."[11] Here the notion of the virtues is beginning to do serious work. It is raising in our mind analogies with the supposed advantages of virtue ethics, and even the prospect of a unification of epistemology and ethics, built around the common notion of a virtue.

When we see how these two features are actually built up, however, a tension emerges between them. This can be seen when we look again at how the intended *unity* (systematicity, simplicity) was actually achieved. It was achieved by our answer to the question "what makes this feature a virtue?" Sosa's answer to this question is a *consequentialist* one. A faculty or practice is a virtue if it promotes truth or diminishes falsehood.[12] It is the relation to truth as an end that unifies the different "virtues."

I want to pause for a moment to consider other answers that might have been offered. In the first place, we might have noticed that Aristotle's account of the moral virtues, or virtues of practical character, is one within which, though it is true to say that the virtues promote the good in the sense that someone with the virtues will do good things, this thought is not to be understood in a consequentialist way. The good does not have the character of a well-understood aim or end, capable of determining how well the agent acted. Indeed the relation between the good and the virtues is more the other way around; the good is whatever someone with the virtues would do. So there is an apparent unity in Aristotle's account of the moral virtues, but hidden diversity.

What really creates the unity in Aristotle's account is his conception of character, of the unity of the virtues and the doctrine of the mean. We know that anyone who lacks a virtue will go systematically wrong. The source of unity is the way in which a good character is a well-knit one, not some end that good character would promote.

When we turn to Aristotle's conception of the intellectual virtues, however, I have to admit that he does seem to link them to truth in the way that Sosa wants. Aristotle does say that an intellectual virtue is a state by which one will most hit the truth.[13]

There are three attitudes we could take to this claim:

1.   We could take it at face value: truth is a unified end, by relation to which the claims of various states of character to be virtues are determined.

2.   We could suggest that 'truth' is no more a unified end than is 'the good,' so that the unity that it imposes is only apparent. Any kind of

redundancy or disquotation or disappearance theory of truth will make it possible for us to make this move.

3.   We could dispute the truth of Aristotle's claim, taking it in the most interesting sense above, and trying to interpret his remarks in a way more in accord with later suggestions of his that the intellectual virtues are defined as those *concerned with* truth and falsity, or those *concerned with* assertion and denial,[14] without supposing that truth, falsity, assertion, and denial are here counting as ends.

I don't want, and am not really competent, to engage in Aristotelian scholarship here.[15] More to the point might be that if we do take his claim at face value as in 1 above, it is probably false. It seems to me that once one asks oneself whether all the intellectual virtues are such because of their tendency to promote truth, the answer has to be no.[16] This need not mean that they have nothing to do with truth, nor indeed that we can be certain of being able to beat off consequentialist attempts to say that what establishes their status as virtues is their relation to the truth, but it means that in some cases at least, we recognize the status of a character trait as a virtue before examining its relation to truth.

Obviously some examples of virtues whose status as such does not derive from their relation to truth would be helpful. First, consider someone who has a suitable intellectual diffidence. This might be thought a virtue in her even though she would actually do better (a consequentialist phrase meaning hit the truth more often) if she stuck to her guns a bit more. Consider also someone who is hard to shift. This too could be a virtue, one that exists in essential tension with the first one. The intellectually virtuous person will have both of these characters, and will thereby be enabled to hit the mean with respect to sticking and yielding in each case, tending towards one side or the other according to the circumstances. Consider now someone who is intellectually tolerant. Though convinced that your research program is going nowhere, he still allocates departmental funds to it. We *might* be able to establish the status of this type of character by showing how it promotes the truth. But this seems likely to be an uphill struggle, just as moral tolerance is hard to establish as a virtue on the grounds that it means that more beneficial actions get done; for this sort of tolerance seems to be exactly a method of ensuring that more bad ones get done. Another example is the virtue of curiosity, which seems to me to be a virtue even though it may not promote truth. It may lead one to be unable to stick to one line of enquiry for long enough. Consider finally an example of Scanlon's in ethics.[17] We go to a restaurant together. You are a great wine and food buff; I am an ignoramus. I know that if I let you order my meal for me, I will get a better meal, but still wish to order my own food. I would rather make my own choices, even if it means eating worse. Similarly in epistemology. You are an expert; I am not. I could just rely on your say-so. But I insist on making up my own mind, even though I know that by doing so I increase the chance of error. In this realm too, I want to make up my own mind and make my own mistakes.

One can imagine the sort of consequentialist scratching around that would hope to establish that somehow this characteristic—which is an intellectual virtue in me—is one that generally, or in the long run, or if practiced throughout the community, promotes truth. My own view is that there is an intrinsic implausibility in such attempts. The status of this characteristic as a virtue is independent of its relation to the promotion of truth; it derives from consideration of the sort of intellectual being one should be.[18]

So far I have suggested that various features commonly considered virtues are not so because of their relation to the truth. But the reply to this might be that they are not related to the truth singly, but all together. If you have them all, you have the best chances of reaching the truth. But I think that this reply only takes us some of the way. It is true that the examples I gave were treated atomistically, and that this is a possible weakness. It may be that two characteristics neither of which would promote the truth separately would promote it if present together. My first example of the need for a suitable combination of stubbornness and diffidence may be of that sort. But the second, that of epistemic tolerance, seems not to be. I can think of no opposing characteristic such that its copresence with tolerance is virtuous because of their joint tendency to promote truth. And I would say the same about the last suggested virtue, that of insisting on making one's own mistakes.

Another reply might be that I have made too much capital out of an unwitting monism in Sosa. Truth is not the only desirable consequence in epistemology, any more than pleasure is the only valuable outcome in ethics. Now I should first admit that Sosa sometimes talks about "truth and the avoidance of falsehood," and there is an established opinion that the latter is a distinct value. We see here what we see in ethics, where it is not held to be simply pleonastic to talk of pleasure and the avoidance of pain. But whether the avoidance of falsehood is distinct from the promotion of truth or not, both of these virtues are clearly "concerned with truth," in some broader sense. And we could say that as well as those, there are also virtues that are not in the same way "concerned with truth" such as those concerned with the search for simplicity, range, and explanatory power. As I said, Sosa does make mention of these in one place. So perhaps he is not the sort of monistic consequentialist that I have been making him appear.

The sort of pluralistic consequentialism that is emerging here is familiar in ethics, and is harder to dispose of than any monism. But an obvious move, if one is looking to unseat it, is to look to the arguments that are used against similar ethical versions and try to rerun them in the present case. For instance, it is said that if the value of a life is to be measured by the extent to which it has promoted these goals, we are being offered lives devoid of (intellectual) fun. Just as we need moral freedom and moral space, we need epistemic freedom and epistemic space, and these forms of consequentialism singularly fail to provide it. Intellectual curiosity is rather like a spur to take a day off from lining up yet more truths and erasing more falsehoods and have a bit of fun for a while—intellectual fun, no doubt, but still fun.

We might add that the desire to learn classical languages need not, for virtue, derive from the desire to acquire more truths; it might derive from the desire to read Aristotle (or poetry) in the original—and this need not be because one will learn more truths this way. What will it be for? Perhaps the search for truth (and all the features that go with truth) should be subordinated to a greater end, the search for wisdom; perhaps it should not. But even if it were, wisdom is not a result like truth, but somehow lying beyond it. Wisdom is a character trait, and an intellectual virtue itself. So if wisdom is an intellectual end, and that end is a virtue, there is no chance of explaining the intellectual virtues in terms of their common end. The sort of external explanation we are offered by the appeal to the promotion of truth is undermined.

Consequentialists standardly try to drive a hard question: What makes all these things virtues? The intention is to rule out any answer but one that appeals to an external good. The desire to be well informed is indeed an intellectual virtue, just as the desire to do good is in ethics. But this should not persuade us that all virtues are like this, or that the right way to show that something is a virtue is to point to the consequences of exercising it.

If the virtues are not unified as a package by their relation to the truth, what does unify them? The answer has to be the nature of a virtuous life, or the sort of character that such a life reveals. This answer is intended to be crafted on the model of the unity of the virtuous practical life in Aristotle. But it should be noted that this is quite a different sort of unity from the one that Sosa provides, and, crucially, it is not a unity that would show up in any manageable simplicity or systematicity in our account of the supervenience base for justification, or for any other evaluative property. Formal foundationalism is an approach that looks for simplicity at the meta-level. But the appeal to the virtues is part of a story that will not provide us with that sort of simplicity. There will, we hope, be a sort of coherence in our eventual story. But even if this gives us unity of a sort, it will not give us system.

There is, however, a standard reply to these suggestions in ethics, which is also available in epistemology. I seem to have talked about the intellectual virtues as a whole, with no restriction to those that are especially concerned with justification. But surely Sosa has been restricting himself to thoughts about justification, which, as a very specific feature, stems entirely from truth-seeking virtues. Maybe there are other epistemic virtues than these, but this possibility does nothing to undermine Sosa's suggestions in the (central but limited) area that is his concern.

I said that this suggestion is standard in ethics, and we will find it helpful to see just how it runs there. This will reveal what is the real point at issue between consequentialist and virtue-based approaches. Suppose that we are persuaded that there are some consequence-related virtues such as benevolence. The benevolent person is a person who aims to make a difference to the world, to make things go better. Our account of these virtues, we therefore assume, is the one given by consequentialists; these virtues are virtues because of their effects. Now, having read Philippa Foot, we are persuaded that there are also virtues that have little or nothing to do with making things go better, for instance those of loyalty and gratitude. These virtues have to be understood in a quite different way, since they are not (or at least do not appear to be) virtues because of their consequences.

The question now is how we are to put together our accounts of the consequence-related and the non-consequence-related virtues. One possible picture has it that the consequentialists are just right about some virtues and wrong about others. But in fact neither side is happy about this compromise. Consequentialists are constantly trying to maneuver so as to absorb the non-consequence-related virtues into their consequentialist perspective, by finding some indirect relation between these virtues and the production of some suitable result. Non-consequentialists also are unwilling to admit that the consequential-ists are right about anything, because they feel that consequentialism is like a cancer: Once one has let it in at all it will grow until it has taken over completely. The crucial question is whether the two camps are right at least about this, that no compromise is intellectually acceptable. And I think that they are. Consequentialists are wise to seek to give a unified account of all the virtues, because otherwise they will find themselves saying that of the virtues, some are virtues for one sort of reason and others are virtues for another. This position is theoretically unstable, and will always be vulnerable to one that manages to give the same account of why this or that feature is a virtue throughout. Similarly, virtue theorists are right to resist the irruption of a second form of explanation of the status of a character trait as a virtue. Their standard form, which asks how the virtues *together* contribute to a good epistemic life, is perfectly capable already of capturing the nature and role of the consequence-related virtues. That they are consequence-related does nothing to show that we should accept a consequentialist understanding of them.

Suppose that we have a list of virtues:

> gratitude
> honesty
> benevolence   things going better for all
> respect for others
> considerateness
> loyalty
> justice
> independence
> etc.

A consequentialist understanding of benevolence will run on a horizontal line, as I have tried to show, by seeking to understand the status of benevolence as a virtue in terms of the consequences that it is a tendency to promote. A "virtue" understanding of benevolence will run on a vertical line, by considering the contribution of benevolence, in the context of all the other virtues, to the life of virtue. One cannot have both of these at once. They just do not fit together. And that is why it is impossible in ethical theory to admit that consequentialists are right about some restricted area. For to admit that they are right there would be to undermine one's picture of the rest. Consequentialism in one place makes it impossible to tell the right story elsewhere, because it involves a theoretical distortion from the beginning.[19]

All this, of course, is from the point of view of virtue theory. And I have tried to put the point as forcibly as I can, in order to show what is at issue between the two approaches, and why it is theoretically unstable to say that we will adopt a consequentialist picture in a limited area where, because the relevant character traits are concerned with the production of certain consequences, a consequentialist story is clearly possible, while admitting that a cognate story may not be available elsewhere. This does however seem to be what Sosa is trying to do.

At the beginning of my discussion of Sosa's suggestion that the epistemic virtues are united by their tendency to promote the truth, which I have argued is a form of consequentialism, I suggested that the appeal to a common tendency to promote truth is at odds with talk of epistemic praise and blame, so that the two aspects of Sosa's use of the notion of an epistemic virtue do not sit well together. I am now in a position to say why this might be. It is because praise and blame, for a true virtue theorist, will be mediated by considerations of the sort of life that surrounds this failure or that success: there will be a holistic aspect to our moral and to our epistemic assessment. This means that it must always distort the matter to consider as separable one's performance in any particular respect, including the production of consequences—to suppose that praise and blame can be allotted so far as this area goes, without looking over our shoulder to see what effects the wider context might have.

In this sense, therefore, I think that 'virtue consequentialism' has feet in two warring camps. There is another sense in which this is true as well, but I am only going to mention this here, rather than to elaborate it, since I am not sure whether it is not in the end the same point again. This is that it is trying to be externalist in its relation to the notion of aptness, where a mere tendency to promote the truth is sufficient, and at the same time to be internalist in its talk of blamelessness and character. These things do not fit well together; or rather, if they do fit well together (as I suppose that in the end they must) we have not yet been shown how they do. The notion of an epistemic virtue, at least as Sosa has handled, does not answer the problem but merely encapsulates it.

I should admit that it is just not clear to me who is in the right of things on these points at the end of the day. I have tried to lay out the reasons I see for taking what one might call Sosa's holding position to be unstable. Evidently it is not as if those reasons are conclusive, in the present state of moral theory, nor are they in epistemology. But they do represent a challenge to any introduction of consequentialism into epistemology, especially when it is presented as a form of virtue theory.

Notes

1. This paper is a rewritten version of one that I presented at the "Author Meets Critics" symposium at the APA Western Division meeting in March 1993. The symposium was on Ernest Sosa's *Knowledge in Perspective: Selected Essays in Epistemology* (Cambridge: Cambridge University Press, 1991). All unattributed references to Sosa's work will be to this volume.

2. Sosa 191.

3. Sosa 153. One could doubt this account of supervenience on the grounds that though the evaluative must supervene, it need not supervene on the non-evaluative. For instance, it is possible that moral properties supervene, but that some of the properties on which they supervene are mental (intentions and the like), and that the mental is itself in some sense evaluative without supervening on the non-evaluative. The same reason could easily apply to epistemic evaluation. In general, if the evaluative can eventually be "brought down" to the non-evaluative, this will be luck, not part of the account of what supervenience is.

4. Sosa 181.

5. I make much more of the difference between these two relations in chapter 5 of my *Moral Reasons* (Oxford: Blackwell, 1993).

6. Sosa 179.

7. Sosa 179.

8. Sosa 178.

9. Sosa 178.

10. Sosa 241.

11. Sosa 291.

12. Here I oversimplify enormously, but not, I hope, in ways that undermine what I am going on to say.

13. *Nicomachean Ethics* 1139b12-13; my translation.

14. *NE* 1139b15: there are five states whereby the soul hits the truth in assertion and denial.

15. If we abandon exact scholarship, and try to move with a broader but still Aristotelian brush, there is still an internal Aristotelian reason for supposing that the relation between the good and the virtues of character is significantly different from that between the true and the intellectual virtues. This is that if we try to oppose the consequentialist answer to the inevitable question "what makes it the case that each of these is a virtue?" by an answer that, instead of pointing to their relation to an extrinsic end, points instead to the unity of a life that displays them all, we commit ourselves to some form of the doctrine of the unity of the virtues. According to this doctrine, if one virtue is lacking, all the others cease to be the virtues they otherwise would be. With this doctrine in hand, we can appeal to the unity of a life that displays them. But it does not seem as if Aristotle would have wished to assert the unity of the intellectual virtues. They are not defined in terms of hitting a mean. Indeed the account he gives of them (e.g., that some are concerned with things that may be or not be, while others are concerned with things that are necessarily) makes it especially hard to suppose that in the absence of one, one lacks all the others. This may be in some way influenced by the fact that the virtues of character are exactly that—character traits—while the intellectual virtues are more like faculties. So I have a problem here with my suggestion that Aristotle would wish to give a similar account of the relation between the good and the virtues of character and that between the true and the intellectual virtues.

16. Sosa does gesture towards this possibility (225), but makes nothing of it.

17. See his Tanner Lectures, "The Significance of Choice," in S. M. McMurrin ed. *The Tanner Lectures on Human Values*, viii (Cambridge: Cambridge University Press, 1988), esp. 178-9.

18. Those who think that this appeal must somehow be resolved into a claim about consequences should read Philippa Foot "Morality, Action and Outcome," in Ted Honderich, ed., *Morality and Objectivity* (London: Routledge and Kegan Paul, 1985): 23-38, and her "Utilitarianism and the Virtues" *Mind* 94 (1985): 196-209.

19. Much of what I have been saying here is derived from the work of Philippa Foot, cited in fn. 18.

7

Sosa on Knowledge, Justification, and "Aptness"

Lawrence BonJour

Knowledge in Perspective[1] is a rich, wide-ranging, and valuable discussion of a broad range of recent epistemological (and anti-epistemological) views, of the Gettier problem, and of a wide variety of more specific topics. It is mandatory reading for anyone with a serious interest in contemporary epistemology. But it is also an undeniably difficult book—due no doubt in part to its being constructed from articles written over a substantial period of time and for the most part only lightly edited in the process of bringing them together. In the present paper, I propose to concentrate on Sosa's own positive epistemological position, though this will mean leaving largely to one side his often compelling criticisms of competing epistemological views, my own included, and ignoring almost entirely his very valuable discussions of the issues growing out of the Gettier problem. This positive position, which he labels "virtue perspectivism," seems to be intended as an improved version of externalist reliabilism, one that retains the basic idea that reliability is the key to epistemic authority while accommodating at least some of the intuitions that support opposing views like coherentism. I will begin with a presentation of the main elements of the view, followed by an investigation of its motivation in contrast to a less sophisticated version of reliabilism. This will put me in a position to raise what I regard as a fundamental problem.

I

We may begin with the two elements of the view that are reflected in the label "virtue perspectivism": the idea of an *intellectual virtue* and the idea of an *epistemic perspective*. Just as a moral virtue is a disposition or capacity that leads for the most part to morally valuable or admirable actions, so an intellectual virtue is a disposition or faculty that leads for the most part to true beliefs, given the subject's normal surroundings. More precisely, a subject S has an intellectual virtue in relation to a field of propositions F, a set of conditions

C, and an environment E if and only if S, when in C and E, is very likely to believe correctly with regard to a proposition that falls into F (287). (There will be more to say later about what will count as acceptable values for these various parameters.) Examples of such intellectual virtues would include perception, memory, and reason, together with, Sosa suggests (215-22), the acceptance of testimony.

It is deriving from such an intellectual virtue that is, for Sosa, the fundamental basis for the positive epistemic status of a belief. Here we must take note of an important terminological, though not merely terminological, point. Although in some of the earlier papers in the collection, Sosa says that beliefs thus derived are epistemically *justified*, he concedes later on that the ordinary meaning of "justified" and its cognates is too closely tied to the idea of argumentative reasons to be correctly usable to designate this essentially externalist conception of epistemic authority. He therefore proposes to substitute the word "apt": "Apt then is what a belief must be to qualify as knowledge in addition to being true (and un-Gettierized)" (255). Thus being epistemically *justified* will be at most only one way of being epistemically *apt*, and justification will cease to be the central concept of epistemology.

We may approach Sosa's view of justification proper (as contrasted with aptness) by turning to the other main idea reflected in the name of the position, the idea of an *epistemic perspective*. Such a perspective is "an account at least in broad outline of the ways in which. . . . beliefs in various categories acquire epistemic justification [or aptness]" (97), consisting of:

> meta-beliefs which positively attribute. . . . object beliefs. . . . to some faculty or virtue, ... and further meta-beliefs which explain how such a faculty or virtue was acquired, and how such a faculty or virtue, thus acquired, is bound to be reliable in the circumstances as (the believer) views them at the time. (136)

Such beliefs could fall into different levels, constituting a meta-perspective, a meta-meta-perspective, and so on, though plainly the number of levels cannot be unlimited.

It is the presence of such an epistemic perspective, according to Sosa, that allows a body of beliefs to be epistemically justified rather than merely apt. Given the connection that he has emphasized between justification and argument, this presumably should mean that the presence of such a perspective enables one to give something like a cogent argument for the truth (or likely truth) of the various beliefs in the body of beliefs, including those derived from such intellectual virtues as perception and memory. How exactly such an argument might work is an issue that we will have to return to later, but the main initial suggestion is that it will turn primarily on an appeal to the *coherence* of the overall body of beliefs, including the various meta-beliefs.

The factors that confer epistemic authority on beliefs thus fall into two radically different categories: aptness, which is essentially external in character; and a coherent epistemic perspective, which is essentially internal. Where both are present in harmony, we have *reflective knowledge*, while aptness alone yields only *animal knowledge*. Where a coherent epistemic perspective is present in the absence of aptness, we have something like a Gettier case (281). Whether the beliefs in this last sort of case should still be said to be justified is an issue on which Sosa seems to be of two minds: sometimes he seems to say that justification is purely internal in character (e.g., 291), while elsewhere he seems to suggest that purely internal considerations do not suffice for justification in any cognitively significant sense where external aptness is absent (e.g., 290).

II

I have already remarked that virtue perspectivism is apparently viewed by Sosa as a development and refinement of externalism in general and reliabilism in particular. Thus a helpful way to understand at least some of the motivation for the view is to employ a simple version of reliabilism as a dialectical foil. Consider then a view that holds simply that a necessary and sufficient condition for a belief to be epistemically justified (or apt)—and hence for it to constitute knowledge, if it is true and if some appropriate anti-Gettier condition is satisfied—is that the belief be produced by a process that is *reliable*, i.e., one that produces an appropriately high proportion of true over false beliefs; I will refer to this contrasting view, perhaps somewhat tendentiously, as "crude reliabilism." It is clear that Sosa believes both that crude reliabilism is generally on the right track and also that it is unacceptable as it stands. What we must therefore try to understand is just what the deficiencies of crude reliabilism are supposed to be, according to him, and how virtue perspectivism is supposed to remedy these deficiencies. In the present section, I will consider three such deficiencies that are explicitly identified by Sosa: "the new evil-demon problem," "the meta-incoherence problem," and "the generality problem." The following section will then consider a fourth problem, one that is less explicit in Sosa's discussion, but arguably more fundamental.

First, what Sosa refers to as "the new evil-demon problem" concerns an alleged counterexample to the claim of crude reliabilism that reliability is necessary for justification (or aptness). The example concerns a person whose beliefs are caused by a Cartesian evil demon in such a way that, although the beliefs are totally or almost totally false, the person's internal perceptual and mental states are entirely indiscernible from those of a normal human being in a normal human environment. In particular, the demon-victim's internal beliefs and other relevant states may be assumed to fit together in an ideally coherent fashion, including the existence of the right sort of meta-beliefs to constitute a coherent epistemic perspective. According to crude reliabilism, the victim's beliefs are nevertheless not justified, because the process that produces them is obviously not reliable. And the problem is that this result seems intuitively wrong. The demon-victim's beliefs are mostly false and would not constitute knowledge, for Gettier-type reasons at least, even if they happened to be true. But his reasoning and reflective thought processes may nonetheless be impeccable from his own internal standpoint, and thus it has seemed to many to be implausible to deny that he is justified, while at the same time according justification to someone who has the good fortune to live in a normal world, but whose internal states are nonetheless quite indistinguishable.[2]

Sosa's response to this problem is to relativize the assessment to the different environments involved. Relative to the demon environment, i.e., the environment he is actually in, the demon victim's "experience-belief mechanisms" are not intellectually virtuous, and the resulting beliefs are not apt; moreover, his beliefs are either not justified at all or else justified only in a sense that has no real cognitive value. Relative to a normal human environment, however, those experience-belief mechanisms are intellectually virtuous, and the beliefs they produce are both justified and apt.

Two apparent difficulties with this solution are worth noting in passing. First, for it to work, the relevant belief-forming capacities or dispositions have to be identified entirely in terms of internally accessible features, i.e., as Sosa puts it, as "experience-belief mechanisms." This obviously leaves out much that might be relevant to the reliability of such a capacity, such as the causal provenance of the experiences in question—after all, the demon victim might well not even have normal sense organs. This goes against the grain of much reliabilist thought and raises the issue of whether a belief-forming capacity can properly be said to be reliable, even in a given environment, when specified only in this rather minimal way. Second, it is doubtful that Sosa's view really accommodates the intuitions that give rise to the problem. For surely the main intuition is that the demon victim's beliefs are justified without qualification in the actual environment that he inhabits, not merely that they are justified in relation to a quite different environment whose relevance to his actual epistemic situation is pretty obscure.

Second, what Sosa refers to as "the meta-incoherence problem" is the problem posed by various alleged counterexamples to the claim of crude reliabilism that reliability is sufficient for justification. Thus we imagine a person whose belief is caused by reliable clairvoyance, but who (a) has massive evidence against the specific belief in question, or (b) massive evidence against his possessing such a power of clairvoyance, or (c) massive evidence that no such power is even possible, or even (d) no evidence either way on any of these points, but also no account of how the belief in question could have been produced in a reliable way. In each case, it is claimed by the proponents of the objection, the belief in question fails to be justified, despite the claim of crude reliabilism to the contrary.[3]

Sosa's solution to this problem[4] again involves an appeal to the distinction between internal justification and external aptness.[5] Though the clairvoyant believer's belief is *apt*, because produced by a reliable cause, it is not *justified*: in the first three cases, the believer's epistemic perspective is incoherent, at least potentially, because of the conflict between his other evidence and the needed claim of reliability for his clairvoyance; while in the fourth case, he possesses no real epistemic perspective at all that is relevant to the belief in question. Thus he possesses animal knowledge, but not reflective knowledge.

Is this an adequate response to the problem posed by the clairvoyance counterexamples in question? I can see no serious objection to saying that the persons in the various cases possess "animal knowledge" (though how exactly this species of knowledge connects with our general intuitions about knowledge is something about which Sosa has perhaps too little to say). We may also agree that he is correct in identifying the deficiency in the various cases as the lack of an adequate epistemic perspective, where the connection that Sosa himself insists on between such a perspective and reasoned or argumentative justification seems to make it fair to restate this point by saying that what the person lacks in each case is any internally accessible *reason* for thinking that his belief is true. What is uncertain, as we will see more fully below, is whether in Sosa's view it is possible for anyone to ever be genuinely better off in this respect, i.e., whether anyone in his view ever really possesses an internal reason for thinking that his belief is true.

Third, the generality problem for crude reliabilism concerns the proper specification of the process whose reliability is to be assessed. The main problem here is that too narrow a specification may lead to a spurious reliability, e.g., by picking out a process that only occurs once and happens by pure chance or luck to lead on that occasion to a true belief, while too broad a specification may lose sight of a genuinely reliable process by melding its results with those of unreliable processes to which it is only very generically related. But while the possibility of these opposite sorts of mistakes is clear enough, it is doubtful whether crude reliabilism can offer any clear and non-arbitrary basis for picking out a specification of the relevant process that somehow strikes a correct balance between these two extremes.

In the context of Sosa's view, the generality problem translates into the problem of identifying proper values for the main parameters that are involved in the idea of an intellectual virtue: the field of propositions F, the conditions C, and the environment E. His solution is that the values of these parameters are constrained by the role that they must play in the generalizations of the epistemic community and in the generalizations of the subject himself, as reflected in his epistemic perspective (284). These values "must be usable by us in attaining a *coherent* view of our own intellectual economy" (292).

There are two relatively obvious problems here. First, it is not at all clear that the constraint in question is enough to solve the generality problem, i.e., not clear that there will not be competing characterizations of our intellectual processes that satisfy this seemingly rather loose constraint but still differ enough to yield widely different degrees of reliability. Second, even if the constraints in question were somehow sufficient to yield a relatively unique specification of our intellectual processes, it is unclear why that specification should be regarded as ideal or optimum in the context of what is still at bottom a reliabilist position. Why, that is, should the demands of our *internal* theorizing be allowed to influence assessments of *external* reliability?

III

While the foregoing problems are cited specifically by Sosa as objections to reliabilism and as motivations for virtue perspectivism, there is a further problem which, although less explicitly identified, may also be more serious. In several places, Sosa raises the issue of how the reliabilist is to identify his reliable sources of belief and justify the claim that they are reliable, without relying on those very sources in a way that appears circular:

> An important component of a reliabilist theory of knowledge would surely be a list of reliable faculties. . . . But how could one justify the addition of a faculty to the list except by use—direct or indirect—of that very faculty? And is that not as viciously circular as declaring a source reliable by accepting its reports at face value and inferring that it issues truth? (95)

Part of the issue here is what to say to advocates of some sort of superstition who make an analogous appeal:

> the superstitious are well placed to respond with a reliabilist justification of superstition that seems, by parity of reasoning, equally effective. "Look," they might exclaim, "look at how reliable superstition is, as shown by all the truths that it delivers." All the truths that it delivers by whose lights? "Why, by the lights of superstition, of course." (197)

Contrary to what Sosa may seem to suggest, the foregoing concern is not in any clear way a problem for the crude reliabilist himself. For him, the basis for justification is reliability, not reason, and thus by the lights of his own view he has no need to identify reliable sources from an internal perspective or justify from that perspective the claim that they are reliable. All that matters is that the sources upon which he relies are in fact reliable. And this applies also, of course, to the imagined controversy with the proponent of superstition (should the crude reliabilist choose to enter into such a reasoned controversy, even though there is no apparent reason why he is required to). If the crude reliabilist is in fact generalizing from reliable sources whose reliability is attested to by those same reliable sources, and the proponent of superstition is in fact generalizing from unreliable sources whose reliability is attested to only by those same unreliable sources, then the former's conclusions are justified (or apt) and the latter's unjustified (or inapt) in the only sense that crude reliabilism recognizes, and from the crude reliabilist's standpoint that is all that needs to be said.

But while the crude reliabilist view is in this way internally consistent and dialectically defensible, it seems all the same quite unappealing. Even if his analyses of justification (or aptness) and of knowledge are conceded for the sake of the argument, it remains the case that on the crude reliabilist's view we have *no reason at all* for thinking that either of those concepts is ever genuinely realized—or, even more fundamentally, for thinking that any of our beliefs are ever true. This result constitutes in itself a very serious version of skepticism, one that is rendered even more unpalatable by the fact that perhaps the most common argument for crude reliabilism is that only such a view makes it possible to *avoid* skepticism.

As the passages quoted above suggest, Sosa would also not be satisfied with this crude reliabilist stance, though whether his reasons are quite the same is not clear. Indeed, a substantial part of the motivation for the requirement of an epistemic perspective is the idea that mere external reliability, relying on one's "animal aptitudes" (282), is insufficient for a fully human brand of cognition:

> Human knowledge is on a higher plane of sophistication, however, precisely because of its. . . . capacity to satisfy self-reflective curiosity. Pure reliabilism is questionable as an adequate epistemology for such knowledge. . . . (95)

What I want to ask in the balance of the present paper is what Sosa's improvement over crude reliabilism in this crucial respect really amounts to, and whether it is sufficient to solve the problem just raised for crude reliabilism.

Contrast then a person whose beliefs satisfy a crude reliabilist theory with one whose beliefs satisfy the requirements of virtue perspectivism. Both persons have a variety of first-order beliefs about the world, including generalizations and presumably also theoretical beliefs based on the beliefs derived from perception, introspection, etc., and all such beliefs are apt in the sense of deriving from sources that are in fact reliable. The obvious difference between the two is of course that the person who realizes virtue perspectivism has, in addition to his various first-order beliefs, the second-order beliefs that constitute his epistemic perspective: beliefs about the sources of his various beliefs, about how these various modes of belief-acquisition were learned or acquired, and about the degree of reliability that results. These second-order beliefs, we may assume, are also apt; and, in addition, they fit together coherently with each other and with the rest of the person's system of beliefs.

But the crucial question that must be asked is: are these perspectival beliefs genuinely *justified* from the person's internal perspective in the epistemologically relevant sense that he has a reason to think that they are *true*? If so, how is such justification supposed to work? And if not, what exactly is their epistemic status supposed to be?

On this critical point, Sosa's account is substantially less explicit and perspicuous than might be desired. I propose, therefore, to resort to an exploration of the apparently available alternatives. I believe that none of them yields a clear account of how the perspectival beliefs can be epistemically justified without at the same time threatening to undercut the basic externalist thrust of Sosa's position.

First, at times Sosa seems to be saying that the internal justification of the perspectival beliefs is *entirely* a matter of their internal coherence, with each other and with other beliefs in the system of beliefs. Thus we are told, for example, that "Reflective justification, our best reflective intellectual procedure, is a matter of perspectival coherence—and necessarily so" (291); and that "The 'justification' of a belief B requires that B have a basis in its inference or coherence relations to other beliefs in the believer's mind" (289). But if the resulting justification is interpreted as epistemic justification of the truth-conducive kind, it is very hard to believe that such a position is tenable, or indeed that it is what Sosa really intends. There are very familiar and seemingly cogent objections to the idea that mere internal coherence could yield a reason for thinking that the beliefs of a system are true, most notably the possibility of alternative, equally coherent systems. And Sosa is of course familiar with these objections and alludes to them at various points, even though his more developed objections to various versions of coherentism are more specific in character. What these considerations suggest is that if the perspectival beliefs are supposed to be justified in the epistemic sense, their justification cannot derive from coherence alone, but must instead derive from a coherence that is constrained in some way by a further condition on some or all of the beliefs that enter into the coherence relation. What might such a further condition be?

Second, one possibility here would be to appeal to coherence with beliefs having some internally recognizable feature that is relevant to likelihood of truth. Here there are two more specific possibilities worth mentioning. The first utilizes the idea of a *cognitively spontaneous belief.* I myself have elsewhere defended a version of qualified coherentism, according to which it is possible to argue on coherentist grounds from within the system of beliefs that certain kinds of cognitively spontaneous beliefs are highly likely to be true.[6] Such a position, if otherwise defensible, would immediately yield an internal justification for some perspectival beliefs and would make it possible to give an internal justification for others by virtue of their coherence with reliable cognitively spontaneous beliefs, as internally identified. But it seems very unlikely that Sosa can have had this sort of possibility in mind without being substantially more explicit about it.

The other, somewhat more obvious possibility under this second general rubric would be an appeal to some version of internalist foundationalism, according to which there are *basic beliefs* that there is some internally recognizable but non-argumentative reason to think are likely to be true. Given an adequate defense of a view of this kind, it would then be possible to provide an internal justification for perspectival beliefs by virtue of their coherence with such basic beliefs. But while there are a number of places in earlier papers in the book where Sosa exhibits sympathy for internalist foundationalism and defends it against various objections, I can find no clear indication that he means to invoke it as an essential part of the internal justification of the epistemic perspective. Moreover, a further difficulty is that a successful defense of a view of either of these last two kinds would seem to go fundamentally against the grain of Sosa's position by making purely external reliability dispensable in relation to justification or aptness (though perhaps not in relation to Gettier-type worries): if it is possible to have a genuinely cogent internal reason for thinking that our beliefs, including our perspectival beliefs are true, then much of the mo-

motivation for externalism, which Sosa like most others defends essentially through an argument by elimination, seems to vanish.

Third, the remaining alternative, the one that I am tentatively inclined to believe that Sosa actually holds, is to appeal to the *aptness* of some of the beliefs in the system, perhaps those deriving from primary sources like perception, introspection, memory, and possibly also testimony, to constrain coherence. (An appeal to the aptness of all the beliefs in the system would seem obviously unavailable as a basis for *internal* justification.) The idea would then be roughly that the basis for internal justification is coherence with a body of beliefs, certain kinds among which are thus apt. Such a view would be a kind of foundationalism, and it is perhaps noteworthy that Sosa remarks in a couple of places (97, 207), though without offering any real explanation, that "perspectival coherentism" can just as well be regarded as a species of foundationalism. But the obvious problem for such a view is to understand how coherence with beliefs that are externally apt can give rise to *internal* justification, i.e., how such coherence yields, any more than pure coherence, an internal reason for thinking that the perspectival beliefs are true. A different way to put what is at bottom essentially the same point is to ask, recurring to Sosa's own example, how a person whose perspectival beliefs are coherent with beliefs that are apt, but which he has no independent reason to think are apt, is in any better position to argue with the proponent of superstition (who may, for all that has been said, also possess an internally coherent epistemic perspective).

The indicated conclusion is that the perspectival beliefs are not internally justified in the distinctively epistemic sense that involves having a reason for thinking that they are true, that their purely internal justification must therefore be of some other sort. I have no clear idea what this other sort of justification might be. But the main problem is that if the person who realizes virtue perspectivism has no reason for thinking that his perspectival beliefs are true, then it becomes very hard to see how Sosa's view is a genuine improvement over that of the crude reliabilist. If mere aptness of first-order beliefs is not enough for the fully human brand of knowledge, how exactly does adding some further meta-beliefs that are apt but not epistemically justified improve the situation? To be sure, these meta-beliefs are also supposed to be coherent with each other and with the first order beliefs, but we have seen no clear account of how internal coherence, which is of little or no significant epistemic value by itself, becomes more valuable when combined with external aptness.

I have space remaining on the present occasion only for a brief look at one further passage in which Sosa raises something resembling the present concern. In a chapter entitled "The Coherence of Virtue and the Virtue of Coherence," he raises the issue of whether coherence might be epistemically prior to reliability in the sense that justification or aptness results from reliability "only if such reliability is noted through a belief that coheres adequately with the adequately comprehensive world view of the subject" (210). Though his response to this issue does not provide any clear answer to the question I have been raising about why exactly the appeal to coherence is supposed to yield genuine justification, it does speak in a way to the collateral worry that an adequate answer to this question would make the externalist appeal superfluous. The response is in effect to challenge the reliability of coherence itself, by imagining possible worlds in which the pursuit of coherence would lead one astray, thus suggesting that even for coherence, it is aptness that is ultimately fundamental.

An adequate treatment of the various issues raised by this suggestion would greatly exceed the allowable bounds of the present paper. For the moment, I must limit myself to pointing out that this sort of response fails to really speak to the basic dilemma that seems to have emerged for Sosa's position, a dilemma that may be restated as follows: Either the appeal to internal coherence can somehow, perhaps when coupled with further internal elements of some sort, provide a genuinely cogent reason for thinking that one's perspectival beliefs (and so also the further beliefs whose reliability they underwrite) are likely to be true, or it cannot. On the former alternative, as Sosa himself seems to suggest, the appeal to external reliability is, as it were, absorbed by the appeal to perspectival coherence and seems to have no independent justificatory function. But on the latter alternative, which I believe to be the one that Sosa actually holds, the internal epistemic perspective turns out to be itself unjustified, and hence the reason for thinking that virtue perspectivism is an improvement over crude reliabilism is apparently lost. In particular, on this latter alternative, it seemingly turns out that on Sosa's view, like that of the crude reliabilist, we have no reason at all for thinking that any of our beliefs are true or apt or justified or instances of knowledge, a result that seems quite unacceptable for one whose primary argument against competing views is that they lead to skepticism.

Notes

1. Ernest Sosa, *Knowledge in Perspective: Selected Essays in Epistemology* (Cambridge: Cambridge University Press, 1991). References in the text are to the pages of this book. This paper was originally presented at the "Author Meets Critics" symposium at the APA Western Division meeting in March 1993.

2. For one version of this argument, see Richard Foley, "What's Wrong with Reliabilism," *The Monist* 68 (1985): 188-202.

3. For the original version of these counterexamples, see my paper "Externalist Theories of Empirical Knowledge," *Midwest Studies in Philosophy* 5 (1980): 53-73. A somewhat modified version is to be found in my *The Structure of Empirical Knowledge* (Cambridge, Mass.: Harvard University Press, 1985), chapter 3.

4. In one passage (237-38), Sosa seems to endorse a different response offered by Alvin Goldman. Goldman's response turns on revising crude reliabilism to require, over and above the reliability of the process by which the belief was actually produced, that there be no further reliable process available to the believer that would, if employed in addition, have led to the belief in question not being accepted. If accepted, Goldman's modification would handle the first three of the four sub-cases just described, but not in any obvious way the fourth. In any case, Sosa offers a different response to this problem elsewhere, one that draws on the resources of his own position rather than relying on Goldman, and it is that response that I propose to focus on here.

5. I am here modifying the wording of Sosa's actual discussion, which is not initially couched in terms of aptness, since the passage under discussion was written prior to his introduction of that term.

6. See part two of *The Structure of Empirical Knowledge*, cited above.

8

Perspectives in Virtue Epistemology:
A Response to Dancy and BonJour

Ernest Sosa

I thank Jonathan Dancy and Laurence BonJour for their gracious comments, and for the good questions they have raised about my work. Although I have learned from nearly all of what they have to say, however, I lack the space to respond fully, and must restrict myself to what seems most important.

I

Dancy raises questions first about formal foundationalism and how it relates to substantive foundationalism; and, secondly, about the doctrine of epistemic supervenience. In doing so he introduces concepts of resultance and of universalizability that turn on a special notion of something making something else be the case. I agree with some of his points and disagree with others, but none seems a real problem for my views.

First, I will lay out very briefly my view of supervenience and normative epistemology as it is found in the collection, early and late, and as I still accept it. By stating very briefly and in quick succession the main components of that view, I hope to make it seem acceptable, and perhaps even uncontroversial.

Epistemic justification is supposed to distinguish knowledge from a lucky guess. 'Aptness' seems a better term for the epistemic status a belief requires in order to be knowledge, but 'justification' is still well entrenched. Here now is a way to think of such justification:

1. Epistemic justification *supervenes.*

The *doctrine of supervenience* for an evaluative property is simply that, for every x, if x has Φ then there is a non-evaluative property (perhaps a relational property) Y such that (i) x has Y, and (ii) necessarily, whatever has Y has Φ.[1]

2. Re epistemic justification, there are three grades of *formal foundationalism:*

first, the supervenience of epistemic justification; second, its explicable supervenience, and, third, its supervenience explicable by means of a simple theory.[2]

Again:

This deeper [formal] foundationalism is applicable to any normative or evaluative property Φ, and it comes in three grades. The *first* or lowest is simply the supervenience of Φ: the idea that whenever something has Φ its having it is founded on certain others of its properties which fall into certain restricted sorts. The *second* is the explicable supervenience of Φ: the idea that there are formulable principles that explain in quite general terms the conditions (actual and possible) within which Φ applies. The third and highest is the easily explicable supervenience of the idea that there is a *simple* theory that explains the conditions within which Φ applies.[3]

3. Coherentism and *substantive foundationalism* both fulfill the highest grade of formal foundationalism:

By coherentism we shall mean any view according to which the ultimate sources of justification for any belief lie in relations among that belief and other beliefs held by the subject: explanatory relations, perhaps, or relations of probability or logic.

According to substantive foundationalism, as it is to be understood here, there are ultimate sources of justification other than relations among beliefs. Traditionally these additional sources have pertained to the special content of the belief or its special relations to the subjective experience of the believer.[4]

4. Formal foundationalism re epistemic justification is acceptable at least because of the intrinsic plausibility of its lowest grade (which, as we have seen, is tantamount to the supervenience of epistemic justification).

So far as I can see, the main reason for accepting formal foundationalism in the absence of an actual, convincing formal foundationalist theory is the very plausible idea that epistemic justification is subject to the supervenience that characterizes normative and evaluative properties generally. Thus, if a car is a good car, then any physical replica of that car must be just as good. If it is a good car in virtue of such properties as being economical, little prone to break down, etc., then surely any exact replica would share all such properties and would thus be equally good. Similarly, if a belief is epistemically justified, it is presumably so in virtue of its character and its basis in perception, memory, or inference (if any). Thus any belief exactly like it in its character and its basis must be equally well justified. Epistemic justification is supervenient.[5]

5. Is there reason to accept a higher grade of formal foundationalism? It is hard to conceive of any very good reason to do so other than that which would be provided by some specific theory that explained the supervenience of justification. Such a theory would provide general principles that when combined with enough factual information about any specific case of a justified belief, would explain how, on what nonevaluative basis (or, at least, non-epistemically-evaluative basis), that belief is justified.

This is a framework uniformly presupposed throughout *Knowledge in Perspective* (KIP). Thus, commitment to the supervenience of justification appears already in the early second paper, which makes it clear that epistemic justification must derive ultimately from the non-epistemic.[6] And the other parts of the framework soon surface repeatedly until the end.

Dancy's critique argues that one cannot succeed in supporting either formal or substantive foundationalism on the basis of supervenience. But in fact formal foundationalism (of the lowest grade) follows trivially from supervenience, being identical to it. Does that give some reason "in favor of" any higher grade of formal foundationalism? Yes, I suppose so, since at least it presents the *possibility* of a higher grade: thus it stimulates our curiosity and challenges us to fulfill that possibility. But nowhere in KIP is it supposed (nor do I think now) that the doctrine of supervenience by itself gives any very good reason to think that we shall ever be able to understand in general terms just how it is that our beliefs come to be epistemically justified.

If supervenience gives no very strong argument to believe in any formal foundationalism beyond the lowest grade, moreover, a fortiori it gives no very strong argument for *substantive* foundationalism. Nor does formal foundationalism provide support for substantive foundationalism as opposed to its rivals. On the contrary KIP recognizes that, for example,

coherentism may also turn out to be formal foundationalism of the highest grade, provided only that the concept of coherence is itself both simple enough and free of any normative or evaluative admixture. Given these provisos, coherentism explains how epistemic justification supervenes on the nonepistemic in a theory of remarkable simplicity: a belief is justified if it has a place within a system of beliefs that is coherent and comprehensive.[7]

Dancy finds in the collection two versions of the doctrine of supervenience:

Version 1   The *doctrine of supervenience* for an evaluative property Φ is simply that for every x, if x has Φ then there is a non-evaluative property Y (perhaps a relational property) such that (i) x has Y, and (ii) necessarily, whatever has Y has Φ.[8]

Version 2   ...the supervenience of Φ is simply the idea that whenever something has Φ its having it is founded on certain others of its properties which fall into certain restricted sorts.[9]

He argues that these are different for two main reasons. First, something (x's having Φ) can supervene without being founded on something else (x's having Y), and can be founded without supervening on it. Second, according to the second version, Φ is said to supervene on properties that fall into certain "restricted" sorts, but there is no such restriction in the first version.

Having distinguished the two versions, Dancy suggests that perhaps confusing the two is what leads to the mistaken view that a grade of formal foundationalism could amount to nothing more than supervenience itself. And he denies that from mere supervenience we could derive any kind of formal foundationalism, or even the more restricting supervenience of the second version above.

To the contrary, I mean the two versions of the doctrine of supervenience as equivalent ways to put what is put less ambiguously by the first. As for the reference to "restricted sorts" in the second version, that requires only *some* "restriction" and is satisfied even if the restriction narrows the relevant class of properties only to properties that are non-normative or non-evaluative.

Indeed it seems to me that Dancy and I are in substantial agreement that the supervenience of the normative and the evaluative might well be so messy that it cannot be fully explained by any simple set of principles (or even by any principles comprehensible by humans). We agree that "there is no *antecedent* reason" to expect otherwise. "But there may be a subsequent reason, namely the discovery that as a matter of fact there is a certain pattern to the ways in which justification results, case by case, and that there can be an explanation of this fact."[10]

In the second part of his paper, Dancy considers the role of the intellectual virtues in epistemology. He notes first my claim that they help to provide a pleasing unity in our view of how beliefs become justified simply by deriving appropriately from the exercise of such a virtue. And he thinks further that they are supposed to help "key our talk of justification into talk of epistemic praise or blame."

Of course if these virtues were motley, the unity they might help provide would be just an illusion. My way of unifying them is to define them as states that help us get at the truth, which also seems to be Aristotle's view, as Dancy points out. But he remains unconvinced, and presents plausible reasons to doubt, that everything it could be reasonable to characterize as an "intellectual virtue" must be truth conducive.

Near the end of his paper Dancy himself provides the best response to his own objection: namely, to focus on those virtues that are especially concerned with epistemic justification, and to hold that *these* must all be truth conducive. But he argues, "for a true virtue theorist there will be a holistic aspect both to our moral and to our epistemic assessment. This means that it must always distort the matter to consider as separable one's performance in any particular respect, including the production of consequences. . . . In this sense, therefore, I think that 'virtue consequentialism' has its feet in two warring camps. . . . [It] is trying to be externalist in its relation to the notion of aptness, where a mere tendency to promote the truth is sufficient, and at the same time to be internalist in its talk of blamelessness and character. These things do not fit well together; or, rather if they do fit well together (as I suppose that in the end they must) we have not yet been shown how they do."[11]

Such issues of externalism and internalism are at center stage in epistemology today, and Larry BonJour has been largely responsible for putting them there. What is more, his paper for this symposium characteristically focuses on such issues. My discussion below is meant to respond to the concerns regarding internalism and externalism raised both by Dancy and by BonJour.

II

BonJour presents the main lines of "virtue perspectivism," my proposed account of human knowledge, and raises what he regards as a "fundamental" problem. The problem is presented by means of a comparison between "virtue perspectivism" and what he calls "crude reliabilism," namely the view that all it takes for a belief to be epistemically justified (or apt) is that it be produced by a reliable process, one that produces a sufficient preponderance of true beliefs.

According to BonJour, crude reliabilism (CR) entails that we have *no reason at all* for thinking that we ever know anything or even that any of our beliefs is justified. And he raises the question of whether virtue perspectivism (VP) offers any advantage in this respect. His answer:

> the main problem is that if the person who realizes virtue perspectivism has no reason for thinking that his perspectival beliefs are true, then it becomes very hard to see how [VP] is a genuine improvement over [CR]. . . . If mere aptness [reliability] of first-order beliefs is not enough for the fully human brand of knowledge, how exactly does adding some further meta-beliefs that are apt but not epistemically justified improve the situation?[12]

And he concludes by suggesting that both on my own view, VP, and on that of the crude reliabilist, CR:

> we have no reason at all for thinking that any of our beliefs are true or apt or justified or instances of knowledge.[13]

However, neither crude reliabilism (CR) nor virtue perspectivism (VP) entails any such consequence. CR simply does not *require* that we have such reasons in order to know. But nothing in CR entails that we never have them. What is more, VP does in fact require that one have reason to think one's first order beliefs true, since it requires that first order beliefs be placed in "epistemic perspective," where one takes note of the sources of one's beliefs (of the first order ones, at a minimum) and of how reliable these are. Thus one's epistemic perspective would classify a typical perceptual belief as a perceptual belief of some relevant sort, and would combine that with an assessment of the reliability of beliefs of that sort. Consider now the following perspectival meta-belief.

MB   B is of perceptual sort Π and beliefs of sort Π are most often true.

Does not MB give one "reason" to think that one's belief B is true?

Accordingly, BonJour's point cannot properly be that according to CR no one has any reason to think they know anything or that any of their beliefs is true or justified, etc. It must be rather that CR would grant to a subject S title to knowledge (perceptual or otherwise) that p in the absence of any such reason.

And his related point against VP must be that it only postpones the unpleasantness. True, VP does require that one have, for first order beliefs such as B, the sort of reason that is provided by a meta-belief such as MB. But according to BonJour,

the crucial question that must be asked is: are these perspectival beliefs [such as MB] genuinely *justified* from the person's internal perspective in the epistemologically relevant sense that he has a reason to think that they are *true?* If so, how is such justification supposed to work? And if not what exactly is their epistemic status supposed to be?[14]

BonJour believes that there are only three possible lines of reply to the questions he has posed for VP, and that none of them is really acceptable when thought through. I agree with him that the three lines of reply he considers are all unsatisfactory but I disagree that they exhaust the possibilities. For they all assume that the only satisfactory internal justification for holding a belief, perspectival beliefs included, would have to involve some reason for thinking the belief true or likely to be true. And BonJour apparently assumes that one needs pervasive justification of that sort in order to have, internally, a full measure of intellectual rationality (or worth or merit). However, if we interpret him in the way apparently intended, then it is evident that although VP will indeed fail, that is only because on the operative assumptions no conceivable epistemology could possibly succeed.

Thus consider again our beliefs B and MB above:

1. MB must itself be epistemically justified in order to constitute a genuine reason for holding B.

2. But in order to be epistemically justified, belief MB requires a belief MMB related to it in the way it is related to belief B (all of these being beliefs by the same subject S at the same time t).

3. Yet for any finite human mind there must be a top rung in the ladder that ascends from B to MB to MMB, etc.

4. And for holding any belief at that top rung—say, belief T—one will *not* have the sort of reason that MB gives one for holding belief B.

5. Indeed if one has a reason at all for holding such a top-rung belief T, it cannot be any reason that involves believing belief T to have some feature in terms of which one might justify holding it. For that would require that one ascend to a higher rung yet, where one might have a meta-belief about that belief T. But *ex hypothesi* our belief T is already a top-rung belief.

To place this result in a wider and perhaps illuminating context, consider a view of practical rationality as follows:

PR   Agent A is rational to Φ at t if and only if A Φs at t because A opts to Φ at t (chooses, decides), and A is rational to so opt.

It is easy to see that PR leads to vicious regress. If the rationality of acting a certain way must derive in the way suggested from the rationality of "opting" to act that way, then the rationality of opting cannot in turn always be understood similarly in terms of the rationality of opting to opt. This sort of view must find some *other* account of the rationality of opting (at *some* level of opting).

And compare now the following view of theoretical rationality:

TR   Subject S is rational to believe P at t if S believes P at t because S believes that his believing P is likely to be correct (given some feature Φ of his believing P at t), and S is rational to believe the latter.

It is equally clear that TR leads to vicious regress. If the rationality of accepting some object-level belief—say, belief that P—must derive in the way suggested from the rationality of believing that one is likely to be right in believing that P, then the rationality of such perspectival beliefs cannot in turn always be understood similarly in terms of the rationality of some higher-level belief. This sort of view must find some other account for the rationality or justification of such beliefs at *some* level of ascent.

We might invoke the internal coherence of S's system of beliefs, including the meta-beliefs that constitute S's epistemic perspective, and propose such coherence as the source of internal rationality or justification for S's beliefs. But there are problems with this. For one thing, beliefs might cohere with each other but fail to cohere with the subject's sensory experiences, in which case some of the beliefs would seem irrational or at least unjustified, or at a minimum would exhibit some intellectual or cognitive failing attributable to the subject herself and not to any imperfection or abnormality in the circumstances. Besides, some infinitely complex, coherent systems of belief have no semblance of the sort of epistemic justification requisite for knowledge. Thus one might believe that there is at least one F in location L, that there are at least two, that there are at least three, etc. And if any such belief is challenged one can defend by invoking its successor. In view of this, and other similar cases, the internal coherence of one's beliefs clearly is not enough by itself; we must require a sort of coherence that satisfies other desiderata as well. For example, it must be coherence not only among one's beliefs, but among one's beliefs *and* experiences. And, further, it must be a coherence that turns perspectival and includes some view of the sources of one's beliefs and of the reliability of these sources.

We think, or hope, that we can explain what distinguishes a system of beliefs (and experiences) that, internally regarded, is intellectually admirable. Presumably our explanation would involve the system's explanatory coherence, its overall simplicity and lack of adhocness and epicycles, and so on. Many characters of popular or philosophical lore rate high in all such respects, however, though their beliefs still fall far short of being knowledge even when true. Think of the brain in a vat for example, or of the victim of the evil demon. Someone already adult when envatted, or when victimized by the evil demon, can be indistinguishable from the best of us in respect of the comprehensiveness and coherence of his beliefs and experiences. However, his contingent beliefs about environing objects and events are far from being knowledge even in those rare cases when they happen to be true.

Only an excessively arrogant philosopher would take such comprehensive internal coherence to exhaust all cognitive or intellectual virtue, even when it encompassed not only beliefs but also experiences. Yet it would be excessively diffident to dismiss it as something of little or no intellectual or cognitive importance. As a philosopher, or just as someone reflective, one aims for such coherence. Of course, one hopes and believes *also* that one has faculties and virtues other than reflective reason: perception, for example, and memory. And these surely go beyond mere internal coherence. But, equally, internal coherence goes beyond such additional faculties, and requires the operation of reason. And this counts for a lot in its own right to most of us. "Why so?"—demands BonJour. Why so? If comprehensive coherence is no guarantee of truth, if indeed it is easy to think of unfortunates, such as the envatted brain, whose internal coherence yields very little truth and hence seems of small cognitive account.

These good questions deserve an answer, and we can begin to answer them by comparing reason with memory. Retentive memory and inferential reason take beliefs already in place as inputs and yields beliefs as outputs—the same belief in the case of retentive memory, and normally a new belief in the case of inferential reason. Now it should be clear that even the most excellent of such transmission faculties will not by themselves guarantee or even make it likely that they will yield much truth. That is going to depend not only on the quality of the transmission but crucially on the quality of the inputs. However, from this fact about transmission faculties, it would be wrong to infer that they are of little or no cognitive worth. They are of cognitive worth because they *combine* with other faculties to increase the total yield of true beliefs far beyond what it would be in their absence.

According to BonJour we need from VP some "clear account of how internal coherence, which is of little or no significant epistemic value in itself, becomes more valuable when combined with external aptness." My proposed account is that coherence-seeking inferential reason, like retentive memory, is of epistemic value when combined with externally apt faculties like perception and memory, because when so combined it, like retentive memory, gives us a more comprehensive grasp of the truth than we would have in its absence.

Certain experience/belief transitions when ingrained in a subject are constitutive of good perception—thus the transition from the sort of visual experience characteristic of a snowball seen in good light to belief that there is such a snowball there. Other such experience/belief transitions are constitutive of good introspection, as when one's headache prompts one to believe that one has a headache. Finally, consider comprehensive coherence in one's system of beliefs. To the degree that it is both present and at least in part responsible for the constitution and persistence of one's belief system, to that degree does it betoken the operation of a commendable faculty of reason. Such comprehensive coherence is not just the product of a brute inference machine, of course, but must rather reflect appropriate sensitivity to factors like adhocness, simplicity, and explanatory power. In any case, however such coherence within one's system of beliefs is to be understood in detail, there is a broader coherence that includes not only such belief/belief connections but also experience/belief connections constitutive of good perception, and conscious-state/belief connections constitutive of good introspection. By including these we obtain a broader conception of the coherence of one's mind, which now involves not only the logical, probabilistic, and explanatory relations among one's first-order beliefs, but also coherence between these beliefs and one's sensory and other experiences, as well as comprehensive coherence between first-order experiences, beliefs, and other mental states, on one side, and on the other beliefs *about* such first-order states (as well as meta-meta-beliefs about these meta-beliefs, etc., for some finite distance up such rungs of a ladder of reflection).

Concerning certain aspects of such broad coherence—e.g., the experience/belief transitions as well as the enumerative and abductive inferences involved—it may well be asked why these should be viewed as adding to the subject's intellectual worth or merit. This challenge needs to be taken seriously, and I would like now to supplement my initial suggestions above by considering two possible responses to it.

First, it might be said that intellectual worth is just necessarily present in such coherence, and that this is a brute necessary fact to be accepted with humble piety. The problem with this approach is that the set of facts involved is motley in the extreme. Thus consider only the experience/belief connections that we regard as coherent. Of course, if we regard these as experience-as-if-P/belief-that-P, then we find a pleasing simplicity and generality. The ugly scatter emerges, however, once we press beyond this and consider the intrinsic character of whatever realizes the subject's experience-as-if-P, and ask why *that* character counts as experience-as-if-P in the first place, and why it should be thought to fit so coherently with belief-that-P.

Attempts to answer that question may easily lead to the *second* response, according to which broad coherence adds to a subject's intellectual merit because it is truth conducive: that is to say, broad coherence is valuable and admirable in a subject because it increases the likelihood that the subject will have true beliefs and avoid false ones.

However, is that not obviously false in the case of the Cartesian demon's victim (and the envatted brain)? Someone in the clutches of the demon (or in the vat) is not really helped along towards the truth by coherence of our broadened sort. For he believes "Here is a snowball" prompted by the white, round image that he sees, but he is actually wrong, and he is equally wrong, again and again, in his many other such beliefs, no matter how coherent they may be with each other and with his experience.

All this I am prepared to grant, but we can perhaps understand it comfortably if we distinguish two sorts of epistemic justification as follows:

> S is "same-world justified" in world W in believing P iff S believes P in W in virtue of a faculty that in W is truth conducive.

> S is "actual-world justified" in world W in believing P iff S believes P in W in virtue of a faculty that *in our actual world* α is truth conducive.

Such relativization and contextualization is pervasive in our ordinary ways of thinking and I see nothing terribly forced or artificial in our appeal to it here. So I claim that: (a) our broad coherence is necessary for the kind of reflective knowledge that our tradition has always taken as a desideratum; and (b) such broadly coherent knowledge is desirable because in our actual world α it helps us approach the truth and avoid error. This is not to deny that there is a kind of "knowledge," properly so called, that falls short in respect of broad coherence— "animal knowledge," as we might call it. It is rather only to affirm that beyond "animal knowledge" we humans, especially those of us who are philosophical or at least reflective, aspire to a higher knowledge. This higher knowledge we might call "reflective," since by definition it requires some appropriate degree of broad coherence including one's ability to place one's first-level knowledge in epistemic perspective. But why aspire to any such thing? What is so desirable, epistemically, about broad coherence? Here again we might appeal to the truth-conduciveness of such coherence, even if, as we well know, a mind *might* be broadly coherent in a world where such broad coherence was *not* truth conducive. *We* can still regard such broad coherence as intellectually valuable and admirable so long as we do *not* regard *our* world as such a world. But then, of course, we *don't*, do we?

In this respect, we are, it seems to me, in just the position of arch-internalist Descartes. The following passage is of crucial importance here:

That an atheist can clearly know that the three angles of a triangle are equal to two right angles, I do not deny; I merely say that this knowledge of his *(cognitionem)* is not true science *(scientia)*, because no knowledge which can be rendered doubtful should, it seems, be called science. Since he is supposed to be an atheist, he cannot be certain that he is not deceived even in those things that seem most evident to him, as has been sufficiently shown; and although this doubt may never occur to him, nevertheless it can occur to him, if he examines the question, or it may be suggested by someone else, and he will never be safe from it, unless he first acknowledges God.[15]

Descartes wants to be able to defend against possible skeptical doubts about his intellectual faculties, not only his faculties of perception, memory, and introspection, but even his faculty of intuitive reason, by which he might know that 3+2=5, that if he thinks he exists, and the like. He believes he can defend against such doubts *only* by coherence-inducing theological reasoning that yields an epistemic perspective on himself and his world, in terms of which he can feel confident about the reliability of his faculties. And these faculties must include the very faculties that he employed in arriving, via his a priori theological reasoning, at his perspective on himself and his world, the perspective that enables confidence in the reliability of such faculties.

Virtue perspectivism (VP) is *structurally* Cartesian, though its content is very different from Descartes's own rationalism. Such rationalism admits only (rational) intuition and deduction (along with memory) as its faculties of choice (or anyhow of top choice) and wishes to validate all knowledge in terms of these faculties. VP is not so restricted, and admits also perception and introspection, along with intuition, as well as inductive and abductive reasoning, along with the deductive reasoning favored by Descartes.

By use of all such faculties, plus testimony, and aided by one's epistemic community, one attains, according to VP, a broad view of oneself and one's environing world. And, if all goes well, then in terms of this epistemic perspective one can feel confident about the reliability of one's full complement of faculties. True, these faculties include the very faculties employed in arriving at the perspective on oneself and one's world that enables confidence in the reliability of such faculties.

Our procedure was viewed as viciously circular by Descartes's critics and is still widely thought vicious even today. Undeniably, it does present a troubling aspect of circularity. However, a closer look may reveal that the supposed viciousness is only an illusion. But I must postpone that to another occasion.[16]

∗This title is a reply to Jonathan Dancy's "Supervenience, Virtue, and Consequences," and Laurence BonJour's "Sosa on Knowledge, Justification, and 'Aptness'," for a symposium on Knowledge in Perspective at the APA Pacific Division meetings of March 1993.

Notes

1. Ernest Sosa, *Knowledge in Perspective* (Cambridge: Cambridge University Press, 1991), 153.
2. Sosa 191.
3. Sosa 181.
4. Sosa 184.
5. Sosa 179.
6. See the definition of full validation, ibid., 30.
7. Sosa 180.
8. Sosa 181.
9 Sosa 181.
10. Dancy 194.

11. Dancy 202-203.

12. BonJour 218. Here BonJour falls in with my distinction between externalist, reliability-bound aptness and internalist, rationality-bound justification. (A fuller account of relevant epistemic statuses would require further distinctions.)

13. BonJour 218.

14. BonJour 219.

15. *The Philosophical Works of Descartes*, trans. Haldane & Ross, vol. 2, 39.

16. See my "Philosophical Skepticism and Epistemic Circularity," *Proceedings of the Aristotelian Society Supplementary Volume* (1994); and compare Barry Stroud's response, "Scepticism, 'Externalism', and the Goal of Epistemology," ibid. And compare also the symposium on proper functionalism among Richard Feldman, Alvin Plantinga, and myself in *Nous* 27 (1993); and the symposium on virtue perspectivism among Richard Foley, Richard Fumerton, and myself in *Philosophical Issues* 5 (1994).

Part III

Responsibility, Motives, and Consequences

9

From Reliabilism
to Virtue Epistemology

Linda Zagzebski

I

One of the problems with reliabilism is that it does not explain what makes the good of knowledge greater than the good of true belief. Previously I have given this objection only to process reliabilism.[1] In this paper I will develop the objection in more detail, and will then argue that the problem pushes us first in the direction of three offspring of process reliabilism—faculty reliabilism, proper functionalism, and agent reliabilism—and finally to a virtue epistemology based on virtue in the ethical sense.

II

A reliable process is good only because of the good of the product of the process. A reliable espresso-maker is good because espresso is good. A reliable water-dripping faucet is not good because dripping water is not good. Reliability per se has no value or disvalue. Its value or disvalue derives solely from the value or disvalue of that which it reliably produces. So the value of the product of a process is transferred to the process that produces it. But the value of the process is not transferred back again to the product. A reliable expresso-maker is good because espresso is good, but the espresso made now is no better because it was produced by a reliable espresso machine. The water dripping now is no better because it was produced by a reliably dripping faucet; and neither is it any worse.

Similarly, a reliable truth-producing process is good because truth is good. But if I acquire a true belief from such a process, that does not make my belief better than it would be otherwise. Of course, since the process is good, I am better off for having it, and I may even be better off for using it now, but that does not add status to any given true belief of mine that it produces. So if Adam

113

has a reliable memory and acquires a true belief about the past as a result of using his reliable memory, his belief is no more valuable epistemically than the belief of Eve, who has an equally reliable memory and who acquires the same true belief about the past, but acquires it by a non-reliable process. Eve may be no worse off than Adam, but the important point is that Adam is no better off than Eve.

This objection is the analogue of one sometimes given to rule utilitarianism. If we assume that maximizing utility is good, rules generalizing from behavior that reliably leads to maximizing utility are also good; but there is no additional good in the fact that a particular act follows such a rule. If a particular act maximizes utility, its value is not increased by the fact that it is a member of a class of acts most of which maximize utility. And if an act does not maximize utility, it does not get value from the fact that it is a member of such a class.

One moral to draw from this is that value can be transferred in one direction only, not back and forth. The value of the product is transferred to the value of a process reliably producing that product, but the product in any given case does not get an extra boost of value from the value of the process. So the value of true belief is transferred to the value of a reliable truth-producing process, but a particular true belief does not get any extra value from being the product of such a process. Hence process reliabilism cannot explain what gives knowledge greater value than true belief. I will call this the value problem.

Evidentialism does not have the value problem. Basing belief on evidence is good not only because doing so reliably leads to the truth, but because there is something epistemically good about seeing the connection between the evidence and the truth. So when a person bases a true belief on the evidence, it is good that she has the truth; it is good that she has evidence; it is an additional good that her true belief is based upon the evidence. The fact that she bases her belief on the evidence is good, not because doing so leads to the truth in general, nor only because it has led to the truth on this occasion, but because on this occasion she has seen the connection between the evidence and the true proposition she believes, and has thereby acquired a level of epistemic status she would not have had otherwise. We recognize this when we say that there is something epistemically valuable about even a false belief properly based on evidence. In contrast, it is problematic to say that there is anything epistemically valuable about a false belief produced by a reliable process. Would we say that the bad-tasting espresso produced by a reliable espresso maker is any better than bad-tasting espresso produced by an unreliable espresso-maker? We do not, nor should we say that the false belief produced by a reliable truth-producing process is any better than the false belief produced by an unreliable belief process. If a reliable process does not give value to a false belief, neither does it add value to a true belief.

Whatever one thinks of evidentialism, then, it cannot be faulted for not identifying a distinct epistemic good in addition to getting the truth. Its problem, in fact, is just the opposite: the two goods it identifies seem to be too far apart. Evidentialism attempts to capture two sources of epistemic good in one concept of justifiedness—truth-conduciveness and rationality. What makes this problematic is that there is no prima facie reason to expect any connection between the two. Perhaps it is obvious that it is rational to base beliefs on evidence, but if that is what it is to be rational, why think that *that* has anything to do with getting the truth? Elsewhere I have called this the alignment problem.[2] I will not go into the alignment problem here, however, since in this paper I am primarily interested in a different class of theories. I assume that reliabilists are right that the value of knowledge in addition to true belief has something to do with truth-conduciveness. But I have argued that it cannot be truth-conduciveness alone. The reliabilist intuition that there ought to be a connection between the rationality (justifiability, warrant) of a belief and its truth is an advantage of the theory. Evidentialism cannot explain the connection; reliabilism builds the connection into its definition of knowledge.

Process reliabilism founders on the value problem. An improvement is, or may be, faculty reliabilism of the sort endorsed by Ernest Sosa. It is possible that the product of a reliable faculty is epistemically enhanced in virtue of being such a product, but that is unclear because the concept of a faculty is vague. If there is a faculty of weighing evidence and forming beliefs based on the evidence, then, given the remarks I have just made about evidentialism, their epistemic value is more than the value of the truth they produce. But, then, they do not get their value solely from their reliability. On the other hand, if a faculty is a psychological mechanism like memory, it does not enhance the believer's epistemic status unless the faculty consists in more than a reliable process. If a faculty is nothing more than a reliable process for generating true beliefs it does not give extra value to its product any more than the espresso machine does. So faculty reliabilism is subject to the same objection I have given to process reliabilism unless there is something more *in* the faculty than an organ/process for producing beliefs. And that something more must have value that is transferred to its product.

The problem for either kind of reliabilism, then, is that whatever makes the product of a reliable faculty good cannot be reliability, but something else. It is reasonable to think that that something else underlies and explains the reliability of the faculty or process. So even though reliabilists are probably right that there is a close connection between reliably formed true beliefs and knowledge, the source of the value of knowledge is something deeper than reliability.

Alvin Plantinga's proper function theory is an attempt to identify something valuable that is deeper than reliability and that explains it. Typically, a reliable faculty is reliable because it is functioning the way it was designed. So Plantinga has proposed that knowledge is true warranted belief where, roughly, a warranted belief is one that is produced by properly functioning faculties in an appropriate environment according to a design plan aimed at truth.[3] This theory has the disadvantage of adding the vagueness of the concepts of proper function and design to the vagueness of the concept of a faculty, but it includes the insight that reliability per se does not epistemically enhance either a particular belief or a believer for having that belief. A properly functioning faculty *is* reliable, but its reliability is grounded in what Plantinga proposes makes it *really* valuable—the fact that it is functioning properly. And it is true, perhaps analytically true, that proper functioning is a good thing, unlike reliability, which, I have argued, is not good in itself. Of course, a reliable espresso machine is almost always a properly functioning one, and a reliably dripping faucet is almost always a malfunctioning one, and one might even say that in the case of espresso machines and water faucets, their function is *nothing but* reliably producing certain products—and not certain other products. But the sense of good in which proper function is good is not the one we want in a component of knowledge. A properly functioning faculty, like a reliable faculty, gets its value from what it does or produces when it is functioning properly. A properly functioning cancer cell is not good even though it is functioning properly *for* a cancer cell. It may be a good cancer cell, but it is not good. Properly functioning nerve gas is not good even though it is functioning as nerve gas is supposed to function. Cancer cells and nerve gas are not good; in fact, proper functioning makes them even worse.

At this point another element of Plantinga's theory becomes crucial. What gives properly functioning faculties additional value in Plantinga's theory is that they are the product of intelligent design that has a certain aim. On this position, a properly functioning espresso machine is good, not only because espresso is good, but because it has fulfilled the purpose of its designer. Perhaps this gives it value in addition to the value of its product. So if my espresso machine is functioning properly it is a good machine because it is doing what it is designed to do. It is not good simply because espresso is good. A malfunctioning faucet is bad because it is not doing what it is designed to do, and its badness is not merely derivative from the badness of dripping water; or so it can be argued.

But is the value of the espresso produced by a machine functioning as it was designed any better than it would be if it were produced by a reliable but undesigned machine, much less an unreliable and undesigned machine? I do not see that it is. Consider three objects used as screwdrivers: one, a properly functioning screwdriver that does a good job of screwing in a screw; the second, a dime, which is not designed to be a screwdriver, but does a perfectly good job of screwing in a screw; the third, an unreliable and malfunctioning screwdriver with a loose handle that nonetheless, on this occasion, screws in the screw perfectly well.[4] If the unreliable and improperly functioning screwdriver drives the screw in straight, the result is just as good as it would be if it were driven in by either the dime or the properly functioning screwdriver. And the screw driven in by the former is just as good as the one driven in by the latter. That is, there would be no reason in any of the three cases to remove the screw and redo the process. If the result is just as good, it makes no difference whether the process was one that usually gets good results, nor does it matter whether the process was one designed to be used in that way. The fact that things and processes operate as designed may be a good thing, but it is a good extrinsic to the product. The product itself is neither better nor worse because it is the work of design.

The conclusion is that neither reliability nor proper function identifies what is epistemically valuable in knowledge in addition to truth, but reliability is a sign of something deeper that *is* valuable. Plantinga's theory of functioning as designed is an attempt to identify what that is. He thinks that what makes the believer reliable is what is really valuable. And given the objection I have just made to Plantinga, we may add that what proper functioning consists in is what is really valuable. And that has to be something intrinsic to the believer or the belief, not something extrinsic. Design is extrinsic.

III

If neither reliability nor proper function is sufficient to explain what makes an instance of knowledge better than true belief, why have so many philosophers thought otherwise? The answer, I think, is that they have misunderstood the moral of Gettier problems. It is often said that the key problem in Gettier cases is that they are instances in which a person's belief is justified (or warranted) and true, but she gets to the truth accidentally. There is only an accidental connection between her state of justifiedness/warrant and her reaching the truth. For this reason it has often been proposed that knowledge ought to be defined as non-accidentally true belief. Since a belief that is the product of either a reliable process, a reliable faculty, or proper function according to a design plan aimed at truth gets to the truth non-accidentally, it may be tempting to think that that is good enough both to avoid Gettier problems and to be an instance of knowledge. I believe it does not succeed in either aim. Elsewhere I have argued that reliabilism and proper functionalism cannot escape Gettier problems,[5] but my point here is that neither theory has identified the ingredient in knowledge that explains what makes it more valuable than true belief. Non-accidentality is not valuable enough to give us the value we think knowledge has.

Gettier cases are in a genre of counterexamples that illustrate what is wrong with a definition by taking extreme cases. In these cases the truth is reached accidentally, and that is sufficient to preclude their being instances of knowledge. But it is a mistake to conclude from *that* that anything short of accidentality is good enough. Of course a belief must be non-accidentally true in order to be an instance of knowledge, but that is only the weakest thing we can say about it. Accidentality is epistemically bad, but it does not follow that non-accidentality in any degree or form is epistemically good. The hard part is to identify a good-making property of a belief or a believer that accounts for the extra value of knowledge in addition to true belief and that also is immune to Gettier problems.

Susan Haack has suggested that an obvious way to modify reliabilism is to substitute reference to processes (or faculties) that we *believe* to be reliable for those that *are* reliable.[6] Presumably, Plantinga's theory could be modified in the parallel fashion. What would make a belief warranted would be that we believe it is the outcome of properly functioning faculties according to a design plan aimed at truth. I think this suggestion is moving in the right direction, but reliabilists and proper functionalists are right to reject it. What a person stupidly, irrationally, or even just mistakenly believes about what reliably leads to truth or functions as part of a design plan is not sufficient to give a true belief the extra value we are looking for. If reliability has anything to do with knowledge at all, it is not simply in virtue of the fact that the believer believes it obtains. Perhaps we should say that the believer must be *aware* of her reliability. But, of course, such awareness also can be irrational or based on a mistake, and that also would make it disvaluable. Perhaps, then, we should say that the believer must be *justifiably aware* of her own reliability. But that is non-explanatory since the issue we are discussing here is the value problem, and one way of putting the issue is to determine what justifiability consists in. It is interesting, though, that reflection on the value problem in reliabilism tends to lead us back to one of the most important features of evidentialism—that what is good about knowledge has something to do with meritorious features of the agent's subjective perspective.

John Greco has moved in this direction in the most recent form of reliabilism, agent reliabilism. According to Greco, an agent's true belief *p* has the value that converts true belief into knowledge just in case his believing *p* results from stable and reliable dispositions that make up his cognitive character.[7] Greco intends this definition to entail the satisfaction of conditions of subjective epistemic justification. A knower's reliability must be grounded in the cognitive dispositions she manifests when thinking in a way motivated by the attempt to get truth. Can agent reliabilism avoid the value problem? As with faculty reliabilism, the answer depends upon the kind of dispositions that make up an agent's cognitive character and why they are reliable. If the value of a cognitive character is no more than the value of its reliability, then the espresso maker analogy can be used against this form of reliabilism as well as the others. Intuitively, character *is* the sort of thing that is valuable apart from reliability. In particular, the motive for truth is valuable not only because it reliably leads to truth, but also because a person with such a motive has a praiseworthy cognitive character. If so, the additional value of knowledge comes from properties of a person's motives or character; reliability per se is not the source of the value. If this is what Greco intends, I would think the theory would be more appropriately named something like "character reliabilism" rather than "agent reliabilism." But if the theory places the value that converts true belief into knowledge on the reliability of the agent's cognitive dispositions rather than on the value of character, the theory falls prey to the argument of this paper.

So far I have argued that knowledge is more valuable than true belief and its value must accrue to the believer for having the belief. A belief produced by reliable or properly functioning processes or faculties or dispositions does not have that extra value unless the reliability and proper function rest on something else that is a valuable epistemic property of the believer. Evidentialism does not have the problem of identifying an extra source of value, and this suggests that evidentialists may be right that the extra source of value is something praiseworthy about the believer's subjective perspective. The evolution of reliabilism from process reliabilism to faculty reliabilism to agent reliabilism leads in the same direction. Greco discusses cognitive dispositions that arise out of the motive for truth and he intends his form of reliabilism to entail subjective justification.

I have not denied that when an agent knows she or the process she uses is reliable and properly functioning. But what makes knowledge valuable is what grounds or explains the reliability and proper functioning of the process and/or agent. The move from processes to faculties to dispositions in reliabilism can be plausibly construed as an attempt to move towards deeper features of the agent's character that underlie and explain her reliability. So the moral we have drawn from the fact that reliabilism and proper functionalism have the value problem is that when I know p, there is something valuable about my belief p or the way it was acquired that explains why it was formed by a reliable and/or properly functioning process/faculty/disposition, and the moral we have drawn from the fact that evidentialism does not have the value problem is that it is somehow grounded in praiseworthy features of the subjective perspective of the believer.

IV

What makes conscious beings act reliably? Of course, they may do so accidentally, but we have already seen that accidentality does not add value. Or they may do so because that is their nature, a nature of which they may not even be aware. But in that case they do not differ from the espresso maker already discussed. Or they may act reliably because that is what they are motivated to do. Elsewhere I have proposed a definition of knowledge in which its primary constituent is the motive for truth and the motive to act in ways that derive from the truth-motive (e.g., being open-minded, intellectually fair, thorough, careful, etc.). Basing knowledge on the motive for truth combines the advantages of reliabilism and evidentialism. Like evidentialism and unlike reliabilism it does not have the value problem because it identifies a good that knowledge has in addition to the good of true belief. Like reliabilism and unlike evidentialism it does not have the alignment problem because it explains the connection between truth and rationality/justifiability. Let us look more closely at how the motive for truth can serve these purposes in defining knowledge.

A motive to get to the truth and to act in ways found to be reliable ways of getting there is a good thing for the same reason a motive to promote human well-being and to act in ways found to be reliable ways of promoting human well-being is a good thing.

We think of promoting well-being as a good thing even if it is done unconsciously. Similarly, we think of getting the truth as a good thing even if it is done unconsciously. That is why it is good to have a true belief no matter how it is acquired. But we think that some ways of promoting human well-being are not as good as others. Most obviously, promoting well-being by accident is not as good as doing so intentionally, and this difference in value is not just one of degree but of kind. Similarly, getting the truth by accident is not as good as doing so intentionally, and again, the difference is not just one of degree, but of kind. Notice that I have contrasted getting the truth accidentally with getting the truth intentionally. But accident and intentional action are two ends of a spectrum of conscious control. There is a wide area in between, and we have already seen that while the moral of Gettier cases and cases of guessing is that accidental success in getting the truth is ruled out of the realm of knowledge, it does not follow that any non-accidental success is good enough for knowledge. Similarly, promoting human well-being by accident is ruled out of the realm of moral praiseworthiness, but it does not follow that any non-accidental promotion of well-being is good enough to deserve moral praise. The intentional promotion of good usually merits the highest praise, but doing good with something less than full conscious intention may be good enough even though doing good by anything more than accident is not always enough.

The concept of motive is useful in this context because motives are connected to the successful attainment of their ends in much more than an accidental way even though they are not always intentional or fully conscious. A person may be motivated to bring about the well-being of others even when she does not consciously think of that as her end on each occasion in which the motive is operative. Similarly, a person may be motivated to get the truth and avoid falsehood even when he does not consciously think of that as his end on each occasion in which that motive is operative. We are conscious of our motives only part of the time, whether in our epistemic or our overt behavior, but our praiseworthiness and blameworthiness for those motives are not limited to those occasions in which we are conscious of them. Rarely do we consciously and deliberatively think that we are motivated to acquire truth when we form beliefs even though it is often the case that the best explanation of our behavior is that that is our motive. Similarly, it is rare that we consciously and deliberatively think that we are motivated to promote human well-being even when the best explanation of our behavior is that that is our motive.

I assume that the motive to get the truth is a good motive in our belief-forming activity and that the motive to promote human well-being is a good motive in our overt acts. What makes these motives good is an important question, one that I address elsewhere.[8] My point here is only that these motives *are* good, and that their goodness is such that it transfers to the goodness of that which it motivates an agent to do. Epistemic behavior motivated by the motive for truth has value in addition to the value of the truth that is thereby attained. Overt behavior motivated by the motive to promote human well-being has value in addition to the value of the well-being that is thereby attained. Success in reaching truth or well-being is not guaranteed in either case, of course, but I assume that when it *is* attained, the behavior that is successful in attaining it gains value that it would not otherwise have. Therefore, behavior that is both motivated to attain some good and is successful in doing so is more valuable than either behavior that is well motivated but unsuccessful in its end or behavior that reaches the end but does not arise out of a motive to reach it.

Finally, behavior that is both motivated to reach a good end and is successful in doing so is more valuable if its success in reaching its end is *due to* the good motive.

An agent who is motivated to promote human well-being and who does so because of some other mechanism than the causal influence of his motivation on his act and the effects of his act is not deserving of the same kind of moral praise as an agent who is similarly motivated and who is successful in promoting human well-being because of the way that motive brings about his act and the way that act brings about human well-being. Similarly, an agent who is motivated to get the truth but who gets the truth on some occasion because of some other mechanism than the way that motive brings about his cognitive acts and their consequences is not deserving of the same kind of epistemic praise as an agent who is similarly motivated and who gets the truth on some occasion because of the motive and the cognitive behavior to which it leads.

If a particular piece of behavior is the cause of a good end on some occasion, this usually implies that behavior of that kind reliably or characteristically leads to an end of that kind. A reliable connection between behavior of a certain kind and a consequence of a certain kind is not all that there is to the relation holding between that behavior and the state of affairs it causes, but it is probably the most common and salient feature of the Because relation. For this reason reliabilists are right to focus on reliability as a critical feature of the relation between believers and truth, but they are wrong if they think it is constitutive of that relation.

In short, my suggestion is this: If a cognitive agent is motivated to get to the truth and acts in ways that are reliable because of that motive, and is successful in reaching the truth *because of* the motive and the reliable processes to which the motive gave rise, that is a cognitive agent who has reached an epistemic state worth having—not just truth, but knowledge. This theory is a form of virtue theory because it identifies the value in knowledge in addition to true belief as based on the agent's motive, a primary constituent of a virtue. It therefore avoids the value problem. The theory also avoids the alignment problem because there is a natural connection between the two values identified in the account of knowledge: the motive for truth and getting the truth. In fact, if I am right that the value of knowledge in addition to truth is that the truth is reached *because* of the motive for truth and reliable cognitive behavior, then there is a definitional connection between the two values as well. In contrast, the evidentialist must explain why there should be a connection between truth and basing beliefs on evidence. It will no doubt turn out, of course, that one of the ways found to be reliable ways of getting to the truth is to base beliefs on evidence, but basing beliefs on evidence gets its value from the fact that that is what truth-motivated persons do.

Reliabilism and proper functionalism made an important turn in epistemology by shifting the focus of epistemic evaluation from evidential relations among propositions to persons and their properties. But both reliability and proper functioning are derivative values. The value of reliability derives from the value of that to which it is reliably connected. The value of proper functioning derives from the value of that which functions properly. The value of functioning as designed is also derivative since it is only as good as the design itself. None of these theories can explain the value that knowledge has in addition to true belief. Ever since Plato, knowledge has been considered a lofty state, one that merits praise for its possessor. Persons are not praised in that way merely for getting the truth. Having reliable faculties/dispositions and using reliable processes may be good *indications* that the epistemic agent deserves praise, but they are not the properties for which the agent is praised. Those properties, I have proposed, are motives to behave in ways that derive from the motive for truth and that lead to behavior reliably connected with gaining truth.

Notes

1. *Virtues of the Mind: An Inquiry into the Nature of Virtue and the Ethical Foundations of Knowledge* (Cambridge: Cambridge University Press, 1996), 301-2.

2. This problem has been called the ratification problem by Susan Haack in *Evidence and Inquiry* (Oxford: Blackwell, 1993), passim. I have called it the alignment problem in "Phronesis and Christian Belief," in *The Rationality of Religious Belief*, edited by Godehard Bruntrup (Dordrecht: Kluwer, 2000). [Revised version, chapter 16, this volume.]

3. *Warrant and Proper Function* (New York: Oxford University Press, 1993).

4. I thank Frank McGuinness for suggesting this analogy to me.

5. The first place in which I gave this argument is "The Inescapability of Gettier Problems," *Philosophical Quarterly* vol. 44, #174 (January 1994): 65-73. A revised version of this paper appears in *Virtues of the Mind*, Part III, section 3. A more recent form of the argument appears in "What is Knowledge?" in the *Blackwell Guide to Epistemology* edited by Ernest Sosa and John Greco (Oxford: Blackwell, 1998).

6. Haack 1993, chapter seven.

7. "Agent Reliabilism," *Philosophical Perspectives*, vol. 13 (1999). Greco uses the term "agent reliabilism" for a larger class of theories than his own, including Sosa's, Plantinga's, and my early theory, but as I will argue, his own version comes closer to solving the value problem than faculty reliabilism or proper functionalism.

8. *Virtues of the Mind*. I present a more detailed defense of the primacy of the value of good motives in *Divine Motivation Theory*, manuscript in preparation.

10

Moral and Epistemic Virtue

Julia Driver

Over the last couple of decades ethicists have demonstrated an increased interest in virtue evaluation, and, indeed, an entire new family of theories has developed centered on virtue evaluation as central or "primary" to ethical evaluation. What these theories seem to have in common is the view that virtue evaluation, rather than act evaluation, is more central to ethical theory. More recently, some epistemologists have argued similarly for epistemology—virtue evaluation should be central, and atomistic evaluation of beliefs as justified or unjustified is not good enough.[1] One could picture a form of virtue epistemology in which justified beliefs are those beliefs an epistemically virtuous person would have. This raises the question of what an epistemic virtue is.

What Is a Virtue?

Linda Zagzebski has argued that one could develop an account of virtue that is unified—that is, which accounts for both moral and intellectual virtue.[2] Thus, the account she offers would be a general account of normative virtue. Indeed, she argues for a particularly bold claim: that "the concept of the moral is too narrow as commonly understood and that it ought to be extended to cover the normative aspects of cognitive activities."[3] Her view is that modern ethical theory is really a system focused on regulating conflict, and is thus artificially narrow in scope for the full purposes of evaluation. If expanded to include intellectual norms, moral evaluation can offer a genuinely unified and general account of virtue. I disagree and will argue that a unified account of virtue is neither doable nor desirable. Additionally, I disagree with her view of what the virtues are because I think her view suffers—not surprisingly—from some of the same faults one sees in accounts of moral virtue generated by similar attempts at developing virtue ethics.

This paper will examine accounts of epistemic virtue in light of structurally similar accounts one sees of moral virtue in the virtue ethics literature. I will conclude by offering the account I believe is the best of the available options, which is not unified, but which does reflect parallels between the two types of evaluation. It is important to keep in mind that there is a distinction between epistemic virtue theory and virtue epistemology. Virtue epistemology, like virtue ethics, holds that virtue evaluation is primary. Virtue theory, on the other hand, is simply concerned with understanding the virtues—whether they are primary or not. This paper concentrates on the accounts of virtue that are given by virtue ethicists and virtue epistemologists, but does not directly address the issue of whether or not virtue ethics or epistemology is feasible.

In the area of virtue ethics, Michael Slote has done the most to try to develop a systematic account.[4] Slote attempts to develop an account that avoids some of the main problems raised for putative virtue ethics. One significant problem is that virtue ethics seems unable to provide *direction*. I call this the 'procedure problem' since it rests on the view that any theory that holds virtue to be primary—as opposed to some rule—will not be able to provide a procedure for action. Slote disagrees. He has argued that virtue ethics can be developed as an "agent-based" moral theory.[5] An agent-based ethics treats moral evaluation of agents as prior to evaluation of acts. Thus, the person's actions will be evaluated in terms of features of the persons. Not all agent-based theories will qualify as exemplars of virtue ethics, however. For example, subjective act utilitarianism might qualify as an agent-based theory since the rightness of an action is determined by its *expected* utility, expectation being internal to agency or an antecedent condition to it.

One way to spell out agent-basing would be to maintain, for example, that the motive of the action determines the action's moral quality. Roughly, if the motive is good then the action is good because it exemplifies virtue that is characterized by having a good motive; if the motive is bad, the action is bad. I have elsewhere presented criticisms of this approach for virtue ethics.[6] One serious problem, for example, will be the difficulty of this approach in specifying what makes a motive good or bad without appealing to external factors such as consequences. Even if, as Slote suggests, good motives will somehow be outward looking—so as to avoid the moral autism objection—one runs up against the problem of the incompetent agent who has made efforts to discover the truth, yet nevertheless goes astray.

Slote's account provides an example of a theoretical approach that I call 'evaluational internalism'.[7] This sort of theory holds that the moral quality of an action or character trait is determined by factors internal to agency, such as motives or intentions. This approach is contrasted with 'evaluational externalism' which holds that the moral quality of actions or character traits is determined by factors external to agency, such as actual (as opposed to expected) consequences. Slote holds that one way to develop a virtue ethics that can incorporate the notion of a right action is to view an action as right if it comes from a good and virtuous motive (and thus exemplifies virtue)—and, roughly, what marks virtue is this disposition to act from a good motive. The virtuous agent is one who has good motives.

Contrasted with Slote's account would be the Aristotelian account of virtue. This account holds that moral virtue involves not merely the proper motivation (e.g., being motivated for the sake of the virtue itself, or having a "good" motive of some sort), but also involves some connection to actual human flourishing—thus, for Aristotle there is an external success condition as well. This account is a "mixed" account since it is neither purely internalist nor purely externalist. The success condition is necessary to help distinguish natural virtue from true virtue. A child, for example, may have a natural virtue in the sense that he wants to do good, but because he lacks practical wisdom, he will consistently fail to actually accomplish the good and may even do things that are harmful.[8] Actual good must be reliably accomplished for the individual to have true virtue, and this requires practical wisdom. Thus, though the virtuous agent acts virtuously for its own sake, there is a definite connection between virtue and production of the good, or human flourishing.

Linda Zagzebski's strategy with intellectual virtue is similar to Aristotle's (indeed, she is explicitly Aristotelian in orientation) since she has both an internal condition with the added success condition: "virtue . . . [is] a deep and enduring acquired excellence of a person, involving a characteristic motivation to produce a certain desired end and reliable success in bringing about that end."[9] Thus, in her view, the agent must be rightly motivated, but must also exhibit a trait that is reliably successful. The scope of the reliability is a bit unclear. She also writes that "A person does not have a virtue unless she is reliable at bringing about the end that is the aim of the motivational component of the virtue."[10] This makes the success limited to the agent, not to the trait systematically. This restriction can lead to various problems. For example, William Alston has pointed out that this would seem to imply that a person who would give freely if she has anything to give, and who in fact doesn't, cannot be considered generous since in her case there is no *actual* good produced.[11] This problem can be avoided on a reliabilist account, and by extension, it can be avoided for Zagzebski's success condition, given that the reliability is of the trait as a whole and not of the trait as embodied in an individual. Thus, if the trait produces good systematically, it is a virtue, even if in a particular instance no actual good is produced.

Moral virtues may have the same general end of aiming at the well-being of others, whereas the end of the intellectual virtues will be truth. Since both of these things are part of a good human life, virtues overall do not differ in their truly ultimate end. Thus, Zagzebski's view, like Aristotle's, is of the "mixed" variety—it has both internal and external factors that are held necessary to virtue. Mixed accounts tend to be intuitively appealing because they represent a compromise between the two theoretical extremes. So, for example, the intuition that agents deserve credit for good motives is preserved while also retaining the intuition that systematic failure is bad, even when agents are well motivated. The well-motivated and ill-motivated incompetents are ruled out automatically. As she notes regarding her account of virtue, reliability is a component of virtue: it's just not the only component since the agent must have the appropriate internal states.

However, these mixed accounts are subject to theoretical problems that afflict both of the pure extremes. The superficial plausibility of the mixed account is purchased at the cost of significant theoretical advantages. By contrast, the view that I would adopt is one that picks the externalist extreme as the paradigm. In ethics, this would tend to be exemplified by a consequentialist account of virtue; in epistemology, by a reliabilist account.[12]

The analogy can be spelled out this way: in epistemology the 'end' is true belief; in ethics it is the good. States conducive to the end are 'virtues'—either intellectual or moral. One difficulty with this approach is that it would hold something like 'perception' to be an intellectual virtue, which seems false. However, this difficulty could be dealt with (albeit possibly in an ad hoc fashion) by restricting virtues to character traits, even in the intellectual arena. Perception is a capacity, not a character trait, and thus would not count as an intellectual virtue, whereas traits like rigor, curiosity, and the like would count as intellectual virtues.

I suggest the following definitions:

> (MV)   A character trait is a moral virtue iff it systematically (reliably) produces good consequences (it systematically produces good producing action).

A trait systematically produces good if its instances tend to produce more good than not. This is an actualist account of moral virtue.

This parallels reliabilism in epistemology which does not view internal states as 'inherently' justifying; a true belief is knowledge if produced reliably, and certain mental qualities are intellectual virtues only if they are such reliable producers of true belief:

> (IV)   A character trait is an intellectual virtue iff it systematically (reliably) produces true belief.

This account rules out simple properties or capacities as counting as virtues. Perception is not an intellectual virtue, though it is a capacity that reliably produces true belief. In this way, the 'will,' so to speak, is important in an account of virtue. However, the 'will' needn't be directed a certain special way for the agent to qualify as having a virtue. Another way to look at it is that, though virtues are traits involving the will, so that a being who lacks a will cannot have intellectual or moral virtues, that will need not be manifested in a certain way. In the moral case consider kindness; for an agent to be truly kind she does need to be able to engage in intentional, purposeful action (helping others); however, this does not mean that to truly possess virtue she must act with a Kantian good will; nor, along subjective utilitarian lines, does it mean that she must consciously try to maximize the good; nor—and here you can pick whatever special quality of the will has been focused upon. Special subjective states are not relevant to the trait's status as a virtue, though to have virtue the being must be capable of intention.

A problem for a reliabilist account of intellectual virtue has been the case of *wishful thinking*. Jonathan Kvanvig puts it this way, by way of discussing a particular account of intellectual virtue as a truth-conducive account:

> It might be, for example, that wishful thinking for a particular person gets that person to the truth; and it might also be that that person has a disposition to believe what is only, for him, wishful thinking.[13]

For Kvanvig, any account that therefore implies wishful thinking is an intellectual virtue is clearly wrong. To avoid the problem, one would add a requirement that the disposition in question be *epistemically significant*. This in part means that the true beliefs must be produced in accord with *right reason*. This in turn means: "an epistemically significant characteristic produces beliefs in accord with right reason just in case that characteristic is a necessarily justification-conferring characteristic, and the belief in question is based on the justification generated by the characteristic in question."[14]

But another way to go, as suggested by Kvanvig, is to abandon an 'atomistic' approach—and insist that the good, or true belief, be produced systematically (and need not be produced in every single case). This would handle the wishful thinking case, since the fact that it seems to work for a particular person is not relevant—does it work systematically? No. What if it did work systematically to produce true belief? Well, then we may well be inclined to change our view of the trait's virtue status. It starts looking a lot better. And the account of moral virtue spelled out here is not atomistic.

This same strategy could be used to defuse the clairvoyance case posed by BonJour as a problem for reliabilist accounts. He asks us to imagine a situation in which a person uses clairvoyance to acquire belief.[15] Suppose that it is reliably successful, not just for the agent, but in general, unbeknownst to us. BonJour invites the conclusion that this is a problem for reliabilism, but by analogy with the moral case it needn't be. Instead, one could argue that clairvoyance is an intellectual virtue, just an unrecognized one. Bonjour believes that what is essentially lacking in an externalist approach is a notion of *responsibility* for one's beliefs which somehow seems relevant to the issue of whether an agent can truly possess knowledge. If the agent is subjectively irrational or epistemically irresponsible, he can't be said to possess knowledge even if the true belief is produced by a trait that quite reliably produces true beliefs. But if one rejects this responsibility as a necessary feature of one's account of knowledge (and intellectual virtue), then one needn't accept the conclusion. Clairvoyance is an unrecognized intellectual virtue. In the moral area similar sorts of 'counterexamples' are offered. Some argue, for example, that if the externalist account is correct, then we are stuck with the possibility that something like selfishness is a virtue. If one accepts Adam Smith's view that this trait leads to good overall, then that's correct. Selfishness would be an unrecognized moral virtue. We would have been mistaken in regarding it as a vice. This conclusion isn't a reduction of the position, however. David Hume pointed out that when we do recognize a trait's bad effects, we tend to change our judgment of it from virtue to vice. That also seems to work the other way around: when we recognize a trait's good effects, our judgment of it improves.

But this isn't the way Kvanvig decides to go. He thinks that truth-conducive accounts are bound to fail because of the evil demon objection:

> Suppose . . . that Joe is maximally virtuous . . . ; not only does he have the abilities and dispositions humanly possible, he is stable regarding them and he bends and relaxes the impact of each depending on the circumstances. But now suppose that he is the unlucky inhabitant of an evil demon world. The demon is evil enough and powerful enough to make sure that most of Joe's beliefs come out false, and that is just what the demon does.

The problem is that in this world Joe, no matter how 'virtuous,' will probably have false beliefs because of the influence of this evil demon. Yet, on the definition offered above, Joe does not possess the intellectual virtues—and, indeed, it would not be possible for anyone to possess them since whatever traits the agent has, the evil demon will make sure that they produce false beliefs. But this seems strongly counterintuitive; and the same sort of case could be made in the moral arena: suppose that there was an evil demon making sure that things actually turn out bad rather than good, no matter what traits the agent has. Surely there could still be virtue, even though *actual outcomes* are always guaranteed to be bad. The evil demon problem is a putative problem not merely for the externalist or reliabilist view, but also for the mixed view, such as Zagzebski's.

Thus, another advantage of the purely internalist approach is the ability to deal with this problem by making virtue completely internal. And Kvanvig, for intellectual virtue, tries a similar strategy. It isn't truth-conduciveness that is so important—rather, it is trying to attain the truth. An account that is 'objective' fails, but 'subjective' versions may succeed since they don't depend on actual outcomes. The resulting definition treats intellectual virtue the following way: among other things it is a trait that is conducive to epistemically warranted belief, where the idea of epistemic warrant is subjective. On this account, Joe had intellectual virtues since these traits lead to justified belief, even if they are not actually true. Since justification is internal, or subjective, it is not affected by the evil demon, which is an external condition. In this way, 'bad luck' is avoided as a problem for the account (in this case, the 'bad luck' of winding up in an evil-demon world). However, 'truth' is still the goal to be achieved. In this way, Kvanvig's suggestion is analogous to the subjective consequentialist, in moral theory, who defines virtue in terms of a disposition to try to produce the good (whether or not it is actually produced).

My main qualm about this approach is that it dispenses with any connection between the agent and the world. There is no connection to the world, unless it is understood that trying to achieve the good or the true is generally successful. This is a move Kvanvig would want to avoid, since it would be incorrect in the evil demon world. The way I favor to avoid the problem is to hold that in an evil demon world Joe doesn't have intellectual virtues—and, indeed, in such a world they are probably not possible.

Consider a problem for the Kvanvig account: Suppose that, unbeknownst to us, imaginativeness is conducive more to false belief than true belief. The imaginative person may aim at the truth, but not achieve it (maybe she is distracted by too many possibilities, for example). If it were discovered that such were the case, then I doubt that we would continue to call the trait an intellectual virtue, even though it does involve aiming at the truth. There has to be some real connection to the world, or what is true.

Linda Zagzebski's account would avoid this difficulty, because, as mentioned earlier, she does place a success condition on virtue. Aiming at the good in the right way and reliably and systematically achieving it are both necessary for virtue. Yet, if *trying* to achieve the true or the good is necessary, this leaves her account of intellectual virtue open to the self-defeatingness problem raised against the consequentialist. The idea is that when one always goes about trying to achieve the good, one misses it. Peter Railton showed that this problem, if a problem at all, is only a problem for subjective accounts of moral quality.[16]

Zagzebski could deny such a problem on empirical grounds. But then her account has problems inherited from the pure internalist approach, exemplified by Slote. How does one come up with a way of evaluating subjective states as epistemically or morally good, independent of the goals that they achieve? In Slote's case, for example, how can one determine whether or not a motive is good? A consequentialist can solve this problem by appealing to consequences. If Zagzebski tries this approach, however, her account collapses into a purely externalist account since the trying to achieve the good or the true is itself good only because the trying is correlated with success. The approach that she does take is not satisfying. She claims that one way to determine "what makes a motivation a good one and what makes a trait a virtue" is to "appeal to experience."[17] By this she means that we, through experience, are somehow able to see the goodness of persons independent of an evaluation of their behavior. For example, the person "may simply exude a 'glow' of nobility or fineness of character," and our determination of the motives of the person simply involves our seeing that the goodness we detect resides in his motivational structure. But this method for determining good motivation doesn't provide a criterion. What makes a motive good or bad remains mysterious.

For this reason I favor the completely externalist account of virtue presented here. What is very radical about this approach is that, on the view that I suggest, *trying* to achieve the truth, or attain a good end, is not necessary for virtue. This is more surprising than the claim that it is merely not sufficient. There may be character traits that are intellectual virtues that do not involve trying to acquire true belief, but that simply involve actually acquiring it. Possibly something like selective inattention to extraneous detail enables the agent to acquire more in the way of true belief without distraction, even though that may not be the agent's aim; his aim is to simply not be distracted. The moral cases are somewhat easier for me: for example, good friends don't seek the good, though they are more likely to achieve it.

Note that this does not dismiss trying to achieve truth as epistemically unimportant. Trying to achieve the truth may be itself a virtue, and thus responsible for our intuition that trying is extremely important—something for which the agent does deserve praise. There will be a close correlation between attempting and succeeding. The claim is that such trying is not praiseworthy in itself, but is so instrumentally.

The external account of human excellence I propose also resembles the account biologists give for 'fitness,' in the sense that both of these are to be understood externally. The fitness of an animal may involve internal states, but the value of those states is determined by reference to the external environment. Sharp teeth are indicators of fitness only in certain environments. Some environments may occur more regularly than others, so we will loosely speak of sharp teeth contributing to fitness; but it is understood that this is merely a norm; that if the context were to shift, the judgment of fitness would shift as well. Thus, fitness is not to be determined by the animals' internal states alone, without reference to the environment. Likewise, human excellence is not to be understood in terms of internal states alone.

But the externalism could itself be problematic. Imagine someone who lived in an empty universe. Call the person the deluded do-gooder (like Moore's deluded sadist). This person forms good intentions to aid others, this person has dispositions to aid others, but these are not dispositions that systematically produce the good, since there is no external good being produced. The agent is wrong when he thinks that he is helping a little old lady across the street; he is wrong when he thinks he is writing out a check to Oxfam and that check will save thousands of lives, and so on. The advantage of internalism is that it will still be committed to regarding this person as morally good, as virtuous, simply because of his states of mind. His connection to the world is irrelevant to his goodness. The externalist, on the other hand, has a problem because the external connection required for goodness is missing.

These sorts of cases pose only a superficial problem for the account. Our intuitions regarding such an agent are formed by the fact that such agents do, in our world, produce good effects. We may simply be using that paradigm in coming to the positive judgment of that agent. We also know that if the agent were to be in a universe of other beings, these traits would have good effect; thus there is a counterfactual connection. Thus it is still correct to say that a trait is a virtue if it does produce good effects, though we are influenced by the counterfactual that the trait in question is a virtue if it would produce good consequences in normal circumstances. This is not the same as saying that virtue *is* determined by outcomes that would be produced under normal circumstances. This would be to privilege our world over other possible worlds arbitrarily. Rather, the suggestion is that our intuitions are influenced by such judgments.

My approach would be to take the externalist extreme exemplified by objective consequentialism in ethics. It lacks the superficial plausibility of

Zagzebski's approach, and it fails to insulate the agent from luck in the way that Kvanvig's approach would. But the mixed view purchases plausibility at the cost of a host of theoretical problems. And the luck problem of the internalist extreme, in the end, doesn't seem compelling when compared with its own set of problems. Luck is a fact of life, and it may be a form of moral and intellectual virtue to humbly accept that there will be such limits to success no matter how well the agent is justified.

The Disunity of Virtue

The account presented thus far is not committed to unifying epistemic and moral virtue, though it recognizes that parallels exist between the two distinct types of evaluation. In this way, the account differs from the attempt by Zagzebski to unify the virtues (once again, taking a cue from Aristotle). One can see why such unity is appealing. Certainly, the attempt to derive morality from rationality has a long history. Zagzebski isn't engaged in this enterprise—as noted earlier she views the moral as primary. In her view, epistemic evaluation is the same as moral evaluation; it is a subset of moral evaluation.

But this runs counter to many intuitions that are evidence that moral and epistemic norms can often be in conflict, so that, indeed, the two are quite different. I have elsewhere argued that there are virtues that require ignorance, or rest on epistemic defect.[18] For example, modesty is a virtue that requires the agent to *underestimate* self-worth, in some respect, and to some limited degree. An agent's charity can sometimes rest upon the agent overestimating the good in others. And impulsive courage can often rest upon an agent failing to recognize the full extent of danger. In such cases, moral goodness is incompatible with epistemic virtue—e.g., being fully aware of one's own good qualities, the bad qualities of others, or the dangers one faces.

Further, it is often noted that being a good parent can sometimes involve epistemic defect to some limited degree. For example, if it were the case that children responded well to praise and if it were also the case that the praise was more effective if actually believed, then there's a good case to be made for the view that a good, nurturing parent who praises his child's accomplishments actually believes the child is doing better than he or she actually is doing (in those cases where the child's performances is not up to the standard of others, for example). I believe that this is probably the case. Most view with some shock the parent who takes a remarkably objective and realistic view of her children, especially in cases where the child is not doing very well. Perhaps because in such cases, the child may be in particular need of support. Being a good parent may involve epistemic defect. Thus, the moral and epistemic virtues seem incompatible.

Zagzebski might argue that, though epistemic virtues are moral, not all moral virtues exemplify epistemic excellence. In the cases mentioned above, the parents may have one kind of moral excellence while exhibiting another type of moral (epistemic) defect, just as a good parent might exhibit some other type of moral failing (e.g., partisanship for one's children). These cases of conflict don't mean that the moral and epistemic are really incompatible in the sense of being different types of evaluation; they simply show that cases can present conflict within the same type of evaluation.

But the cases I have in mind make a stronger point: It isn't simply the case that a person can have a moral virtue while lacking some intellectual virtue. Rather, these cases illustrate situations in which the moral and intellectual virtues are incompatible, that an agent *cannot* have the moral and the epistemic virtue at the same time, and this is not something Zagzebski explicitly addresses when she discusses her claim that the virtues are unified.

But there is a difference between claiming that one has provided an account of the virtues that is unified and claiming that the virtues themselves are unified. She could be making the first claim without making the second claim. I take it that the idea is that on her account moral virtues are concerned with pursuit of the good, and epistemic virtues with pursuit of a particular good, knowledge. Whenever I pursue knowledge, I pursue the good, broadly speaking, though perhaps not in the way that some other virtue does, such as generosity or kindness.

However, if this is the kind of unification we are talking about—two phenomena are unified if they share the same very broadly construed goal—we have a very weak unification theory. One could then give "unified" accounts of virtue and food, both of which are important to the good human life.

So the thesis really needs to be more robust than this. Moral and epistemic virtue are the same, since they both provide critical norms. She notes that we blame people who make epistemic errors, such as hasty generalization and claims "Such criticism is closer to *moral* criticism than the criticism of bad eyesight or poor blood circulation."[19] Since we don't blame people for the latter, epistemic criticism takes the form of blame, just as moral criticism does. Thus, the two are unified in that they both provide norms regulating when it is appropriate to praise and blame someone regarding their behavior.

But it should be noted that we sometimes, and indeed often do, make critical comments about someone's intellect without blaming them. It depends on our view of their responsibility for the epistemic defect. Someone may be stupid, yet the stupidity not her responsibility. Perhaps she was born with an intellectual deficit, for example. But when the person is guilty of a moral failure, we do not regard that as something that can be due to the natural lottery. Given the person is a normal adult, rational *person*, she is expected to act morally. There is a built-in responsibility for action. Thus, there does seem to be a difference in how we praise and blame when invoking epistemic versus moral norms. We are more forgiving of epistemic defect.

We also have cases that seem, at least intuitively, to cut against this view. For example, she notes that there are persons who seem to have a host of intellectual virtues without having much in the way of what we'd call moral virtues. And we can also speculate that there are people who have moral virtue without much in the way of intellectual virtue. The latter sorts of cases

Zagzebski would dismiss. These are not true virtues—at best they are natural virtues. But the first are more problematic for her. We are all familiar with cases of the seemingly brilliant person who uses her brilliance for evil ends. Intuitively, we want to be able to make claims like "She has the virtue of intelligence, but the vice of cruelty."

The two modes of normative evaluation run parallel to each other, like train tracks and roads. Like tracks and roads there will be structural similarities, and possibly even intersections. But the two modes are not the same sort of thing except in a very attenuated sense: Yes, moral and epistemic virtue claims are often used to praise; but this doesn't make them the same thing in that the sort of praise is different. Models of the intellect are held up as examples of admirability that do not necessarily have anything to do with the moral, and, indeed, may conflict with it. These intuitions run strongly counter to the claims that the unification theorist would make.

Of course, intuitions may be sacrificed when the theoretical advantage is large enough, and the sacrifice small enough. But, as I've hoped to show, the case for theoretical advantage has not been made.

✳An earlier version of this paper was read at the 20th World Congress of Philosophy Meetings in Boston, August 1998. I thank the members of that audience for their questions and comments.

Notes

1. This option is becoming more attractive as writers such as Ernest Sosa discuss it as a serious possibility. See *Knowledge in Perspective* (Cambridge University Press, 1991).

2. Linda Zagzebski, *Virtues of the Mind* (Cambridge University Press, 1996), 255 ff.

3. Zagzebski 255. She also notes in the precis of her book, forthcoming in *Philosophy and Phenomenological Research*, "Intellectual virtues are a subset of moral virtues and justification not just a normative property; it is a moral one" (p. 4, manuscript of precis).

4. Other writers, such as Rosalind Hursthouse [see, for example, "Virtue Theory and Abortion" in *Virtue Ethics*, edited by Michael Slote and Roger Crisp (Oxford University Press, 1997)], have attempted to develop or suggest an account of virtue ethics that avoids some of the main problems raised by writers like Robert Louden. However, since Hursthouse focuses on the issue of what would make an action right within virtue ethics, and is not offering an independent account of virtue, I will not focus my discussion on her work.

5. "Agent-based Virtue Ethics," in Slote and Crisp.

6. "Monkeying With Motives: Agent-Basing Virtue Ethics," *Utilitas*, vol. 7, no. 2 (November 1995): 281-8.

7. Andrew Moore has suggested that a more felicitous phrase would be 'antecedentism' so as to not confuse my terminology with that employed by philosophers of mind. The idea is that what is important about this approach to evaluation is that it is factors antecedent to traits and actions that determine their moral quality (these are factors such as motives and intentions). The contrasting approach to antecedentism, which I call 'evaluational externalism' would hold that virtue-making features are the

consequences of the traits or dispositions rather than their antecedents.

8. See *Nicomachean Ethics* (1144b8-12): "it is true that children and beasts are endowed with natural qualities or characteristics, but it is evident that without intelligence, these are harmful . . . as in the case of a mighty body which, when it moves without vision, comes down with a mighty fall because it cannot see."

9. *Virtues of the Mind,* 137.

10. *Virtues of the Mind,* 136.

11. See Alston's "Virtue and Knowledge," forthcoming in *Philosophy and Phenomenological Research.*

12. Others have noted the similarity between consequentialism in ethics and reliabilism in epistemology. See, for example, Sosa (1991).

13. Jonathan Kvanvig, *The Intellectual Virtues and the Life of the Mind* (Rowman Littlefield, 1992), 116.

14. Kvanvig, 118.

15. Lawrence BonJour, "Externalist Theories of Empirical Knowledge," *Midwest Studies in Philosophy V* (Minnesota, 1990): 53-73.

16. "Alienation, Consequentialism and the Demands of Morality," reprinted in *Friendship: A Philosophical Reader,* edited by Neera Badhwar (Cornell, 1993).

17. *Virtues of the Mind,* 83.

18. "The Virtues of Ignorance," *The Journal of Philosophy,* vol. 86 (July 1989): 373-84.

19. *Virtues of the Mind,* 5.

11

An "Internalist" Conception
of Epistemic Virtue

James Montmarquet

An interest in the "epistemic" (or intellectual) virtues may have any number of motivations. My own lie primarily in the notion of "doxastic responsibility." The idea, briefly, is that if we are going to have a robust notion of responsibility for belief,[1] the epistemic virtues ought to play a role in this regard (just as the moral virtues have been widely supposed to lie at the foundation of judgments of moral praise and blame and, to that extent, of *moral* responsibility). In this paper, my aim is, first, to characterize the epistemic virtues from an "internalist" viewpoint (explaining what the latter term would mean in this connection) and, second, to show how these virtues, so conceived, provide the aforementioned "robust" account of responsibility for belief.

A Non-Causal, Teleological View

On a likely non-internalist ("externalist") conception, the epistemic virtues would be any truth-conducive capacity of a person [cf. Sosa (1991) and Goldman (1992)]. Even more broadly characterized, they would be any capacity productive of truth or some other epistemically valuable item—like knowledge or understanding. Insofar as such capacities would include items not subject—at least not directly subject—to judgments of responsibility, such accounts are evidently not motivated by this concern.[2] So, for instance, such truth-conducive capacities as power and speed of recall or visual acuity are not ones for whose exercise we can be held responsible—except in quite an indirect way (e.g., for not taking steps earlier to improve one's acuity). By contrast, then, an *internalist* account of the epistemic virtues, as I want to conceive it, will be interested in qualities whose exercise is more directly subject to our control—like devoting "careful attention" to what one perceives. (Notice, one can be commanded to "Start paying more careful attention now!"—but hardly to "Start seeing better now!") One immediate question, however, is whether there is any theoretically interesting way to *pick out* such virtues—or whether one must be content to find them scattered among the wider set of presumed epistemically valuable qualities. I will try to show that there is such a way.

What I termed the "externalist" view may be understood as one type of *teleological* conception of these traits, where "teleological" would mean that something is classed an epistemic virtue because of *some* relation it has to epistemically desirable ends. In the case of externalist views, the relevant relation here is causal; but, as we shall see, there can be an internalist, teleological conception of the epistemic virtues. Now one fairly fixed point for any discussion of the virtues and vices (moral or epistemic) is Aristotle's dictum: that it is on the basis of displaying virtue or vice that we are to be *praised or blamed.* But this, notice, raises a difficulty. If the relevant relation between the epistemic virtues and these epistemically desirable ends *is* causal (as the externalist claims), it is not clear how these virtues can *also* be suitable loci of praise and blame. For, again, one is not to be blamed for poor visual acuity. The question, then, is how the epistemic virtues can *both* be distinguished in terms of their distinctive end(s) and be a locus of praise and blame? To give up their connection to praise and blame seems out of the question—if we want these qualities to bear some significant connection to the moral virtues (and if we do not, why even call them "virtues"?). Yet to give up their teleological character entirely seems equally unappealing. Surely, their value must be in *some* way related to such epistemically desirable ends as truth, knowledge, or understanding. It is not as though these qualities are good— *irrespective* of any such end. The very term *epistemic* virtues would surely imply otherwise.

How to proceed, then? One readily applicable way of achieving a measure of end-relatedness without running afoul of Aristotle would be to appeal to some such notion as *trying.* Trying is pre-eminently an end-related notion (there is no such thing as "just trying" irrespective of any end or goal); at the same time, trying raises no apparent problems of responsibility or control. We can assuredly be praised for our efforts in regard to truth, knowledge, or understanding and we can surely be blamed for our lack of effort in this regard. Trying, in short, is subject to our (relatively direct) control.

But where to go now? The *danger,* I think, of an appeal to "trying" is that of reducing the quite rich and interesting array of epistemically desirable qualities to a single, rather attenuated (if pure) notion: of "making a suitable effort in regard to truth (or, again, other epistemically desirable ends). If that mere "exertion of effort" is *all* there is to epistemic virtue, one might well doubt its importance or centrality to epistemology.

Fortunately, there is a way of avoiding this kind of reduction—which is to exploit the following consideration regarding the epistemic virtues (in fact, regarding the virtues generally). While there are few (if any) desirable qualities such that merely trying to exert them is sufficient for a full (or ideal) level of exhibition of them, there is a distinction to be drawn between those qualities such that trying *is* sufficient for a reasonable (or adequate) level of their exhibition, and those for which trying is not thus sufficient.

Consider some examples. Unfortunately, trying to be intelligent is not sufficient for being intelligent at all. Likewise, trying to exhibit mathematical (or physical) dexterity is hardly sufficient for even the most minimal levels of achievement in these. By contrast, trying to be generous, or courageous, or sympathetic are all of them sufficient—at least *while* such effort is being exerted—for a reasonable or adequate level of exhibition of these traits. So, for instance, a person not much given to generosity may, in the course of trying to be generous, still give less than would an ideally generous person to the man at the door collecting for the heart fund. But if he is really trying to be generous—and not just, as it were, pretending to try or deceiving himself into thinking he is genuinely trying when he is not—he must be giving some reasonable amount (relative to what he has), thus exhibiting some reasonable level of generosity. Likewise, a person who is trying to stand his ground and not run away from danger is, at least for that period, being brave (or reasonably so). True, once he "loses his courage" and starts running, he is no longer so—but, by the same token, at that point he is no longer even *trying*. At most, he *was* trying—but couldn't "keep it up." Again, one who is trying to be sympathetic may still fall well short of the kind of deep sympathy of which some people are capable, but at least while he was trying to be sympathetic, he would be achieving at least a reasonable level of this virtue.

Two additional points before turning more specifically to the epistemic virtues. First, notice that I am not resting my case simply on the point that one who is "trying his best" cannot be faulted for his efforts. Even if this is true, my point is a different one, which is that the exhibition of the virtue *itself* is being achieved in these cases—if only for a limited period of time and to a limited extent. Second, I am not claiming that such explicit trying is a *necessary* condition of any virtue exemplification. Presumably, it is not.[3] Certainly, from an Aristotelian perspective, the need explicitly to try to be sympathetic, for example, might bespeak a less than full possession of the relevant "habits" characteristic of sympathetic people (who do not have to do any such "trying").

Turning now to the case of the epistemic virtues: it is apparent that some truth-conducive qualities pass, and that some do not pass, this test. Thus, take what might be classified as the overarching (internalist) epistemic virtue: one's being motivated to pursue truth.[4] Of course, if I am trying to pursue truth, it will follow that I *am* so motivated (at least, to some reasonable extent, while I am trying). A more revealing case, however, would be the virtue of "open-mindedness." If at any given point I am trying to be open-minded, I may not be wholly succeeding (closed-mindedness is not so easily overcome as that), but I will be succeeding, again, to some reasonable extent—*while* I am trying. Open-mindedness involves a certain receptiveness to ideas that are new, or unfamiliar, or that run contrary to one's already held convictions. Perhaps no one succeeds in being ideally open-minded; in fact, one could be "open-minded" to a fault.[5] But how can one separate "exhibiting receptiveness" and "making a genuine effort to be receptive?"[6]

Or consider the virtue of "care": the disposition to be careful in one's belief acquiring and retaining activities. Here, too, in striving to be careful, say, in examining someone's argument, one is certainly exemplifying, at least to a fair degree, this virtue—even if there are things one is simply missing and even if these omissions are due to deficient powers of attention (thus "care")—as opposed to such other factors as a lack of knowledge of the subject matter or lack of powers of reasoning. Again, in such a case, one will be exhibiting the virtue of care—even if one's powers of carefulness are not as great as those of many others. (Of course, if one's attention just "wanders" during a certain stretch of time, then one is not exhibiting care—and, by the same token, not even trying to do so.)

Before moving on to contrast the epistemic virtues and *vices*, we might pause a moment to summarize and clarify some of what we are saying. My view is not that all genuine epistemic virtues, or even that such virtues as open-mindedness, are, in an unqualified sense, "internal" or "modes of trying." Even in such cases as open-mindedness, recall, I am conceding that it (i.e., its *full* exemplification) would have "external" elements, not directly accessible even to one's best efforts. The idea, rather, would be best put as follows. Certain virtues like open-mindedness have a significant "internal" core to them, sufficient to warrant their attribution on the basis of trying to exemplify them. These virtues have in common an underlying motivation in regard to truth (or some other epistemically desirable goal), even though they differ in specific focus (open-mindedness involves a different focus than care; intellectual courage involves a different focus than impartiality, and so forth).

What, then, of the epistemic *vices?* Part of what distinguishes these, I want to suggest—again, from an internalist point of view—is a certain type of *symmetry* with the case of the epistemic virtues. For an important class of the virtues, we have pointed out that "trying" is sufficient for succeeding; for the vices corresponding to these virtues, let us now observe, "trying" is *self-defeating,* thus sufficient for not succeeding. The general reason for this might be put as follows. These epistemic vices—like wishful, inattentive, or too-hasty thinking—involve some characteristic *failure* to attend to truth or truth-related considerations. When one tries, however, to fail in these regards, the very nature of one's wrongdoing shifts to something else. In order to *try* to be gullible, for example, one would have to try to believe things one takes to be beyond the bounds of proper standards of credibility; but even if one could do this (which hardly seems possible), it would be a remarkable exercise in doxastic control, quite lacking in the naive, accepting attitude characteristic of true gullibility. In a similar way, trying to be careless in one's thinking would be like trying to have an "accident"; one might achieve the result, but not in the right way. Blameworthiness in regard to epistemic vice, then, cannot be a matter of one's having tried to exemplify that vice[7]; rather, it would be a matter of some suitable lack of effort in regard to the corresponding *virtue*. It would be a matter of negligence, rather than intentional "wrongdoing." To be sure, exhibiting a vice like closed-mindedness would involve more than a lack of suitable effort; one's closed-mindedness might involve all sorts of dispositions (e.g., a tendency for one's mind to wander when information running contrary to a favored belief was being presented). The claim here is simply that it is the lack of effort that is *blameworthy*.

This inaccessibility of the epistemic vice to direct effort, I might observe here, is important in understanding the sense in which belief (and the exertion of our intellectual faculties generally) is "less free" than action (and the corresponding exertion of our moral or practical faculties). Notice, in the latter case we are quite able to exert ourselves regarding certain vices, at least—and not just regarding the corresponding virtues. One can try to be, and succeed in being, selfish as well as generous; one can try to be *evil*, as well as good. To be sure, not all virtue/vice pairs may admit of this. It is not exactly clear, for instance, that one can try to be (and thereby succeed in being) *impatient* (or cowardly).[8] Still, in the case of the more narrowly *moral* virtues and vices (one who is impatient or cowardly is not exactly immoral) an obvious and, I think, important contrast remains. Insofar as we are able (and, thus, under many circumstances) free to exert ourselves in regard to these, the case of morality remains quite different from that of the epistemic virtues.[9]

The Epistemic Virtues and Truth-Conduciveness

I have offered a teleological, but not a causal, account of the epistemic virtues, in which their suitability to judgments of praise and blame distinguishes these virtues (and their corresponding vices) from an externalist, causal account. But there is a further argument to be made against such a causal view.

To begin, we consider the following "skeptical" possibility. Suppose we were to discover that the world is actually a place in which the qualities— partiality, closed-mindedness, intellectual cowardice, etc.—we presently take to be epistemic vices are truth-conducive (and that the qualities we had previously taken not to be truth-conducive were actually so). Now, in describing the *previous* state of affairs, what should we say? We could say that the qualities we previously took to be vices had all along been virtues (and that the qualities we previously took to be virtues had all along been vices)—and that we had simply not known this.[10] But such a proposal meets with this telling objection: that it severs the aforementioned ("Aristotelian") connection between the virtues and vices and any reasonable notion of praise and blame. For surely we are not wanting to say that, all along, we should have been *blaming* people for being open-minded (and praising them for being closed-minded, etc.). Nor would it seem reasonable, beginning now, retrospectively to extend such judgments of blame and praise. To be sure, henceforth we may reasonably call these previously believed vices "virtues" (and the corresponding previously believed virtues "vices"), but that is not to say that we should revise our *past* judgments. We have, then, a further reason to reject any quick and easy equation of the epistemic virtues with truth (or knowledge or understanding) conduciveness. For, obviously, what has changed is not whether these qualities are truth-conducive, but something more like whether it is "reasonable" to understand them as so. (Before it was not reasonable; upon this great discovery, it is so.)

Even this last claim, however, is a tricky one. If reasonable judgments are ones that a "reasonable" person would make, and a reasonable person is, among other things, one possessed of the epistemic virtues, then it remains unclear whether a closed-minded person (before this great discovery) was reasonable or not. But let us now reconsider our skeptical scenario from an *internalist* perspective. We have said that one cannot (successfully) try to be closed-minded, but suppose we did find out that closed-mindedness was a virtue? In that case, we would be tempted, I suppose, to *make ourselves* closed-minded by appropriate, *in*direct means (taking drugs designed to induce this, and so forth). Such a project, however, raises at least two serious questions. First, even if there were good evidence that closed-mindedness were a virtue, would a truth-desiring person really want to adopt such means? (Suppose that the evidence had been misleading; we would *need* open-mindedness to see our way through this evidence—just as we needed open-mindedness to come to accept the original evidence against this.) Second, there is a question as to whether this kind of closed-mindedness, while truth-conducive, would actually be, have been exemplified as, an epistemic virtue. By way of analogy, notice that generosity induced, and fortified, by a "generosity drug" would not indicate that one was a "moral person." To that extent, it would not be, or have been exemplified as, a moral virtue.

Moreover, turning to what I described earlier as the "overarching" epistemic virtue—one's being motivated to pursue truth—the case is even clearer. Even if this were discovered not to be truth-conducive, it is not as though the opposite motivation could intelligibly replace it as a virtue. Again, one could take a drug to ensure that one would not be particularly interested in truth, but it is unclear that the resulting state could be termed "epistemically virtuous"—except insofar as it was the result of a truth-related wish to induce this state. But, of course, if it *were* the result of such a motive, the project itself would be suspect (as this motive, by hypothesis, is not truth-conducive).

My conclusion, then, is that these apparent virtues—open-mindedness, impartiality, love of truth, and the like—while we can only claim that they are contingently related to the attainment of such epistemic goals as truth and knowledge, are *constitutive of*, and not just instrumentally related to, the project of free and responsible intellectual inquiry. If it were discovered that these virtues were not truth (or knowledge, etc.) conducive, it is not as though the newly recognized "virtues" of closed-mindedness, partiality, and aversion to truth could take their place in this project. Rather, it would seem that the very enterprise of responsible search for truth (certainly as we know it) would be unrecognizably transformed. To put the same point in a different way, one might say that if there are any internalist epistemic virtues at all, they include the ones we presently take to be virtues.

Epistemic Responsibility

Having now offered an account of how the "internalist" epistemic virtues might be picked out (without appealing to their alleged truth-conduciveness), I want to say something more about their *internality*. In what sense are these virtues "internal"? A brief answer to this question will lead to my next main topic: our responsibility for belief.

These virtues are "internal," first, in the sense that one typically has some kind of *access* to whether or not one is exemplifying them. In fact, our account offers one quite strong reason *why* such access would be available. Since we presumably do have access to what we are trying to accomplish and since, as we have argued, trying is sufficient for exemplifying these virtues to some reasonable degree, it follows that we have access to whether or not we are exemplifying them. Of course, since we may exemplify them *without* trying, such access is by no means guaranteed, but that is no problem. If one is expected to do *x*, it suffices that one can *x* at will. It does not matter that, on some occasions, one might *x* involuntarily.

Our access to these epistemic virtues, however, is not limited to *whether* one is exemplifying a certain virtue, but extends, as well, to the specific "virtuousness" of one's doing this. Insofar as the various epistemic virtues are, so to speak, different modes of one's making an effort to find truth, one cannot separate one's access, e.g., to whether one is being open-minded and to whether one is making an effort to find truth. Insofar as I am aware of the one, I will be aware of the other.

Second, we can say that these epistemic virtues are "internal" in their dependence on—or sensitivity to—the *will*. We have already explained how the choice *between* epistemic virtue and vice is not, as such, subject to the will, but this should not cause us to lose sight of the basic idea that trying to be more open-minded, less gullible, more impartial, less subject to wishful thinking very much is subject to the will.

Let us now turn to *belief*—and our responsibility for belief. Now, what links responsibility for the epistemic virtues to doxastic responsibility, on the account I propose, will simply be this: insofar as these virtues—themselves subject to the will—are involved in our belief forming and retaining activities, the latter activities, too, are subject to the will. Here, however, some further explanation is required.

First, we need to remark upon this distinction: between the completeness of one's control over something and the *directness* of such control. Doxastic responsibility, I will concede, is not complete (as it is limited to certain modalities of belief), but this does not mean it is merely indirect. Failure to note this point of difference may easily lead one to the incorrect conclusion that our responsibility for belief is merely indirect, but this, I shall argue, is not so.[11]

To begin, consider the example of care—as applied not to belief but to an ordinary physical action like carving wood. Notice, control over an aspect of this activity is not the same as indirect control over it—via a more direct control over that aspect. Carving wood carefully (cf. Ryle 1949, 137-38) is not a matter of performing inner acts of "exerting care" which will, one hopes, cause alterations in one's physical movements (in the way that movements of one's hands on the steering wheel, one hopes, will cause appropriate movements in one's automobile). Rather, care is exhibited as a *way* of carving, not a way of exerting changes in one's carving.

The same point, moreover, can be made with respect to other modalities of physical action: thus the simple case of running quickly. In running, a person may certainly exert control over the speed with which he is running. At the same time, he will typically not be exerting control over many of its other modalities. The key point, though, is just this. One may affirm *both* that one's running and that one's running quickly are subject to one's direct control; it is not as though direct control with respect to the latter must imply indirect control with respect to the former.

Let us apply these points, then, to the case of belief and the epistemic virtues. Again, the idea would be that these virtues involve, at most, *modalities* of the belief forming and retaining process. We have, I have pointed out, direct control over these modalities—and in so doing have *partial* (read: not indirect) control over the processes of which they are modalities.

More particularly, inasmuch as we can have direct control over whether we are trying to exhibit care, or impartiality, or due attentiveness—beliefs formed under appropriate circumstances can be subject to an appropriate normative assessment. At the very least, they can be assessed according to the virtues or vices they involve.[12]

One final point in this connection. It is commonly alleged against "internalist" epistemologies that these founder on the reef of "doxastic involuntarism": that because belief is not directly subject to the will, we cannot base our epistemologies on norms that would, in effect, require that such control exist.[13] The reply to this, however, is straightforward. Even though a belief might not be producible at will, this does not mean that it could not be found "blameworthy" if it were formed in a particularly unvirtuous way, say, out of sheer wishful thinking; nor would this mean that one's *not* forming it could not be similarly criticized (if this failure were due to wishful thinking or some other vice).

Epistemic Blameworthiness

The previous section provided the basis for an internalist account of doxastic responsibility. Here I want to indicate at least one way of completing such an account—and then criticize two non-internalist accounts in the current literature.

I am especially interested in what makes a belief epistemically *blameworthy*, as this question has not only a direct bearing on the ethics of belief, but bears indirectly on the ethics of action, as well. Thus, what would otherwise be justifiable action can be morally blameworthy insofar as it is based on an epistemically blameworthy belief, e.g., in William Clifford's (1877) case of renting a leaky boat to some emigrants, who go to their deaths.[14] Evidently what makes this act morally wrong is that the agent should have believed that the boat was unsafe—i.e., was *epistemically* blameworthy in believing the opposite. We shall say, then, that a belief is epistemically blameworthy just in case its adoption expresses some epistemic vice on the subject's part—i.e., some shortfall of epistemic virtue (conceived internally) sufficiently great as to be culpable under the circumstances.

Of course, we have not tried to say how *much* of a shortfall is required or to explain in what way this is circumstance-relative. Certainly, one's culpability for exhibiting some vice like wishful or too-hasty thinking will depend on how favorable circumstances are for engaging in the kind of minimally virtuous thinking that would have prevented such vices from manifesting themselves. I have discussed this matter elsewhere (1993); here perhaps it suffices to say that, in terms of this looseness, accounts of moral blameworthiness in terms of the moral vices will be similarly inexact on matters of degree.[15]

My case, then, is that this is really the right type of approach, not that it can be worked out in anything like absolute precision. To bolster this case, let us turn to the kind of non-internalist account of epistemic responsibility many would seemingly favor. On this type of account, one would understand responsibility for belief in terms of those actions which might causally affect one's beliefs. Thus, it has been maintained—see, e.g., Kornblith (1983), Smith (1983)[16]—that we may be blameworthy for what we believe in virtue of our failure to take appropriate *actions*, say, by way of gathering appropriate evidence, checking on possible counter-evidence, and so forth. But even if we accept the point that most blameworthy beliefs do involve such failures of action and investigation, there remains a more basic problem. Typically, one who culpably abstains from gathering needed evidence does so in the culpable *belief* that such efforts are not needed. Typically in the process of convincing himself of what he should not believe he also convinces himself that he has enough evidence to support this culpable belief. Now, if the latter belief (that one has enough evidence) were *not* itself faulty, one could hardly fault someone failing to gather (more) evidence. After all, there are many occasions in which we are entirely justified, and certainly blameless, in failing to seek, or giving up the search, for more evidence. We may hope, then, to characterize epistemically blameworthy actions in terms of a notion of epistemically blameworthy belief, but the reverse project seems a nonstarter.

There is at least one other broadly externalist approach possible, which does not appeal to action. Insofar as externalists tend to think of "objective justification" in terms of the reliability of one's belief acquisition process, they would be liable to think of epistemic blamelessness (or "subjective justification") in terms of the reliability of the process of one's acquiring beliefs *about* one's belief-acquisition process. Thus, Alvin Goldman defines "weakly justified belief," which he equates (1992, 131) with "blamelessly" held belief, as follows:

A belief is 'weakly justified' (but not 'strongly justified') if (a) it is arrived at by an insufficiently reliable method/process MP; (b) the subject S does not believe MP is unreliable; (c) S neither possesses, nor has available a reliable method/process for determining the unreliability of MP; and (d) there is no method or process S believes to be reliable which, if used, would lead S to believe that MP is unreliable.

Suppose, though, that S does have in his possession a reliable method for determining the unreliability of the one he is using, but that, given the limitations of his knowledge, he cannot really be faulted for failing to use this method. In that case, intuitively, S should count as at least "weakly justified" in his belief. Now, Goldman may reply that this is offered only as a sufficient condition of weak justification, but this reply gives us scant reason to think that his approach can be extended—without major amendment—to yield anything like a *full* account of this. We do need to be able to say, in such cases as the latter, that the subject is not to be faulted; and Goldman offers us no assistance here.[17] Even as a sufficient condition, however, there are problems to be noted in reference to the beliefs involved in clauses (b) and (d). Suppose that S arrives at a belief following unreliable method M. Suppose, further, that except for wishful thinking S would have perceived the unreliability of M. And suppose, still further, that whereas there is a method by which S would have arrived at a proper belief in the unreliability of M, S (also out of wishful thinking) does not believe in the reliability of this method. Here, certainly, S should *not* qualify as even weakly justified, but by Goldman's account he would.

Consideration, then, both of the "actional" and the Goldman account should help to increase our confidence in a "virtue" oriented account of doxastic responsibility. For the main difficulty identified in each of the first two accounts seemingly points to the necessity, or desirability (at least), of this type of virtue orientation. In the "actional" case, the problem concerned the possibility that one's culpability would reside in the belief grounding one's failure to take appropriate evidence-gathering actions, rather than in those actions themselves. But reside *how*? One very plausible answer is simply that the culpability resides in the beliefs and values that constitute the agent's intellectual laziness: one doesn't look for more evidence because one is not sufficiently concerned with truth to have the energy required for such undertaking. Intellectual laziness is obviously, though, an epistemic vice.[18] In Goldman's case, the relevant diagnosis and cure are, I think, equally clear. The main problem here was that one might possess a reliable means of determining the unreliability of one's method, but be blameless for failing to use it since one lacked the requisite knowledge. When, though, would one be *blameworthy* for failing to use some epistemic device available to one (or in one's possession)? Presumably, when one's failure reflects some kind of vice—like inattention, wishful thinking, or the like.

Summary: Epistemic and Moral Virtue

One might suppose that an internalist conception of epistemic virtue would seek to minimize, or argue against the existence of, any fundamental differences between the epistemic and moral virtues. After all, the hallmark of this view, at least as presented here, is the strong status it gives to something very much *like* a moral responsibility for belief. Our analysis, however, has shown that matters are more complicated than either an assimilationist position (like Zagzebski's; see note 9) or a strong, externalist anti-assimilationist position would have maintained. In fact, on our analysis, there will be a *three*-fold distinction cutting across the moral/epistemic divide as follows.

(A) There will be qualities (virtues and vices), certainly epistemic ones and presumably moral ones as well, *not subject to our direct control at all*. On my analysis, recall, these will be qualities such that trying to exemplify them is not sufficient for doing so (at all). Again, visual acuity would be an epistemic example of such a trait. Certain powers of, say, creative or imaginative moral thinking might be a good example of a moral virtue of this sort.

(B) There will be certain virtues, epistemic and moral, that are *subject to our direct control, but whose corresponding vices are not*. All of the (internalist) epistemic virtues treated here will fall into this category, but arguably certain broadly moral virtues as well. Thus: our previous examples of patience and courage. These, on our analysis, will also be classifiable as qualities such that trying to exemplify them is sufficient for exemplifying them (to a reasonable degree, etc.); the contraries of these qualities, however, will be such that trying to exemplify them is self-defeating. In this case, in contrast to (A), exhibition of a given trait can be directly required.

(C) There will be certain moral virtues—benevolence, generosity, truthfulness, and justice—such that *we are able both to exemplify them and exemplify their contraries at will*. In this case, trying will be sufficient to exemplify them, as will trying to exemplify their contrary. So, for instance, not only is trying to be generous, as noted earlier, sufficient for being so on a given occasion; trying to be ungenerous (selfish) will be sufficient for being that.

What emerges, then, is a *hierarchy* of evaluatively relevant qualities of persons, which largely *cuts across* the supposed epistemic/moral divide. At the lowest level will be those "externalist" traits subject only to our indirect control. At the middle level will be the "internalist" epistemic virtues and perhaps certain broadly moral virtues. At the summit, will be certain narrowly moral traits.

Notes

1. In keeping with the discussion below, a "robust" notion may be understood along these lines. Our responsibility for what we believe, while it is not complete, is not merely indirect, i.e., is not merely a consequence of our direct responsibility for something that in turn has a causal influence on what we believe. This distinction between direct and complete doxastic control is later elaborated in the section on "Epistemic Responsibility."

2. On his own motivation for an externalist conception, Sosa (1994, 31) observes that the move to "virtue epistemology" (as opposed to forms of non-virtue reliabilism) has the signal advantage of stressing the role and importance of the *knower* as a kind of ultimate epistemic subject.

3. Cf. Audi (1995), 459 ff.

4. On the relation between this virtue and the other more particular epistemic virtues see my (1993, Chapter 2).

5. In that case, one might be, for instance, a kind of "doxastic chameleon" who too readily took on the various belief systems with which he successively came into contact. Even if this did not amount to "gullibility" (itself surely an epistemic vice), it would mark a lack of internal coherence—one could even say "integrity"—to his doxastic life.

6. It is instructive to compare, in this connection, Linda Zagzebski's (1996) more externalist treatment of open-mindedness with my own. For Zagzebski (177), an open-minded person must actually *succeed* in the following endeavor. She must actually *be* "receptive to new ideas, examining them in an even handed way and not ruling them out because they are not her own." (She adds: "merely being motivated to act in these ways in not sufficient.") Again, though, if I am trying to be receptive, am I not being *somewhat* so? Could a person try and utterly fail at receptiveness? To be sure, one could try to be receptive, and not succeed in accepting some new ideal. But, of course, receptiveness is not the same thing as *acceptance*. One can be commanded to be open-minded in regard to a certain speaker, but hardly to be "accepting" of what they say.

7. Not only can one not try to exemplify such vices, one cannot even *knowingly* do so (while trying to accomplish something else).

8. Certainly, one can try to *act* impatiently. But impatience seems to involve certain constituent *beliefs* (typically to the effect that "this is just not moving along as fast as it should") which are not producible at will.

9. Thus when Zagzebski offers an account in which the epistemic virtues are simply to be classed as among the moral virtues (1996, 158ff), I demur to this extent. Moral good and evil are not quite analogous to epistemic good and "evil." The latter do not compete for the attention of the human will or soul in the same way that the former do. See the summary section for a much more articulated statement of how I see the distinction between the moral and epistemic virtues.

10. On this point, Zagzebski, I would think, gets into some difficulty. She insists (185)—correctly, let us allow—that henceforth we should judge these qualities virtues. But, as I suggest in the text, this does not address the difficult problem for an externalist theory (even a modified externalist theory of the sort she proposes) of what judgments we should make about the *past*. Here Zagzebski can say that unvirtuous past inquirers who were fortuitously exemplifying such "virtues" as closed-mindedness were still not truly virtuous because their *motivation* was wrong—i.e., not knowledge-directed (cf. 137, 167). But she will still be in difficulty concerning the reverse case of the apparently virtuous, knowledge-directed inquirer who, through no apparent fault of her own, is exemplifying what are later revealed to be vices. This case, I would maintain, defeats even Zagzebski's moderate externalism.

11. See, for instance, Zimmerman's (1997), my reply (1999), and the more extensive discussion of this matter in my (1993).

12. The question of whether they might be subjected to some other, more "deontological" assessment—in terms of rules governing what ought one to believe—is, in this connection, a red herring. For it suffices, surely, that one belief may be found blameworthy (or blameless, or possibly praiseworthy), based on the qualities of intellectual character it implicates, but more on blameworthiness in the next section.

13. See Alston (1986) for a very careful statement of this point of view.

14. I make the case much more fully in my (1993) that moral responsibility for action often turns on epistemic responsibility for some belief on which the action is predicated.

15. In the most detailed version of such an account, Brandt (1958) relativizes blameworthiness and the exhibition of vice to what the "standard" is in those circumstances. What, then, constitutes blameworthy cowardice would depend on how the typical agent, or how the typical agent relevantly similar to this one, would act. I see no reason why a theory of epistemic blameworthiness could not utilize Brandt's framework, even with its considerable indeterminacy.

16. I discuss the specifics of Smith's theory much more extensively in my (1995).

17. A sufficient condition alone (especially one that fails to get at what seems a crucially important necessary condition) is liable to yield a very limited understanding. This would be akin to characterizing knowledge in terms of mathematical certainty.

18. Is it an *internalist* vice? I don't see why not. Notice, it is not clear whether one can try to be intellectually lazy in such contexts. For this requires some appreciation that one's evidence *is* insufficient.

References

Alston, William (1986). "The Deontological Conception of Epistemic Justification," in *Epistemic Justification* (Ithaca: Cornell University Press).

Audi, Robert (1995). "Acting From Virtue," *Mind* 104: 449-71.

Clifford, William (1877). "The Ethics of Belief," reprinted in Gerald D. McCarthy, ed., *The Ethics of Belief Debate* (Atlanta: Scholar's Press, 1986).

Goldman, Alvin (1992). "Strong and Weak Justification," in *Liasons: Philosophy Meets the Cognitive Sciences* (Cambridge, Mass.: MIT Press).

Kornblith, Hilary (1983). "Justified Belief and Epistemically Responsible Action," *Philosophical Review* 92: 33-48.

Montmarquet, James (1993). *Epistemic Virtue and Doxastic Responsibility* (Lanham, Md.: Rowman & Littlefield).

——— (1995). "Culpable Ignorance and Excuses," *Philosophical Studies* 80: 41-49.

——— (1999). "Zimmerman on Culpable Ignorance," *Ethics* 109: 842-846.

Ryle, Gilbert (1949). *The Concept of Mind* (New York: Barnes and Noble).

Smith, Holly (1983). "Culpable Ignorance," *Philosophical Review* 92 (1983): 543-71.

Sosa, Ernest (1991). *Knowledge in Perspective* (Cambridge: Cambridge University Press).

——— (1994). "Virtue Perspectivism: A Response to Foley and Fumerton," *Philosophical Issues* 5: 29-50.

Zagzebski, Linda (1996). *Virtues of the Mind* (Cambridge: Cambridge University Press).

Zimmerman, Michael (1997). "Moral Responsibility and Ignorance," *Ethics* 107: 410-26.

12

Regulating Inquiry:
Virtue, Doubt, and Sentiment

Christopher Hookway

I. Reasons for Belief and Action

Ethics and epistemology deal with different parts of our normative practice. Each tries to understand our ways of applying normative standards in a different area of life, to conduct and to the search for knowledge. We should expect parallel issues to arise in the two cases, and we should hope that ideas and resources that have been valuable in one field will have fruitful application in the other. One way in which this can benefit epistemology is through helping us to formulate important new epistemological problems and thus to reach a better grasp of the questions that epistemological theorizing should take as its focus. Virtue epistemology, as I understand this position, is an attempt to obtain such benefits by exploiting insights drawn from virtue ethics. The insights we hope for are of at least three kinds: it should help us to escape from an excessively reflective or intellectualistic picture of epistemic evaluation; it should alert us to the possible role of states similar to character traits in the ways in which we revise our beliefs and carry out investigations; and it should alert us to the role of emotions and sentiments in our attitudes towards our beliefs and inquiries. And we can also anticipate that it will lead to a revision in our ways of formulating fundamental epistemic questions.[1]

The remainder to this section poses a question about reasons for belief which parallels some problems that are familiar in the study of practical reason. We then discuss in a general way how a virtue-based approach to epistemology might lead us to address these questions (section II). Against this background, we turn to the role of emotional and other affective states in epistemic evaluation, focusing particularly on issues about the nature of the state of *doubt* (sections III and IV). The final section returns to the issue about reasons, suggesting how it should be viewed in the light of the preceding discussion.

The idea of a *reason* has two aspects: *normative* and *motivational*. A reason for an action reveals why it is a rational or good action to perform; and my awareness of it can explain why I performed the action. My possession of a reason to believe some proposition can explain both why I believe it and why I am right to do so. These facts raise some questions about the relations between these features: can I recognize the normative force of some consideration without acquiring at least some defeasible motivation to perform the action or acquire the belief? One kind of internalism about reasons ('belief-internalism') denies that this is possible; the corresponding externalist view claims that it is (Stratton-Lake 1999: 78). Any philosophical psychology that is adequate to make sense of the phenomena of normativity must account for the relations between recognizing the normative force of considerations and being motivate to act or believe in accordance with those norms. Distinguish three states of affairs:

(1) Given p is the case, it would be best to perform action a.
(2) When I accept p is the case, I explicitly acknowledge that it would be best to perform a.
(3) In virtue of my recognition that p is the case, I am motivated to do a.

(1), we may take it, gives the truth condition for the proposition acknowledged in (2), which provides guidance in (3). The possibility we are considering is that (2) may be true while (3) is not: I might explicitly acknowledge the normative force of some proposition that does not affect my conduct.

Before considering some epistemic examples, it is important to notice that such cases can fall into two kinds, only one of which threatens the kind of internalism that we began by discussing. It is natural to suppose that such cases will involve a form of irrationality, perhaps *akrasia*: normative judgments fail to engage with the will as they normally do. As I act, I can be fully aware that I am acting wrongly or irrationally and that I feel no motivation to act rationally and well. My act may be one that I cannot identify myself with—I am drawn to act as I believe I should not. Even if all is not as explicit as this, it seems that the existence of a gap between my normative judgments and my motivations signals a kind of irrationality. But there are other cases where the fact that my explicit normative judgment is overridden is a sign of greater wisdom, of a sensitivity to the demands of reason that is not conscious or reflective but that reveals a richer awareness of rational demands than is manifested in my conscious reflections. Much rational behaviour is automatic, the product of skills, capacities, and judgments whose functioning may be impaired by the attempt reflectively to interfere with their operations. My reflective normative judgment may not be the only normative 'judgment' in play. When instinctive judgment leads me not to trust someone whose reliability seems to be supported by my conscious reasons, this may not always be a sign of irrationality.

Can we find such cases in the epistemic realm? The application of the idea of 'motivation' to a state-like belief is problematic. We need to find the appropriate analogue of what I called 'internalism.'[2] Here are three examples, the first suggested by one of our non-epistemic examples. Patricia Greenspan considers the case of instinctive mistrust of a salesman that may be warranted, resulting from a sensitivity to the ways in which he has presented himself, where conscious belief that he is not be trusted would not be justified. I could not assert that the person I was dealing with was unreliable: epistemically, I should, perhaps, give him the benefit of the doubt. Indeed all the evidence I possess—perhaps based on testimony of those who have previously had dealings with him—may support his reliability. My instinctive mistrust may just be irrational prejudice with no secure foundation; but it could be sensitivity to character and behaviour which would guide my further thoughts and inquiries in ways that are beneficial. I am, very reasonably, not ready to accept all that he tells me, perhaps suspending judgment on his claims about his products unless they are supported by something other than his assurances (1988, chapter one). Of course, in such cases, the fact that I feel this instinctive mistrust is something that should be available to conscious reflection. I can acquiesce in this instinctive mistrust or I can attempt to resist it. The two reactions express different attitudes to my automatic and instinctive responses.

Second, imagine someone who acknowledged the force of Copernican reasons for displacing the Earth from the center of the universe; but, let us suppose, they cannot do it. In polite scientific company, they might assert the true Copernican doctrine, but, it is evident, they do not 'really believe this.' They lack the natural tendency to accept consequences of this commitment; they welcome evidence that points the other way; their unguarded behavior reveals confidence that Copernican theory will one day be overthrown. Acknowledging that they ought to believe *p*, in some sense, and some degree, they do not. Once again, there are two cases. Copernican results may be regarded an anomaly: a more subtle and less conscious sensitivity to reasons makes us aware that our current limited understanding of these matters is insufficient basis for judgment. Alternatively, this is an embarrassing block to the 'motivational' effect of reasons that may occasion embarrassment. As before, we must recognize great variety both in the aetiology of beliefs and in our sensitivity to the demands of reason (cf. Rorty 1983).

The third example will be a focus for some of our later discussion. Readers of Descartes's first *Meditation* or other skeptical arguments must take a view of the reasons for *doubt* that are offered. Beginners often find no fault in skeptical challenges, yet are unable genuinely to suspend judgment concerning the disputed propositions. Habits of inference, perception, and belief formation produce belief where, they insist, doubt seems the proper response. Acknowledged reasons for doubt lack 'motivational' force. The significance of these phenomena is controversial. Some assert that the instinctive refusal to doubt reveals sensitivity to reasons we cannot report on. Attacking Cartesian approaches to epistemology, Peirce proclaimed that we should not doubt in philosophy what we do not doubt 'in our hearts.' This suggests that when intellectual reflection lacks 'motivational' force, then my beliefs and doubts display a sensitivity to reason that is missed by my search for intellectual reflection and confirmation. Others insist that our continued belief is irrational, even if we should be grateful for this enforced epistemic akrasia.

The bearing of these examples upon our initial puzzle about internalism is ambivalent. Someone sympathetic to externalism might find confirmation for her position: we consciously and sincerely assent to normative propositions while lacking any serious tendency to conform to them. An alternative reaction denies that conscious reflection is our only way of 'accepting' normative propositions. In some of these cases, our adherence to normative standards is reflected in our instinctive or automatic reactions, in the unreflective exercise of judgment, without being manifested in our tendencies consciously to accept propositions that articulate them. We might combine these two stances. We recognize the *normative force* of reasons and standards when we acknowledge that they determine how we ought to conduct our inquiries and form our beliefs. Whether this recognition possesses *motivational force*, whether it will actually influence the ways in which inquiries and deliberations are conducted, will depend upon how it is related to ways of accepting norms that are manifested in our instinctive or automatic reactions. Consciously adopted norms need not be necessarily tied to motivation since they can lack a link to habits of automatic or habitual normative behavior. This is the Aristotelian idea that I wish to explore in this paper.

II. Virtues

The appeal of talk of virtue when discussing evaluation is clear: It takes seriously states such as habits, dispositions, and competencies that provide evaluations using standards whose content is not transparent to the evaluator. Generosity enables our responses to others to be shaped by sensitivity to special features of particular cases. This need involve no explicit reasoning using standards and distinctions that are understood or endorsed. Indeed, we may be unable to understand exactly why we act as we do. We explain how someone responds generously by saying that she was well brought up and is of good character; perhaps she has cultivated the virtues carefully and responsibly through her life up to now. There is no reason to suppose that reflection or philosophical reflection could change someone who lacked generosity. This would require educating the sensibility, acquiring new habits, and developing an ability to see the predicaments of others in a new way. The generous response has three important features: how the response is arrived at is rarely accessible to us; it is not subject to reflective control; but it reflects *character*—and for this reason, we are responsible for our responses.

This view reflects a distinctively 'Aristotelian' conception of virtue. Virtues are *traits of character*, which *regulate the ways in which we carry out deliberations*. Traits of character are relatively stable and broad, flexible dispositions to attach weight to distinctive kinds of considerations in planning our conduct and in acting. Their primary manifestation is in the process of practical decision making itself. Virtues affect what we notice and what seems important; they influence the questions that arise to us and the doubts that seem to matter. The benevolent person finds that the needs of others provide her with reasons to act; someone who is courageous finds that considerations of personal

attaching weight

danger do not intrude upon practical deliberation more than is appropriate. When applied to epistemic evaluation, this approach should focus on the process of theoretical deliberation, on how we reason and reflect when concerned with matters of fact (Hookway 1994). Just as virtue ethics investigates how to live well by asking what it is to be good at practical reflection, so virtue epistemology studies what it is 'to believe well' by examining what it is to be good at theoretical reflection or 'inquiry.' Intellectual courage, freedom from prejudice, a concern with reaching the truth for its own sake: all these can be characteristics that guide our deliberations and enable us to inquire well.

When understood in this manner, virtues must have two main features. They are states of the character that *motivate* us to deliberate, act, or believe in distinctive ways, and that have a role in explaining our actions and deliberations, revealing ways in which we are guided by considerations that are neither transparent to reflection nor under our explicit intellectual control. But secondly, if these states are virtuous, they do this by providing sensitivity to the demands of *reason*: they enable us to deliberate well, and thus promote *good* action and belief. Virtues have a role in directing or regulating deliberations and inquiries; and their role in this process of regulation explains our practical and theoretical successes. Making sense of how there can be such character traits is a substantive task, and this paper makes only a small contribution to carrying it out.

It is often complained that thinking about epistemic virtue in this way brings with it an unwelcome commitment to doxastic voluntarism, to the idea that beliefs can be subject to the will (see, for example, Sosa 1991, final chapter): Theoretical reasoning must produce belief just as practical reasoning produces action—through something like decision. Although voluntarism has its defenders, it is a controversial doctrine which many find wholly implausible. However the Aristotelian conception of an epistemic virtue is not, in fact, committed to this view. Even if belief formation is not a matter for decision, both theoretical and practical deliberation *involve* decisions: I can choose to collect more evidence, to check a train of reasoning, to try to think of more relevant alternatives to a proposition I am disposed to believe. Theoretical inquiry involves acts of observation and experiment and decisions about where to look and about which experiments to conduct. Belief can be the product, direct or indirect, of such decisions. The questions facing 'Aristotelian' virtue epistemology are: how far does talk of virtues illuminate this process of deliberation? and how far does it enable us to understand some of the distinctive phenomena of epistemic rationality and irrationality? (Hookway 1994; Zagzebski; Montmarquet).

Sosa himself favored a different 'Platonic' conception. We possess faculties and competencies, for example, memory, perception, inductive reasoning. Just as we may speak of *sharpness* as the virtue of the knife, so we may speak of different kinds of context bound reliability as virtues of these different faculties. Perhaps justified belief is belief produced by faculties that possess the appropriate *virtues*. The reliability of memory is analogous to the sharpness of a knife. The contrast between two virtue approaches is easily exaggerated. Sosa's system of virtuous faculties is accompanied by an 'epistemic perspective': a sort of folk epistemology, a view of the nature, strengths, and limitations of our faculties. Theoretical deliberation is informed by this; and this is where the more Aristotelian approach locates *its* battery of epistemic virtues. The approaches share a belief in the normative authority of non-reflective parts of our nature: in virtuous 'faculties' or in habits and sensitivities that regulate our use of the products of our faculties. The Aristotelian approach may be uneasy about Sosa's ontology of *faculties*, but it need not be so. I mention the contrast to emphasize that my sympathies lie with the 'Aristotelian' approach, and to question how sharp the opposition need be.[3]

III. How to Think about Doubt

Virtues, we have said, enable us to respond to reasons: they provide a sensitivity to rational requirements in particular cases, and they are usually motivating. Although they can guide conduct through regulating deliberation and inquiry, their operation is not transparent to consciousness or open to reflective self-control. How can this connection to motivation be understood? And what stand should a defender of epistemic virtue theory take towards the issue of belief internalism which I formulated in the first section of the paper? One conclusion of this paper is that we can (only?) make sense of the operation of epistemic virtues by allowing sentiments and emotions a fundamental role in epistemic evaluation.[4] This section prepares for this conclusion by introducing an example, one that is relevant to the third of the issues about belief and motivation which I explained in section I: how should we understand the role of states such as *doubt* in our cognitive economy?

Doubt stands in an interesting relation to some more familiar epistemic concepts such as justification. Justification is a many sided concept, but one of its manifestations ties justified belief to notions of responsibility: I am justified in believing *p* so long as I am responsible in continuing to do so. My beliefs are justified when I believe what I ought.[5] It seems evident, then, that if I ought to doubt a proposition, I am not justified in believing it; if I ought to doubt it, then it is not the case that I ought to believe it. Doubt is distinct from disbelief, from belief in the negation of the proposition. Doubt is a sort of evaluation of its epistemic status. When I doubt some matter, then I acknowledge that I ought not to form an opinion on its truth value without further evidence or inquiry. When I deem a proposition dubitable, I acquire a commitment to investigating the matter further whenever I am required to have an opinion on the matter. If it is doubtful whether my car contains gasoline, I should not go on a long journey without checking the gauge. It is in this spirit that Charles Peirce described doubt as an 'uneasy' state whose role is to prompt inquiry (see Hookway 1998).

In accordance with the remarks made in the first paragraphs of this paper, it is clear that we can find something doubtful in two ways:

- We can consciously affirm that the proposition in question is one that should not be accepted on the basis of the information that is currently available.

- We can *feel* doubt in the proposition. In relevant circumstances, we are motivated to inquire into the matter, and we have a tendency not to trust items of information that depend upon the doubted proposition.

As we saw, people often respond to skeptical challenges in the first ways but not in the second. They affirm that the proposition is worthy of doubt, but they are unable to feel any doubt: the doubt does not motivate further inquiry. 'Doubt-internalism' is the view that I cannot doubt a proposition without feeling some motivation to inquire into it. Our supposed skeptic's attitude towards Cartesian doubt seems to be a counterexample to doubt internalism. We can avoid this only by claiming that someone who merely sincerely assents to the claim that some proposition should be doubted, and who feels no doubt, or is not motivated to inquire into the matter, does not really hold that the proposition is dubitable.

When pragmatist philosophers discuss these phenomena, they adopt a strategy that is amenable to a virtue epistemology. We possess batteries of what they call *habits:* propensities that guide conduct and determine the will. The word may be unfortunate for we normally take habits to be rigid, inflexible ways of behaving, and it is unclear that this connotation should attach to the pragmatist use of this notion. I shall continue to use the word while allowing that habits may be flexible and adaptable and may even require judgment for their exercise in particular cases. These include habits of inductive reasoning, standards of plausibility, habitual ways of estimating what is uncontroversial and what needs of defense. They are reflected in our reasoning and deliberation, and the patterns that result need not correspond to any principles that we can formulate or acknowledge. Even when I do formulate principles of epistemic rationality when defending my views, these operate against the background of habits of interpretation and inquiry that guide their use. Moreover these are mostly habits of *evaluation*. We trust our habitual responses to provide strategies of inquiry and beliefs with positive epistemic values. Confidence in our ability to inquire responsibly requires trust in our habits of cognitive evaluation, although, of course, they can let us down. Some of these cognitive habits ground our capacity to find beliefs or propositions *doubtful*. We automatically find ourselves doubting propositions in the face of surprising evidence or as a result of critical reflection. Cognitive rationality and epistemic responsibility require a presumptive, but defeasible, trust in our cognitive habits. And, as part of this, it requires such a confidence in our judgments of when something is open to doubt.

An account of inference and inquiry with these features seems required by the view that cognition is regulated by epistemic virtues and vices. It introduces a distinction between the epistemic standards that we *believe* we are following and those that we actually *do* follow, the latter being manifested in habitual responses. Of course it is still possible that I am right in my reflective judgment that I *ought* to conform to standards which, my behavior shows, I do not really conform to. 'Real' doubts engage appropriately with the automatic or 'habitual' evaluations that guide our investigations and deliberations; thus they have *motivational force*. The remainder of the paper explores in more detail this notion of motivational force, arguing that it requires many of our epistemic evaluations to be carried by sentiments or emotions.

IV. Affective States and Motivation

Let us consider an everyday example: My confidence that it will be a nice day is shaken when I hear an unfavorable weather forecast. How might this produce a doubt with 'real motivational force'? I may immediately abandon my fair weather beliefs. If this involves sincerely saying that I no longer know that it will be nice, that is compatible with much of my practice being unaffected by the new information. I continue to plan a hike or a sailing trip; I still urgently prepare to water the garden, and so on. And my doubt may prompt some actions (reaching for the telephone to check the forecast) without affecting many other activities to which it is relevant. Alternatively, I may find myself reopening questions whose resolution had depended upon my belief about the weather; I acquire a conditional disposition to check the weather as soon as it becomes relevant to one of my projects.[6] If the doubt engages with my habits of inference and cognitive evaluation, then it will produce other unreflective evaluations in its wake. Questions occur to me whose relevance depends upon there being uncertainty about the state of the weather; I am motivated to investigate them when this uncertainty becomes an obstacle to my pursuit of my goals.

If this is the case, I shall suggest, we have to accept that many epistemic evaluations are manifested in emotional or sentimental reactions. Perhaps doubt is analogous to (or maybe involves) anxiety or fear. We can acknowledge risk and danger in two ways: in the reflective judgment that our situation is dangerous or in responding to the situation with fear. Just as I can judge a proposition to be doubtful while feeling no real doubt of it, so I can judge a situation to be dangerous while lacking this disposition to feel fear. Or I could feel fear in my predicament, my responses showing that I find it dangerous, while I consciously (and perhaps sincerely) assert that it involves no danger. When such cases arise, we often assign greater weight to the conscious judgment: the lack of fear is a flaw in my makeup; or the fear where I believe there is no danger is irrational. But this need not always be the case. In another paper (1998) I discussed the example of a skilled hill walker who is ready to trust his sense that the situation is dangerous, to trust his experience and expertise, although unable to articulate the clues that he relies upon and to defend the instinctive judgments that guide his behavior. In such cases the judgments of danger that he makes have three important features:

- They are rational. They respond to evidential and other appropriate clues, and, so long as the walker is experienced and skilled, provide a better guide to his situation than would a judgment made on the basis of reflective reasons and principles.
- They essentially involve a motivational component. A desire to leave the hills may be part of the fear or anxiety. The feeling of fear does not provide a dispassionate judgment of danger which may fail to engage with the agent's motivations. Indeed the agent's best source of information about the evaluation he has made is likely to be based upon an awareness of these motivational tendencies.
- They 'spread' and thus influence other motivations. The walker's feeling of fear or anxiety will lead (again through processes of which he is not consciously aware) to related appropriate evaluations of related phenomena. He may cease to trust the judgment of those who confidently proclaim that the hills are safe; he may anxiously look out for handholds at crucial points of his journey, and so on. This tendency to 'spread,' I take it, is one of the marks of those evaluations that are carried by emotional reactions. Moreover they tend to draw our attention to considerations that are relevant to dealing with our predicament.

This helps us to see how an emotional or felt recognition of danger can have considerable value to us.

Recall the example from Patricia Greenspan that was introduced in section I. The behavior and demeanor of a salesman may prompt my instinctive mistrust. Although I could not defend my claim that he is unreliable—I would not be able to justify it to other people—it may still result from my experienced sensitivity to his ways of presenting himself, a sensitivity that is, in fact, a useful source of reliable information. Although 'epistemically' I should give him the benefit of the doubt, my instinctive suspicion can guide my thoughts and inquiries in ways that are beneficial. I am, we might say, wise not to accept all that he tells me. It is compatible with this, of course, that these instinctive reactions can lead me wrong—that I am not always wise to listen to my heart's reasons. The important point is simply that often (but not always) I know more than I can say.

This example shows how tacit, habitual wisdom can guide our evaluations of propositions and methods of inquiry. It can do this because it has an affective tinge: it 'spreads,' influencing other evaluations of how much weight should attach to propositions. Moreover the phenomenology of this epistemically relevant knowledge is distinctive: I am aware of my standards through seeing what I am willing to accept, through noting when I recoil from trusting someone's testimony and so on. I cannot simply reject or disregard these evaluations because they spread through and influence my other evaluations. Even if I decide that my suspicion is unwarranted, I may not be able to prevent it from influencing and coloring my other judgments and evaluations. Indeed they do this in a way that helps to hold them in place, for example by producing suspicion of opinions and sources that appear to challenge them. And this, we have seen, can both be a source of insight and a source of error and prejudice.

If these claims are correct, then doubt has a dual character. I can doubt a proposition through a conscious reflective judgment that the available evidence does not warrant belief. I can also do so by being anxious of it and of all that depends upon it, by treating it and its progeny with suspicion. In each case, my doubt can help to shape my beliefs and regulate my inquiries, but they do so in rather different ways. In the first case, my doubt may influence my beliefs only when I remember it, and my memory engages with my desires to root out sources of falsehood. Unless I am attentive, my natural belief in a proposition may remain effective, shaping what I find plausible and what is surprising to me. In the second case, where the doubt is located in habits of inference and evaluation, it shapes my feelings and attitudes towards beliefs, inquiries, and sources of knowledge and does not always need the assistance of reflective deliberation in order to do so. This suggests that states like belief and doubt do not constitute unitary phenomena: If I consciously affirm doubt in p but habitually trust my (probably warranted) confidence that p, then the question whether I really doubt the proposition may have no straightforward answer. The same may go for belief and for other epistemic evaluations.

V. Reasons and Motivation

We can now return to a question about reasons that was alluded to at the beginning of this paper: Do reasons *have* to motivate? This is a many-sided issue and we have restricted our attention to 'belief-internalism': If I accept that I have reason to doubt or believe some proposition, must I be motivated (to at least some degree) to doubt or believe the proposition in question? The qualification is necessary because reasons can have different weights and because they are often defeasible, carrying a ceteris paribus qualification. We are all familiar with cases where action, belief, doubt, and so on fail to conform to acknowledged reasons, and important issues in the explanation of irrationality concern how this is to be accounted for.

We have already noticed that talk of 'motivation' may seem out of place in connection with belief, once voluntarism has been rejected. However, as we have seen, there are at least two ways in which a notion of motivation can have application within this area. First, reasons for doubt, reasons to question or scrutinize, are fundamental to epistemic evaluation and are fairly straightforwardly reasons to perform activities of distinctive kinds. Inquiry is an activity, and many fundamental epistemic norms concern how inquiry should be conducted. Epistemic rationality requires us to be motivated to ask the right questions and to conduct our inquiries in the right way. Second, although 'motivation' may sound slightly odd when used to describe such cases, the impact of reasons 'spreads': Doubts prompt further doubts as well as prompting desires directed at inquiries. Beliefs produce further beliefs through inference, and this can all happen without being controlled by a controlling process of reflection. This spreading depends upon largely tacit bodies of skills, competencies, and habits that reflect and form our epistemic characters. One kind of internalist about epistemic reasons holds, presumably, that a proposition does not provide me with reason to doubt unless it is integrated with these motivational tendencies. When people worry about the impotence of Cartesian doubts (for example), they are disturbed by exactly this lack of motivational force. Perhaps I do not 'really accept' normative claims unless they possess this kind of integration.

Emphasizing the dual character of doubt (and belief) makes possible a somewhat ambivalent attitude towards the question whether reasons must motivate. When we acknowledge reasons intellectually and explicitly, then we acknowledge their normative force. Perhaps we can do this, and do it sincerely, even if our acceptance is not integrated with the body of habits and dispositions that grounds the motivational force of our reasons. In other cases, our acknowledgment of the normative impact of a reason for doubt or belief is inseparable from our motivational tendencies. I have tried to suggest that this view of the matter is required to make sense of the facts of epistemic rationality. Moreover it offers strong support for an approach to epistemic rationality that has many points of analogy with Aristotelian ideas of virtues.

Notes

1. The particular approach to virtue epistemology that I favor has been influenced by my reading of the American pragmatists, especially Peirce and Dewey. Chapters eight to eleven of my *Truth, Rationality and Pragmatism* (Hookway 2000) present historical studies that complement the content of this paper. Another scholar who is alert to the continuities between virtue epistemology and the pragmatist tradition is Guy Axtell (1996).

2. Which should not be confused with the notion of internalism which is used in constructing theories of justification. It is unclear whether (and if so, how) the two internalisms are related.

3. Gilbert Harman has recently argued that, in the light of research in social psychology, we should abandon the idea that people possess characters, traits, and virtues and thus abandon much of our 'folk morality' (Harman 1999). I cannot discuss these arguments here and will proceed on the assumption that virtue talk is respectable.

4. The example discussed here is examined in much more detail in Hookway (1998). The fact that virtue-based approaches to epistemology make it possible to take seriously the role of emotions in epistemic rationality is also a theme in Zagzebski 1996: 31ff, 126ff.

5. This notion of justification is sometimes described as a 'subjective one': I can be fully responsible in accepting a proposition on the basis of evidence that (as a matter of fact and unbeknownst to me) does not actually make the proposition probable.

6. As Gilbert Harman (1986) has emphasized, we are not good at this. Beliefs have a form of inertia: we tend to hold on to them when the evidence on which they were based is discredited.

References

Axtell, G. 1996. "Epistemic Virtue-talk: the Reemergence of American Axiology?" *Journal of Speculative Philosophy* X, no. 3: 172-98.

Greenspan, P. 1988. *Emotions and Reasons*. New York: Routledge.

Harman, G. 1986. *Change of View*. Cambridge, Mass.: MIT Press.

———— 1999. "Moral Philosophy Meets Social Psychology: Virtue Ethics and the Fundamental Attribution Error." *Proceedings of the Aristotelian Society*, XCIC: 315-31.

Hookway, C. 1994. "Cognitive Virtues and Epistemic Evaluation." *International Journal of Philosophical Studies*, 221-27.

———— 1998. "Doubt: Affective States and the Regulation of Inquiry." *Canadian Journal of Philosophy*, Supplementary volume 24: 203-26. Reprinted as chapter ten of Hookway, 2000.

———— 2000. *Truth, Rationality and Pragmatism: Themes from Peirce*. Oxford: Oxford University Press.

Montmarquet, J. 1993. *Epistemic Virtue and Doxastic Responsibility*. Lanham, Md.: Rowman & Littlefield.

Rorty, A. 1983. "Akratic Believers." *American Philosophical Quarterly*, vol. 20: 175-84.

Sosa, E. 1991. *Knowledge in Perspective*. Cambridge: Cambridge University Press.

Stratton-Lake, P. 1999. "Why Externalism is Not a Problem for Ethical Intuitionists." *Proceedings of the Aristotelian Society*, XCIX: 77-90.

Williams, B. 1979. "Internal and External Reasons," reprinted in Williams, *Moral Luck*. Cambridge: Cambridge University Press, 1991.

Zagzebski, L. 1996. *Virtues of the Mind*. Cambridge: Cambridge University Press.

Part IV

Special Interest Topics in Virtue Theory

13

Critical Thinking, Moral Integrity, and Citizenship:
Teaching for the Intellectual Virtues

Richard Paul

Educators and theorists tend to approach the affective and moral dimensions of education as they approach all other dimensions of learning, as compartmentalized domains, and as a collection of learnings more or less separate from other learnings. As a result, they view moral development as more or less independent of cognitive development. "And why not!" one might imagine the reply. "Clearly there are highly educated, very intelligent people who habitually do evil and very simple, poorly-educated people who consistently do good. If moral development were so intimately connected to cognitive development, how could this be so?"

In this paper, I provide the outlines of an answer to that objection by suggesting an intimate connection between critical thinking, moral integrity, and citizenship. Specifically, I distinguish a weak and a strong sense of each and hold that the strong sense ought to guide, not only our understanding of the nature of the educated person, but also our redesigning the curriculum.

There is little to recommend schooling that does not foster what I call intellectual virtues. These virtues include intellectual empathy, intellectual perseverance, intellectual confidence in reason, and an intellectual sense of justice (fairmindedness). Without these characteristics, intellectual development is circumscribed and distorted, a caricature of what it could and should be. These same characteristics are essential to moral judgment. The "good-hearted" person who lacks intellectual virtues will act morally only when morally grasping a situation or problem does not presuppose intellectual insight. Many, if not most, moral problems and situations in the modern world are open to multiple interpretations and, hence, do presuppose these intellectual virtues.

We are now coming to see how far we are from curricula and teaching strategies that genuinely foster basic intellectual and moral development. Curricula are so highly compartmentalized and teaching so committed to "speed learning" (covering large chunks of content quickly) that they have little room for fostering what I call the intellectual virtues. Indeed, the present structure of curricula and teaching not only strongly discourages their development but also strongly encourages their opposites. Consequently, even the "best" students enter and leave college as largely mis-educated persons, with no real sense of what they do and do not understand, with little sense of the state of their prejudices or insights, with little command of their intellectual faculties—in short, with no intellectual virtues, properly so-called.

Superficially absorbed content, the inevitable by-product of extensive but shallow coverage, inevitably leads to intellectual arrogance. Such learning discourages intellectual perseverance and confidence in reason. It prevents the recognition of intellectual bad faith. It provides no foundation for intellectual empathy, nor for an intellectual sense of fair play. By taking in and giving back masses of detail, students come to believe that they *know* a lot about each subject—whether they understand or not. By practicing applying rules and formulas to familiar tasks, they come to feel that getting the answer should always be easy—if you don't know how to do something, don't try to figure it out, ask. By hearing and reading only one perspective, they come to think that perspective has a monopoly on truth—any other view must be completely wrong. By accepting (without understanding) that their government's past actions were all justified, they assume their government never would or could do wrong—if it doesn't seem right, I must not understand.

The pedagogical implications of my position include these: cutting back on coverage to focus on depth of understanding, on foundational ideas, on intellectual synthesis, and on intellectual experiences that develop and deepen the most basic intellectual skills, abilities, concepts, and virtues. A similar viewpoint was expressed by Whitehead:

> The result of teaching small parts of a large number of subjects is the passive reception of disconnected ideas, not illuminated with any spark of vitality. Let the main ideas which are introduced into a child's education be few and important, and let them be thrown into every combination possible. The child should make them his own, and should understand their application here and now in the circumstances of his actual life. From the very beginning of his education, the child should experience the joy of discovery. The discovery which he has to make is that general ideas give an understanding of that stream of events which pours through his life. (*The Aims of Education*, p. 14)

To accomplish this re-orientation of curriculum and teaching, we need new criteria of what constitutes success and failure in school. We need to begin this re-orientation as early as possible. Integrating teaching for critical thinking, moral integrity, and citizenship is an essential part of this re-orientation.

Teaching for "Strong Sense" Skills

The term "critical thinking" can be used in either a weak or a strong sense, depending upon whether we think of critical thinking narrowly, as a list or collection of discrete intellectual skills, or, more broadly, as a mode of mental integration, as a synthesized complex of dispositions, values, and skills necessary to becoming a fairminded, rational person. Teaching critical thinking in a strong sense is a powerful, and I believe necessary, means to moral integrity and responsible citizenship.

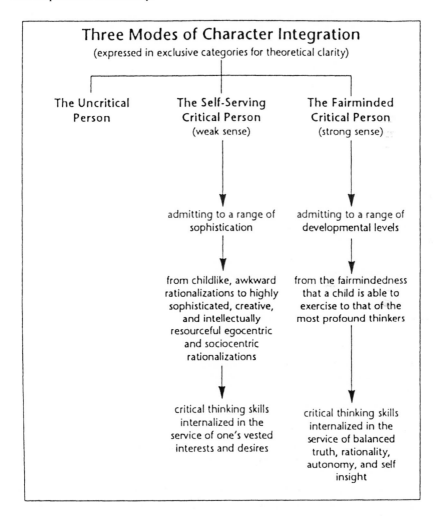

Three Modes of Character Integration
(expressed in exclusive categories for theoretical clarity)

The Uncritical Person	The Self-Serving Critical Person (weak sense)	The Fairminded Critical Person (strong sense)
	admitting to a range of sophistication	admitting to a range of developmental levels
	from childlike, awkward rationalizations to highly sophisticated, creative, and intellectually resourceful egocentric and sociocentric rationalizations	from the fairmindedness that a child is able to exercise to that of the most profound thinkers
	critical thinking skills internalized in the service of one's vested interests and desires	critical thinking skills internalized in the service of balanced truth, rationality, autonomy, and self insight

Intellectual skills in and of themselves can be used either for good or ill, to enlighten or to propagandize, to gain narrow, self-serving ends, or to further the general and public good. The micro-skills themselves, for example, do not define fairmindedness and could be used as easily by those who are highly prejudiced as those who are not. Those students not exposed to the challenge of strong sense critical thinking assignments (for example, assignments in which they must empathically reconstruct viewpoints that differ strikingly from their own) will not, as a matter of abstract morality or general good-heartedness, be fair to points of view they oppose, nor will they automatically develop a rationally defensible notion of what the public good is on the many issues they must decide as citizens.

Critical thinking, in its most defensible sense, is not simply a matter of cognitive skills. Moral integrity and responsible citizenship are, in turn, not simply a matter of good-heartedness or good intentions. Many good-hearted people cannot see through and critique propaganda and mass manipulation, and most good-hearted people fall prey at times to the powerful tendency to engage in self deception, especially when their own egocentric interests and desires are at stake. One can be good-hearted and intellectually egocentric at the same time.

The problems of education for fairminded independence of thought, for genuine moral integrity, and for responsible citizenship are not three separate issues but one complex task. If we succeed with one dimension of the problem, we succeed with all. If we fail with one, we fail with all. Now we are failing with all because we do not clearly understand the interrelated nature of the problem nor how to address it.

The Intellectual and Moral Virtues of the Critical Person

Our basic ways of knowing are inseparable from our basic ways of being. How we think reflects who we are. Intellectual and moral virtues or disabilities are intimately interconnected. To cultivate the kind of intellectual independence implied in the concept of strong sense critical thinking, we must recognize the need to foster intellectual (epistemological) humility, courage, integrity, perseverance, empathy, and fairmindedness. A brief gloss on each will suggest how to translate these concepts into concrete examples. Intellectual humility will be my only extended illustration. I will leave to the reader's imagination what sorts of concrete examples could be marshalled in amplifying the other intellectual virtues.

Intellectual Humility: Having a consciousness of the limits of one's knowledge, including a sensitivity to circumstances in which one's native egocentrism is likely to function self-deceptively; sensitivity to bias, prejudice, and limitations of one's viewpoint. Intellectual humility depends on recognizing that one should not claim more than one actually knows. It does not imply spinelessness or submissiveness. It implies the lack of intellectual pretentiousness, boastfulness, or conceit, combined with insight into the logical foundations, or lack of such foundations, of one's beliefs.

To illustrate, consider this letter from a teacher with a master's degree in physics and mathematics, with twenty years of high school teaching experience in physics:

After I started teaching, I realized that I had learned physics by rote and that I really did not understand all I knew about physics. My thinking students asked me questions for which I always had the standard textbook answers, but for the first time it made me start thinking for myself, and I realized that these canned answers were not justified by my own thinking and only confused my students who were showing some ability to think for themselves. To achieve my academic goals I had to memorize the thoughts of others, but I had never learned or been encouraged to learn to think for myself.

This is a good example of what I call intellectual humility and, like all intellectual humility, it arises from insight into the nature of knowing. It is reminiscent of the ancient Greek insight that Socrates was the wisest of the Greeks because only he knew how little he really understood. Socrates developed this insight as a result of extensive, in-depth questioning of the knowledge claims of others. He had to think his way to this insight.

If this insight and this humility are part of our goal, then most textbooks and curricula require extensive modification, for typically they discourage rather than encourage it. The extent and nature of "coverage" for most grade levels and subjects imply that bits and pieces of knowledge are easily attained, without any significant consideration of the basis for the knowledge claimed in the text or by the teacher. The speed with which content is covered contradicts the notion that students must think in an extended way about content before giving assent to what is claimed. Most teaching and most texts are, in this sense, epistemologically unrealistic and hence foster intellectual arrogance in students, particularly in those with retentive memories who can repeat back what they have heard or read. *Pretending* to know is encouraged. Much standardized testing validates this pretense.

This led Alan Schoenfeld, for example, to conclude that "most instruction in mathematics is, in a very real sense, deceptive and possibly fraudulent." He cites numerous examples including the following. He points out that much instruction on how to solve word problems in elementary math

> is based on the "key word" algorithm, where the student makes his choice of the appropriate arithmetic operation by looking for syntactic cues in the problem statement. For example, the word "left" in the problem "John had eight apples. He gave three to Mary. How many does John have left?" . . . serves to tell the students that subtraction is the appropriate operation to perform. (p. 27)

He further reports the following:

> In a widely used elementary text book series, 97 percent of the problems "solved" by the key-word method would yield (serendipitously?) the correct answer.
>   Students are drilled in the key-word algorithm so well that they will use subtraction, for example, in almost any problem containing the word 'left'. In the study from which this conclusion was drawn, problems were constructed in which appropriate operations were addition, multiplication, and division. Each

used the word 'left' conspicuously in its statement and a large percentage of the students subtracted. In fact, the situation was so extreme that many students chose to subtract in a problem that began "Mr. Left."

Schoenfeld then provides a couple of other examples, including the following:

I taught a problem-solving course for junior and senior mathematics majors at Berkeley in 1976. These students had already seen some remarkably sophisticated mathematics. Linear algebra and differential equations were old hat. Topology, Fourier transforms, and measure theory were familiar to some. I gave them a straightforward theorem from plane geometry (required when I was in the tenth grade). Only two of eight students made any progress on it, some of them by using arc length integrals to measure the circumference of a circle (Schoenfeld, 1979). Out of the context of normal course work these students could not do elementary mathematics.

He concludes:

In sum: all too often we focus on a narrow collection of well-defined tasks and train students to execute those tasks in a routine, if not algorithmic fashion. Then we test the students on tasks that are very close to the ones they have been taught. If they succeed on those problems, we and they congratulate each other on the fact that they have learned some powerful mathematical techniques. In fact, they may be able to use such techniques mechanically while lacking some rudimentary thinking skills. To allow them, and ourselves, to believe that they "understand" the mathematics is deceptive and fraudulent.

This approach to learning in math is paralleled in all other subjects. Most teachers got through their college classes mainly by "learning the standard textbook answers" and were neither given an opportunity nor encouraged to determine whether what the text or the professor said was "justified by their own thinking." To move toward intellectual humility, most teachers need to question most of what they learned, as the teacher above did, but such questioning would require intellectual courage, perseverance, and confidence in their own capacity to reason and understand subject matter through their own thought. Most teachers have not done the kind of analytic thinking necessary for gaining such perspective.

I would generalize as follows: Just as the development of intellectual humility is an essential goal of critical thinking instruction, so is the development of intellectual courage, integrity, empathy, perseverance, fairmindedness, and confidence in reason. Furthermore, each intellectual (and moral) virtue in turn is richly developed only in conjunction with the others. Before we approach this point directly, however, a brief characterization of what I have in mind by each of these traits is in order:

Intellectual Courage: Having a consciousness of the need to face and fairly address ideas, beliefs, or viewpoints toward which we have strong negative emotions and to which we have not given a serious hearing. This courage is connected with the recognition that ideas considered dangerous or absurd are sometimes rationally justified (in whole or in part) and that conclusions and beliefs inculcated in us are sometimes false or misleading. To determine for ourselves which is which, we must not passively and uncritically "accept" what we have "learned." Intellectual courage comes into play here, because inevitably we will come to see some truth in some ideas considered dangerous and absurd, and distortion or falsity in some ideas strongly held in our social group. We need courage to be true to our own thinking in such circumstances. The penalties for non-conformity can be severe.

Intellectual Empathy: Having a consciousness of the need to imaginatively put oneself in the place of others in order to genuinely understand them, which requires the consciousness of our egocentric tendency to identify truth with our immediate perceptions or long-standing thought or belief. This trait correlates with the ability to reconstruct accurately the viewpoints and reasoning of others and to reason from premises, assumptions, and ideas other than our own. This trait also correlates with the willingness to remember occasions when we were wrong in the past despite an intense conviction that we were right, and with the ability to imagine our being similarly deceived in a case at hand.

Intellectual Good Faith (Integrity): Recognition of the need to be true to one's own thinking; to be consistent in the intellectual standards one applies; to hold one's self to the same rigorous standards of evidence and proof to which one holds one's antagonists; to practice what one advocates for others; and to honestly admit discrepancies and inconsistencies in one's own thought and action.

Intellectual Perseverance: Willingness and consciousness of the need to pursue intellectual insights and truths in spite of difficulties, obstacles, and frustrations; firm adherence to rational principles despite the irrational opposition of others; a sense of the need to struggle with confusion and unsettled questions over an extended period of time to achieve deeper understanding or insight.

Faith in Reason: Confidence that, in the long run, one's own higher interests and those of humankind at large will be best served by giving the freest play to reason, by encouraging people to come to their own conclusions by developing their own rational faculties; faith that, with proper encouragement and cultivation, people can learn to think for themselves, to form rational viewpoints, draw reasonable conclusions, think coherently and logically, persuade each other by reason and become reasonable persons, despite the deep-seated obstacles in the native character of the human mind and in society as we know it.

Fairmindedness: Willingness and consciousness of the need to treat all
viewpoints alike, without reference to one's own feelings or vested interests,
or the feelings or vested interests of one's friends, community, or nation;
implies adherence to intellectual standards without reference to one's own
advantage or the advantage of one's group.

The Interdependence of the Intellectual Virtues

Let us now consider the interdependence of these virtues, how hard it is to
deeply develop any one of them without also developing the others. Consider
intellectual humility. To become aware of the limits of our knowledge we need
the *courage* to face our own prejudices and ignorance. To discover our own
prejudices in turn we must often *empathize* with and reason within points of
view toward which we are hostile. To do this, we must typically *persevere* over
a period of time, for learning to empathically enter a point of view against which
we are biased takes time and significant effort. That effort will not seem justified
unless we have the *faith in reason* to believe we will not be "tainted" or "taken
in" by whatever is false or misleading in the opposing viewpoint. Furthermore,
merely believing we can survive serious consideration of an "alien" point of
view is not enough to motivate most of us to consider them seriously. We must
also be motivated by an *intellectual sense of justice.* We must recognize an
intellectual *responsibility* to be fair to views we oppose. We must feel *obliged* to
hear them in their strongest form to ensure that we do not condemn them out of
our own ignorance or bias. At this point, we come full circle back to where we
began: the need for *intellectual humility.*

Or let us begin at another point. Consider intellectual good faith or integrity.
Intellectual integrity is clearly difficult to develop. We are often motivated—
generally without admitting to or being aware of this motivation—to set up
inconsistent intellectual standards. Our egocentric or sociocentric side readily
believes positive information about those we like and negative information
about those we dislike. We tend to believe what justifies our vested interest or
validates our strongest desires. Hence, we all have some innate tendencies to use
double standards, which is of course paradigmatic of intellectual bad faith. Such
thought often helps us get ahead in the world, maximize our power or
advantage, and get more of what we want.

Nevertheless, we cannot easily operate *explicitly* or overtly with a double
standard. We must, therefore, avoid looking at the evidence too closely. We
cannot scrutinize our own inferences and interpretations too carefully. Hence, a
certain amount of *intellectual arrogance* is quite useful. I may assume, for
example, that I know just what you're going to say (before you say it), precisely
what you are really after (before the evidence demonstrates it), and what
actually is going on (before I have studied the situation carefully). My
intellectual arrogance makes it easier for me to avoid noticing the unjustifiable
discrepancy in the standards I apply to you and those I apply to myself. Of
course, if I don't have to empathize with you, that too makes it easier to avoid

seeing my duplicity. I am also better off if I don't feel a keen need to be *fair* to your point of view. A little background *fear* of what I might discover if I seriously considered the consistency of my own judgments also helps. In this case, my lack of intellectual integrity is supported by my lack of intellectual humility, empathy, and fairmindedness.

Going in the other direction, it will be difficult to maintain a double standard between us if I feel a distinct responsibility to be fair to your point of view, understand this responsibility to entail that I must view things from your perspective in an empathic fashion, and conduct this inner inquiry with some humility regarding the possibility of my being wrong and your being right. The more I dislike you personally or feel wronged in the past by you or by others who share your way of thinking, the more pronounced in my character must be the trait of intellectual integrity in order to provide the countervailing impetus to think my way to a fair conclusion.

Defense Mechanisms and the Intellectual Virtues

A major obstacle to developing intellectual virtues is the presence in the human egocentric mind of what Freud has called "defense mechanisms." Each represents a way to falsify, distort, misconceive, twist, or deny reality. Their presence represents, therefore, the relative weakness or absence of the intellectual virtues. Since they operate in everyone to some degree, no one embodies the intellectual virtues purely or perfectly. In other words, we each have a side of us unwilling to face unpleasant truth, willing to distort, falsify, twist, and misrepresent. We also know from a monumental mass of psychological research that this side can be *powerful,* can dominate our minds strikingly. We marvel at, and are often dumbfounded by, others whom we consider clear-cut instances of these modes of thinking. What is truly "marvelous," it seems to me, is how little we take ourselves to be victims of these falsifying thoughts, and how little we try to break them down. The vicious circle seems to be this: because we, by and large, lack the intellectual virtues, we do not have insight into them, but because we lack insight into them, we do not see ourselves as lacking them. They weren't explicitly taught to us, so we don't have to explicitly teach them to our children.

Insights, Analyzed Experiences, and Activated Ignorance

Schooling has generally ignored the need for insight or intellectual virtues. This deficiency is intimately connected with another one, the failure of the schools to show students they should not only test what they "learn" in school by their own experience, but also test what they experience by what they "learn" in school. This may seem a hopeless circle, but if we can see the distinction between a critically analyzed experience and an unanalyzed one, we can see the link between the former and *insight,* and the latter and *prejudice,* and will be well on our way to seeing how to fill these needs.

We subject little of our experience to critical analysis. We seldom take our experiences apart to judge their epistemological worth. We rarely sort the "lived" integrated experience into its component parts, *raw data, our interpretation* of the data, or ask ourselves how the interests, goals, and desires we brought to those data shaped and structured that interpretation. Similarly, we rarely seriously consider the possibility that our interpretation (and hence our experience) might be selective, biased, or misleading.

This is not to say that our unanalyzed experiences lack meaning or significance. Quite the contrary, in some sense we assess *all* experience. Our egocentric side never ceases to catalogue experiences in accord with its common and idiosyncratic fears, desires, prejudices, stereotypes, caricatures, hopes, dreams, and assorted irrational drives. We shouldn't assume a priori that our rational side dominates the shaping of our experience. Our unanalyzed experiences are some combination of these dual contributors to thought, action, and being. Only through critical analysis can we hope to isolate the irrational dimensions of our experience. The ability to do so grows as we analyze more and more of our experience.

Of course, more important than the sheer *number* of analyzed experiences is their *quality* and *significance*. This quality and significance depends on how much our analyses embody the intellectual virtues. At the same time, the degree of our virtue depends upon the number and quality of experiences we have successfully critically analyzed. What links the virtues, as perfections of the mind, and the experiences, as analyzed products of the mind, is *insight*. Every critically analyzed experience to some extent produces one or more intellectual virtues. To become more rational it is not enough to have experiences nor even for those experiences to have meanings. Many experiences are more or less charged with *irrational* meanings. These important meanings produce stereotypes, prejudices, narrowmindedness, delusions, and illusions of various kinds.

The process of developing intellectual virtues and insights is part and parcel of our developing an interest in taking apart our experiences to separate their rational from their irrational dimensions. These meta-experiences become important benchmarks and guides for future thought. They make possible modes of thinking and maneuvers in thinking closed to the irrational mind.

Some Thoughts on How to Teach for the Intellectual Virtues

To teach for the intellectual virtues, one must recognize the significant differences between the higher order critical thinking of a fairminded critical thinker and that of a self-serving critical thinker. Though both share a certain command of the micro-skills of critical thinking and hence would, for example, score well on tests such as the Watson-Glaser Critical Thinking Appraisal or the Cornell Critical Thinking Tests, they are not equally good at tasks which presuppose the intellectual virtues. The self-serving (weak sense) critical thinker would lack the insights that underlie and support these virtues.

I can reason well in domains in which I am prejudiced—hence, eventually, reason my way out of prejudices—only if I develop mental benchmarks for such reasoning. Of course one insight I need is that when I am prejudiced it will seem to me that I am not, and similarly, that those who are not prejudiced as I am will seem to me to be prejudiced. (To a prejudiced person, an unprejudiced person seems prejudiced.) I will come to this insight only insofar as I have analyzed experiences in which I was intensely convinced I was correct on an issue, judgment, or point of view, only to find, after a series of challenges, reconsiderations, and new reasonings, that my previous conviction was in fact prejudiced. I must take this experience apart in my mind, clearly understand its elements and how they fit together (how I became prejudiced; how I inwardly experienced that prejudice; how intensely that prejudice seemed true and insightful; how I progressively broke that prejudice down through serious consideration of opposing lines of reasoning; how I slowly came to new assumptions, new information, and ultimately new conceptualizations).

Only when one gains analyzed experiences of working and reasoning one's way out of prejudice can one gain the higher order abilities of a fairminded critical thinker. What one gains is somewhat "procedural" or sequential in that there is a *process* one must go through; but one also sees that the process cannot be followed out formulaically or algorithmically, it depends on principles. The somewhat abstract articulation of the intellectual virtues above will take on concrete meaning in the light of these *analyzed experiences*. Their true meaning to us will be given in and by these experiences. We will often return to them to recapture and rekindle the insights upon which the intellectual virtues depend.

Generally, to develop intellectual virtues, we must create a collection of analyzed experiences that represent to us intuitive models, not only of the pitfalls of our own previous thinking and experiencing but also processes for reasoning our way out of or around them. These model experiences must be charged with meaning for us. We cannot be *indifferent* to them. We must sustain them in our minds by our sense of their importance as they sustain and guide us in our thinking.

What does this imply for teaching? It implies a somewhat different content or material focus. Our own minds and experiences must become the subject of our study and learning. Indeed, only to the extent that the content of our own experiences becomes an essential part of study will the usual subject matter truly be learned. By the same token, the experiences of others must become part of what we study. But experiences of any kind should always be critically analyzed, and students must do their own analyses and clearly recognize what they are doing.

This entails that students become explicitly aware of the logic of experience. All experiences have three elements, each of which may require some special scrutiny in the analytic process: *1)* something to be experienced (some actual situation or other); *2)* an experiencing subject (with a point of view, framework of beliefs, attitudes, desires, and values); and *3)* some interpretation or conceptualization of the situation. To take any experience apart, then, students must be sensitive to three distinctive sets of questions:

1) What are the raw facts; what is the most neutral description of the
    situation? If one describes the experience this way and another
    disagrees, on what description can they agree?

2) What interests, attitudes, desires, or concerns do I bring to the situation?
    Am I always aware of them? Why or why not?

3) How am I conceptualizing or interpreting the situation in light of my
    point of view? How else might it be interpreted?

Students must also explore the interrelationships of these parts: How did my
point of view, values, desires, etc. affect what I noticed about the situation? How
did they prevent me from noticing other things? How would I have interpreted
the situation had I noticed those other things? How did my point of view,
desires, etc. affect my interpretation? How *should* I interpret the situation?

If students have many assignments that require them to analyze their
experiences and the experiences of others along these lines, with ample
opportunity to argue among themselves about which interpretations make the
most sense and why, then they will begin to amass a catalogue of critically
analyzed experiences. If the experiences illuminate the pitfalls of thought, the
analysis and the models of thinking they suggest will be the foundation for their
intellectual traits and character. They will develop intellectual virtues because
they had thought their way to them and internalized them as concrete
understandings and insights, not because they took them up as slogans. Their
basic values and their thinking processes will be in a symbiotic relationship to
each other. Their intellectual and affective lives will become more integrated.
Their standards for thinking will be implicit in their own thinking, rather than in
texts, teachers, or the authority of a peer group.

Conclusion

We do not now teach for the intellectual virtues. If we did, not only would we
have a basis for integrating the curriculum, we would also have a basis for
integrating the cognitive and affective lives of students. Such integration is the
basis for strong sense critical thinking, for moral development, and for
citizenship. The moral, social, and political issues we face in everyday life are
increasingly intellectually complex. Their settlement relies on circumstances and
events that are interpreted in a variety of (often conflicting) ways. For example,
should our government publish misinformation to mislead another government
or group that it considers terrorist? Is it ethical to tolerate a "racist" regime such
as South Africa, or are we morally obligated to attempt to overthrow it? Is it
ethical to support anti-communist groups that use, or have used, torture, rape, or
murder as tools in their struggle? When, if ever, should the CIA attempt to

overthrow a government it perceives as undemocratic? How can one distinguish "terrorists" from "freedom fighters"?

Or, consider issues that are more "domestic" or "personal." Should deliberate polluters be considered "criminals"? How should we balance off "dollar losses" against "safety gains"? That is, how much money should we be willing to spend to save human lives? What is deliberate deception in advertising and business practices? Should one protect incompetent individuals within one's profession from exposure? How should one reconcile or balance one's personal vested interest against the public good? What moral or civic responsibility exists to devote time and energy to the public good as against one's private interests and amusements?

These are just a few of the many complex moral, political, and social issues that virtually all citizens must face. The response of the citizenry to such issues defines the moral character of society. These issues challenge our intellectual honesty, courage, integrity, empathy, and fairmindedness. Given their complexity, they require perseverance and confidence in reason. People easily become cynical, grow intellectually lazy, or retreat into simplistic models of learning and the world they learned in school and see and hear on TV. On the other hand, it is doubtful that the fundamental conflicts and antagonisms in the world can be solved or resolved by sheer power or abstract good will. Good-heartedness and power are insufficient for creating a just world. Some modest development of the intellectual virtues seems essential for future human survival and well-being. Whether the energy, the resources, and the insights necessary for this development can be significantly mustered remains open. This is certain: We will never succeed in cultivating traits whose roots we do not understand and whose development we do not foster.

14

Virtue Theory
and the Fact/Value Problem

Guy Axtell

The 20th Century Context of the Problem

If description of mental processes and evaluation of agents and their beliefs are rightly to be considered as complementary concerns on any plausible construal of the epistemological project, then this relationship cries out for explanation. For the complementarity of these concerns is hardly straightforward: One cannot epistemically evaluate a belief without knowing how it was formed, a largely if not wholly a scientific question; on the other hand, epistemic norms are and must be used to evaluate our scientific beliefs and theories, and apparently then require a basis at least partly independent of scientific matters of fact.

This *aporia* pits the proponent of naturalized epistemology, which asserts a continuity of epistemology and the cognitive or "special sciences," against the non-naturalist as the traditional champion of epistemology's normative functions. To be sure, there is middle ground in this dispute, the prospect for a pragmatic or "normative naturalism." Consider the naturalistic turn in epistemology from a historical perspective. Various solutions to the Fact/Value problem have been posed under the rubric of "epistemology naturalized." Some are eliminative of epistemology's normative tasks, and those that are not eliminative hold that the development of normative epistemic standards depends closely on psychology and the cognitive sciences. Eliminative solutions are not new. Before the turn towards naturalized epistemology, the logical empiricists had their own eliminative solutions. They attempted to reduce epistemology not to psychology, but to logic; not to the synthetic, but to the analytic. The rational reconstruction of scientific decision-making was not thought of as a normative undertaking, but was rather glossed as simply part of "the logical analysis of the language of science."[1] The turn away from logical analysis in the 1960s and towards a naturalism that entailed a conception of the "supervenience" of normative criteria on natural fact arose partly in response to explicit forms of non-naturalism. But it responded more directly to the failure of logical empiricism to arrive at criteria of scientific theory-choice by way of the analytic method of *conceptual analysis*. As has been the case many times already in the twentieth century, the Fact/Value problem was transformed with this newer, naturalized conception of the epistemological project, only to reappear in a new form.

Most of us think of ourselves as good naturalists now, and while the naturalistic turn was at first identified with eliminative approaches for some thinkers, we find it hard to think of those "closet intuitionists," the logical empiricists as naturalistic. The point that they, too, sought to eliminate evaluative language from "the logic of science" should, then, serve as a reminder that the logical empiricist legacy may still exude a residual influence over us. This is an influence by which we tend to perceive the only viable naturalistic models as those that, if not eliminative of normative tasks of epistemology, at least show epistemic evaluation to be sharply contrasted with other evaluative uses of language. At the dawn of a new century, we may still labor under the residue of deep "metaphilosophical" assumptions of a sharp separation between two kinds of judgment, and therefore also between their corresponding forms of philosophical analysis. In the logical empiricist system of thought, the objectivity of epistemological rational reconstructionism, and of "the language of science" in general, was in no small part predicated on its contrast from the presumed subjectivity (or non-cognitive status) of ethical judgment and "the language of morals." David Carr has recently made a closely related point when he wrote, "Thus it is well-known that whilst prescriptivists are willing to concede the possibility of a descriptive sense of goodness or value in the non-moral realm they nevertheless insist that these terms must have a non-descriptive 'evaluative' sense in the moral sphere."[2] In still broader terms, this disparity is what Alan Gewirth, in identifying a primary dogma of empiricism, thought of as being behind the unholy combination of a "normative science and a positive ethics"; it is similar to (and also motivates) the combination of "metaphysical realism and moral relativism" that Hilary Putnam has identified and criticized in thinkers such as Bernard Williams.

It is often said that the logical empiricists were foundationalists. But it is worthwhile noting that they were also skeptics, only quite selectively so. They utilized many arguments taken directly from the tropes of the ancient skeptics, and advanced them against the idea of moral knowledge, or of an "ethico-cognitive parallel" (Reichenbach). The rhetorical point of such contrasts was to show that skepticism undermines claims to the objectivity or rationality of ethical judgment, but not to that of scientific judgment. I am concerned with the upshot of these metaphilosophical assumptions, and we need not rehearse in any detail the arguments that contributed to the breakdown of this logical empiricist worldview and the rise of naturalized epistemology. Let it be enough to say, first, that these arguments came both from inside and outside the empiricist camp, with figures such as Thomas Kuhn and W. V. Quine sitting ambiguously but intriguingly on its borders; and second, that these arguments involved divulging the implicit intuitionism of the logical empiricists in their treatment of rational reconstructions of scientific decision-making and other aspects of epistemic evaluation. The upshot, as I understand it, is closely akin to what Putnam calls the "companions in guilt" argument against the above-mentioned combination of metaphysical realism and moral relativism. More specifically, a skeptic's slant on that breakdown and the lessons to be taken from are essentially this: *Tu Quoque!* You yourself do it! You (filthy Anglo) logical empiricists are our companions in guilt, for your rules or supposed algorithms of rational reconstruction are really, as Kuhn argued, "values at work" in science; and if your skeptical arguments succeed, as you claim, in undermining the objectivity of ethical judgment in the choice of normative ethical theory, then they prove far *too much* for your own good, for they equally well impugn the objectivity of scientific judgment in theory choice!

Quine's neo-pragmatic approach to language led him to see that Carnap's distinction between the analytic and the synthetic, another edifice of this logical empiricist program, was contextual, not absolute. Quine's way of handling the normative dimension of epistemology was generally eliminative, as is famously captured in his description of epistemic normativity as merely "a branch of engineering," implying its reducibility to a purely instrumental form of reason. But this view, part of Quine's conception of epistemology reduced to psychology, may simply beg many of the interesting questions raised in Kuhn's work on "cognitive values." Might it not invite the equally trenchant reply of the Deweyan pragmatist—that the distinction between instrumental and intrinsic value is also (and for many of the same reasons) not absolute, but a matter that can be determined only contextually?

One point more to make before we can relate this discussion back to the Fact/Value problem. Barry Stroud, an epistemologist and noted scholar of the history of skepticism, writes as follows:

> Scepticism is most illuminating when restricted to particular areas of knowledge
> . . . because it then rests on distinctive and problematic features of the alleged
> knowledge in question, not simply on some completely general conundrum in the
> notion of knowledge itself, or in the very idea of reasonable belief.[3]

If it is correct that skepticism makes its greatest challenges when so addressed to particular spheres, this highlights the poverty of the sharp separations and asymmetries in thinking about evaluative language that characterized the metaphilosophical views of twentieth century logical empiricism. The scientistic strategy of division—of persuasive definition and of contrast between scientific epistemology and "mere" evaluative language, whether in the positivist or even the Quinean naturalistic mode—is a dangerous game. For it plays into the hand of the most serious forms of skepticism. When that strategy can no longer be carried through, when it becomes apparent that an unacknowledged intuitionism has been present from the start, the skeptical upshot remains. Not only does it remain, but it reflects back with still greater force upon the one whose strategy it was to employ the skeptic's tropes in order to affect the desired contrast. And not the recognition of evaluative components in scientific reasoning, but the perceived philosophical *implications* of that recognition, is part and parcel of our era's excessive skepticism about the viability of epistemology as a normative discipline. The question of "the place of normativity in naturalized epistemology" is just the contemporary version of the older unsolved positivist quandary about "the place of values in a world of facts," and our current inability to come to grips with it, I suggest, reflects equally poorly on *our* ability to understand knowledge and valuation under a single, unified philosophical perspective.

To summarize my point now in a positive manner, while the science/non-science distinction remains of importance, there is distinct advantage in a metaphilosophical approach that redresses the excessive asymmetries characterizing empiricist thought regarding the relationship between epistemic and other forms of evaluative discourse. This relationship between epistemic and other kinds of evaluation must be of deep concern in any naturalistic philosophy broad and pragmatic enough to address itself to the human agent as both a reasoner *and* a valuer. If there is to be a less utopian approach to the Fact/Value problem than eliminativism, it can only take place around a new consensus on the need for a more symmetrical treatment of epistemology and ethics as central normative subdisciplines of philosophy.

The issues that I have raised in providing this retrospective look at the Fact/Value problem are issues of a metaphilosophical nature. This is the level at which I see contemporary virtue theory beginning its reconstructive account of human agency. Although it was a backbone of his critique of logical empiricism, Kuhn's term "cognitive values" is rarely heard today, and most epistemologists are concerned with knowledge and justification generally, rather than scientific theory choice. But Kuhn's essential lesson has not been lost, only transformed during the turn to naturalistic epistemology. Increasingly in recent years, there is growing mutual interest and overlap between those doing work on ethical and on intellectual virtue. Many problems central to ethical agency, problems that have been addressed in virtue ethics such as the relationship between "responsibility" and "luck," are reappearing across subfields of philosophy as problems equally relevant to a conception of epistemic agency. Virtue theorists understand the justification of beliefs to be related to intellectual virtue in a way substantially analogous to the way that the rightness of acts relates to moral virtue. If these analogies between ethical and epistemic evaluation prove strong, it will invite if not demand an account of human agency unified enough to be applicable to fields.

In the language of virtue epistemology the search for an unified account of ethical and epistemic evaluation is simply the search for a unified account of the virtues. Or at least the latter is a substantial step towards the former. Some have suggested these as primary goals of contemporary virtue theory. But the perceived prospects and advantages of a unified theory of the virtues are matters of contention, even among virtue epistemologists. I believe that its prospects are strong, and that there can be grounds for a meeting of minds on the sound form such an account should take. Though I may not get far in developing such an account here, I hope to clear some ground that allows virtue epistemologists of various persuasions to see the advantages of such a "unified account" as part of a response to the perennial Fact/Value problem. To begin this ground-clearing project, the next two sections of this paper will address some of the issues that virtue epistemologists debate among themselves, and some of the ways that dispute becomes exasperated. Examining how oppositions about the definition of intellectual virtue are understood by virtue epistemologists will help to clarify which differences are substantive, and which are likely explainable as the result of divergent interests in the complex topic of epistemic agency. In the final two sections we will then reverse course, exploring the extent to which there is hidden complementarity behind oftentimes sharply expressed differences. We will there examine the shared goal of a "mixed externalist" account of epistemic justification, and how this goal can itself be seen as one step in establishing the form and function of a viable unified account of the virtues.

Virtue Reliabilist and Virtue Responsibilist Epistemologies

The best-known version of virtue epistemology, that of Ernest Sosa, is a form of epistemic reliabilism, and that is the identification that virtue epistemology basically has for many philosophers.[4] But reliabilism has been criticized from within the fold of virtue theory for assuming a quantitative, maximizing goal, and for not promoting a "genuinely aretaic" approach.[5] To see how these objections arise, consider Sosa's proposed definition of intellectual virtue as "a quality bound to help maximize one's surplus of truth over error." Here intellectual virtues are defined in terms of their truth-conduciveness, so that the aim of truth is taken as conceptually prior to and independent of the concept of a virtue. Jonathan Dancy's characterization of the reliabilist view as "virtue consequentialism" seems quite fitting. This characterization, however, and especially Sosa's one-time description of his account as "epistemic rule-utilitarianism" (which term he borrowed, perhaps unfortunately, from Roderick Firth) have raised questions in the minds of others who take virtue theory as a non-consequentialist approach.[6]

Sosa's broader virtue theory, which to date remains largely implicit, endorses a strategy for defining both intellectual and ethical virtue. To quote again, "Intellectual virtues are . . . ingrained modes of intellectual procedure that tend to give us truth, just as practical virtues are ingrained modes of practical conduct that tend to yield what is good." Sosa has defended this view by arguing both its support in classical Greek virtue theory, as well as its advantageousness and desirability from the perspective of contemporary philosophic naturalism. But as we will see, he is challenged on both these fronts of classical support and contemporary desirability. These challenges are usually framed and developed in the work of a strain of virtue epistemology that I'll term "virtue responsibilism" in order to clearly mark it off from Sosa's branch, which I'll hereafter refer to as "virtue consequentialism" or (to make the contrast with responsibilism clearer in some contexts) "virtue reliabilism." Sosa intends his truth-linked definition of the intellectual virtues to respond to a demand for normative criteria of justified belief, as beliefs formed through the instancing of one or more intellectual virtues. This demand for normative criteria is part of the perceived incentive for a consequentialist or goal-linked account of the virtues, since virtue theory is often considered more difficult to maintain if virtues are treated as primary rather than as derived.[7] Indeed, it is often claimed by consequentialists in ethics that if Aristotle did intend to make the virtues of character primary, and definitive of the end (*eudaimonia*) itself, then his account suffers from circularity.

On Sosa's account, intellectual virtues are *any* truth-conducive cognitive faculty or stable cognitive disposition, including genetically-granted ones such as the various perceptual faculties, and the transmission faculties of deduction and memory. Virtue responsibilists dispute such definitions.[8] The responsibilists' departure from Sosa comes in thinking of virtues as accruing to their possessor rather than to the faculties themselves. If justified belief is in part a matter of epistemic responsibility, as right action is a matter of ethical responsibility, then attributions of virtue are more appropriately assigned to persons than to faculties. Linda Zagzebski, like several other critics of Sosa including Jonathan Dancy, points out that the account of intellectual virtues as faculties like memory, sight, etc. runs counter to Aristotle's account of virtue. Virtue for Aristotle is a *hexis*, a *state* or disposition acquired either by habit (ethical virtues) or teaching (intellectual virtues); it is one that is "in accordance" with but not "by" nature. This should be enough to dispel such an identification of genetic faculties or natural capacities with intellectual virtues, Dancy and Zagzebski have both argued.

Sosa's way of responding to these objections is to argue that such a definition, while perhaps not Aristotelian, is recognizably "still Greek": Plato in particular recognized anything with a function, such as the eye, as having virtues germane to it. This broader Platonic sense of virtue, then, recognizes non-moral goods, and brings with it an attached sense of praiseworthiness for an object (like an eye or a knife) that follows from its being *good of a kind*, i.e., good at promoting that object's function. Sosa can also point out that intellectual virtue is presented quite differently than ethical virtue even in the context of Aristotle's thought. The latter are seen as dispositions to choose the mean or to deliberately desire the mean. By contrast, intellectual virtue for Aristotle is a disposition to hit the truth, and Aristotle therefore has a straightforwardly consequential definition for intellectual virtue, whatever his views about moral virtue. So to quote Sosa's direct response, "as Dancy himself acknowledges, if one tries to oppose the consequentialist answer and to more closely assimilate the relation of the *good* and the virtues of character to the *true* and the intellectual virtues, we commit ourselves to some form of the doctrine of the unity of the virtues. . . . But it does not seem as if Aristotle would have wished to assert the unity of the intellectual virtues. They are not defined in terms of hitting a mean, and the account he gives of them (some concerned with things necessary, others with things that may be or not be) makes it difficult to suppose that in the absence of one, one lacks all the others" (chapter 8).

Dancy (chapter 7) concedes that when one turns to Aristotle's account of the intellectual virtues, "he does seem to link them to truth in the way that Sosa wants. Aristotle does say that an intellectual virtue is a state by which one will most hit the truth" (*NE* 1139b12-13). But Dancy then makes the same move as Zagzebski and the virtue responsibilists: he opts to pass over Aristotle's apparent asymmetries between the two kinds of virtue, and to treat the intellectual virtues in the way that he sees Aristotle treating the ethical ones. For Dancy a genuinely aretaic epistemology requires a pluralistic and *holistic* conception of the goals of our intellectual life. The consequentialist retorts, "What makes all these things virtues, if not the goal (or function) which they promote?" There must be some characteristic unitariness to the intellectual virtues, or we could not know that in identifying virtues as such, we are not merely "picking out a motley crew," as Sosa puts it. Dancy's answer: "There is an apparent unity in Aristotle's account of the moral virtues, but hidden diversity. . . . The source of unity is the way in which a good character is a well-knit one, not some end which good character would promote." Somewhat like John McDowell, Dancy is saying that praise and blame, for a true virtue theorist, will be mediated by consideration of the entire sort of life that surrounds this failure or that success: "there will be a holistic aspect to our moral *and* to our epistemic assessment."

This claim clearly draws upon Aristotle's ethics as its model, extending this model to include intellectual virtue; it draws more specifically on Aristotle's indication (again explicitly only within his ethics) of an internal rather than an external relationship of means to ends, which serves to distinguish ethical virtue from skill, and moral and evaluative from productive reasoning. A skill is causally separable from the outcome it is used to produce, but an ethical virtue cannot likewise be conceived as separate from the ends of truth and justice; these latter are part of what we *mean* by that human flourishing that honesty or fairness serve to promote; they are *constitutive* of those ends rather than just causally productive of them. Responsibilists like Dancy and Zagzebski have also noted that the reliabilists' epistemic goal of maximizing true beliefs and minimizing false ones is not as easily discernible as it may appear: it may well be two goals, at times in tension with each other. We need to find a proper balance of strength and security in our practices of belief acquisition, at times perhaps even committing ourselves to brave error in order to enhance understanding. Maximizing true beliefs ("Jamesian reliability") will depend upon the virtue of *intellectual courage*, while minimizing false ones ("Cartesian reliability") leans on the virtue of *intellectual caution*. If so, this would certainly support Dancy's claim that there is hidden diversity in the *epistemic* as well as in the ethical goal.

Both reliabilist and responsibilist virtue epistemology is sometimes presented to us as being "strongly Aristotelian." Unfortunately, Aristotle's thought may be misused as a means of arguing and mediating this in-house dispute among virtue epistemologists, just as it often is in disputes among contemporary virtue ethicists. Yet what we have found is that, for reasons of contemporary concern, virtue reliabilists and virtue responsibilists both depart from Aristotle in more ways than they admit. Consider that neither group splits the field of virtues in the Aristotelian manner, offering a consequentialist account in one area and a non-consequentialist account in the other. *Both,* in other words, want more symmetry in their own accounts than Aristotle's appears to provide. They both take leave from Aristotle's account of intellectual virtue, yet in revealingly different ways. The one attempts to understand all virtues as he sees Aristotle understand the *intellectual virtues,* and the other prefers drawing the model from Aristotle's ethics or *virtues of character.*

To be more specific, the virtue reliabilists utilize the account they find in Aristotle's treatment of intellectual virtues, yet they broaden the notion of virtue beyond states acquired either by habit or by teaching. They do not distinguish teleology from consequentialism, and while they draw analogies between ethical and epistemic evaluation, these analogies are typically quite thin because unlike responsibilists, they rarely express their own views on ethical evaluation directly. The responsibilists, on the other hand, express a robust sense of the primacy of the virtues, and this makes virtue theory in their eyes a more unique philosophical alternative. Their account of intellectual virtue exhibits a strong affinity with Aristotle's account of the relationship of virtues and *eudaimonia* in his ethics. In fact they sometimes argue for subsuming the intellectual virtues *under* the moral virtues (Zagzebski), or at least for a far more holistic conception of our epistemic goal than Aristotle's own account supports. Sometimes for instance it has been suggested that *eudaimonia* should be thought of as *common goal* of both the ethical and intellectual life.[9] As a mark of their similarity with ethical virtues, several responsibilists including Zagzebski and Montmarquet have tried to provide a conception of the unity of the intellectual virtues analogous to Aristotle's conception of the doctrine of the mean. Along with these differences from Aristotle, they also sometimes build into their conceptions of intellectual virtue the same kind of strong motivational requirement that Aristotle makes for the ethical virtues. Here again the responsibilist's treatment of the relationship between the virtues appears to evoke a stronger symmetry between the ethical and intellectual than Aristotle intended. If consistently developed, the model here is not Aristotelian but neo-Aristotelian, in that it creates a subclass of "ethical virtues pertaining to intellect." The Greek thinker would not have understood the idea of a kind of ethical virtue that pertains to the intellectual sphere (intellectual courage, conscientiousness, fairness, trustworthiness, etc., all *intellectual analogous* of acknowledged ethical virtues).

It is fine that the virtue responsibilist wants to throw emphasis upon this kind of disposition, a kind that Zagzebski rightly points out seems to have "fallen into the gap between ethics and epistemology" and been neglected to some extent in both fields. But the concern comes when responsibilists insist that this newly recognized class of dispositions is definitive of intellectual virtue. There are good reasons for thinking this approach to defining the virtues is overly restrictive. Let's call habits and dispositions of this kind (ethical virtues pertaining to intellect or better, to intellectual *activity*) CT virtues, for critical thinking. Thinking is, after all, an activity. It seems misguided to *define* intellectual virtue in terms of this class of CT virtues, as responsibilists do when they insist that only *acquired* traits can count as virtues, or when they place strong motivational constraints on *all* intellectual virtues. Why? Theoretically, such a definition *displaces* the broader, reliabilist class of faculties and dispositions to hit the truth (we could call these "cognitive virtues," retaining "intellectual" as the cover term for both kinds); at the same time, Zagzebski's model places all CT and the specifically ethical virtues that they are analogues of under a general conception of virtue as a disposition to act morally. This is the position that subsumes or assimilates the virtues, the model of "a virtue epistemology based on virtue in the ethical sense." In essence, such a model is not neo-Aristotelian, but rather non-Aristotelian.

By contrast, the non-assimilationist model of virtue that my suggested terms would indicate—with "cognitive" virtues ("passive" faculties such as the perceptual) on the one side and "specifically moral" and "CT" virtues on the other—could likely be seen as neo-Aristotelian. But as I said above, there is nothing (except hopefully clarity) to be gained by such labels. The more important point is the simplest and most practical: that in order for virtue epistemologists to share a broad range of interests, they need to begin with a broad enough definition of intellectual virtue. I think this is also the case with respect to definitions of virtue theory itself, and it is to debate over that issue we can turn next.[10]

What Virtue Theory Is (and Is Not)

In *Virtues of the Mind* (1996) Zagzebski's main objections to Sosa are that "his model of moral theory is act-based, and his definition of virtue is consequentialist." By these charges she has alleged that Sosa's approach does not really constitute a virtue theory. I will briefly rebut those arguments here. The latter of these charges breaks down into two separable issues, the relationship of virtues to rules, and the relationship of virtues to goals, both of which are discussed by Zagzebski. I will briefly take the three desiderata of a virtue theory in what seems the most straightforward manner.

The relationship between virtues and rules

The most sound criteria for distinguishing a virtue theory that Zagzebski proposes is in terms of relationships of priority between virtues to rules. This is a potentially strong desiderata, in that it gives us a typology based upon deep-level *formal relationships*. On this construal, all and only virtue theories in ethics define rules (rightness) in terms of the source of an action in an ethical virtue; and by analogy, all and only virtue theories in epistemology define rules (justification) in terms of the source of a belief in an intellectual virtue. This desiderata is very closely related to the *change in the direction of analysis*, that Greco uses to define virtue theory. He says virtue theories in epistemology define justification by the source of belief in intellectual virtue, rather than defining intellectual virtue as a disposition to believe rightly. By this criterion, however, Sosa's approach surely constitutes a virtue theory, since his definitions of knowledge and justification in terms of their ground in intellectual virtues demonstrate the conceptual priority he gives to the virtues in relationship to rules.

The relationship between virtues and ends

Another important consideration, an extension of the same formal approach, comes from looking at the relationship between virtues and goals or ends. In *Virtues of the Mind,* Zagzebski says that this relationship distinguishes different forms of virtue theory: "The question of which comes first, end or motive, is the point at issue between a virtue theory that is happiness-based [goal-based] and an agent-based theory of the form I have called motivation-based."[11] Those that give priority to the goal, and define virtues in terms of conduciveness to that goal, are what she calls "Good-based" virtue theories. The priority relationship here would be of the form 1. End (truth), 2. Virtue, 3. Rules (justification). Those that reverse the place of the end or goal, seeing virtue as derivative from or definitive of the goal, are what she calls "motivation-based" virtue ethics. Their order of organization would be 1. Virtue, 2. Rules, 3. End (or possibly 1. Virtue, 2.End, 3. Rules). For Sosa, the intellectual virtues are defined in terms of their truth-conduciveness, an objective matter viewed as independently attributable to cognitive processes. For Zagzebski on the other hand, truth is treated as a derivative concept in much the same way that the *good* is a derivative concept in her ethics.

Zagzebski certainly wants to argue that the form of virtue theory she calls motivation-based is best able (or perhaps even uniquely able) to account for the value of the motive to seek knowledge, and the greater value of knowledge when compared with the value of true belief. On Zagzebski's preferred motivation-based account, the goodness of virtues is based on the goodness of the agent's motives, and this form of goodness is conceived as intrinsic, not derived. These are interesting questions, but separate, it seems to me, from the question of whether "Good based" theories can constitute a form of virtue theory. Since in her book she allows that there is room *within* virtue theory to accommodate different views of the relationship between the virtues and the *Good,* to say as she sometimes appears to that Sosa's account is not a form of virtue theory *because* its definition of virtue is consequentialist would clearly reflect inconsistency on her part. By her own criteria, "virtue consequentialism" is consequentialism and virtue theory both.

The distinction between belief-based and agent-based accounts

Given what we've said about the distinction between Good and Motivation-based virtue theory, Zagzebski's argument that Sosa's approach is not a form of virtue theory because "his model of moral theory is act-based" is equally curious. The differences between act and agent-based accounts are interesting their own right, and she is correct that (Chisholmian) deontological and consequentialist theories is epistemology have structural similarities with act-based ethics" (8). These are reasons to think that virtue consequentialism is a belief-based and not strictly speaking an agent-based theory. But using this as a desiderata to show that Sosa's virtue consequentialism is not a virtue theory again illustrates how Zagzebski's categories are inconsistently applied in *Virtues of the Mind.*

Arguably this way of dividing the field is not exactly correct even in its characterization of normative ethical theories. That question aside, Zagzebski appears to agree strongly with Christopher Hookway in desiring to de-emphasize the centrality of the issue of justification in epistemology in order to make issues of active agency the primary focus. As Hookway puts this responsibilist claim, "The primary focus is on how we order activities directed at answering questions and assessing methods of answering questions; it is not upon the epistemic status of beliefs."[12] I would suggest that it is really matters of interest and emphasis that are at the root of this matter, not the desiderata for virtue theory itself. Once again the conclusion is that the ways of dividing the field under criteria (a) and (c) give us different results. Having begun with the desiderata of section (a), Zagzebski can't consistently use the distinction between belief-based and agent-based theories to argue that virtue consequentialism is not a form of virtue theory.[13]

Mixed Accounts of Justification

In the previous two sections we discussed some of the dividing points between virtue reliabilism and virtue responsibilism, focussing around their respective understandings both of intellectual virtue and of virtue theory. We have found, I believe, that the cause of many of these disputes is primarily the alternative interest and focus of the two strains. This raises the expectation that these in-house disputes can be mediated, and are due as much to confusion as to substantive philosophical differences. In this section, then, I would like to focus and build upon an important shared emphasis in these two strains of virtue epistemology.

Virtue epistemologists share a broad range of assumptions that bring them together with interest in an intellectual virtue-centered account of epistemic agency. An account of epistemic agency will necessarily involve both descriptive and evaluative concerns; it will also involve consideration of both "passive" and "active" agency. At the most passive end of the spectrum are the functions of processes like those of the human perceptual faculties, and the beliefs they may causally entail; at the most active end are dispositions that are acquired either by habituation or teaching, and which are reflected in "chosen acts" that influence the rational acceptance of propositions. Justification is a particularly difficult issue in epistemology, in part because in discussing it we often cut across divisions that should be kept clear. Some pertinent examples are the division between evaluation of beliefs and evaluation of agents, between the criteria of justification and the conduct of inquiry, between belief and the act of propositional acceptance, between objective evidence supporting a belief and the agent's own evidence, and between passive and active agency. The problems engendered by cutting across these distinctions haphazardly have been abundantly evident over the past three decades in the epistemological debates over "internalism" and "externalism" in epistemology.

Virtue epistemologists often stumble in dealing with these distinctions as well. Nevertheless, virtue epistemology may present unique potential for developing an account of epistemic agency that pays proper respect to these divisions. Consider justification as one important aspect of such an account of agency. One of the assumptions virtue epistemologists share, which I regard as definitive of their unique philosophical approach, is the need for a "dual component" conception of justification, sometimes also called a "mixed externalist" account of justification. This is one that integrates constraints on an agent's faculty reliability with constraints on the agent's responsibility in gathering and processing evidence. So to cite but three instances, Ernest Sosa writes that in his virtue perspectivism, a proposition is evident or reflectively known (from the K point of view) to a subject "only if *both* he is rationally justified in believing it *and* is in a position to know (from the K point of view) whether it is true."[14] Linda Zagzebski defines knowledge and justification through a "dual-component" account of intellectual virtue, which builds into the conception of the virtues themselves both "a characteristic motivation to produce a certain desired end and reliable success in bringing about that end."[15] Greco also describes his as a "mixed theory": "The main idea is that an adequate account of knowledge ought to contain both a responsibility condition and a reliability condition. Moreover, a virtue account can explain how the two are tied together. In cases of knowledge, objective reliability is grounded in epistemically responsible action."[16]

Despite their differences, these three thinkers have been most explicit proponents of a "mixed" account of justification. All three see this as a pre-eminently "Aristotelian" characteristic, since Aristotle placed both motivational and success constraints on the attribution of virtue to an agent. It has also been perceived as a characteristic that contemporary virtue theorist should well embrace for its advantages in facing and overcoming the internalist/externalist opposition in epistemology. Zagzebski's "dual-component" account of the virtues, for example, has twin aspects of *success* and *motivation.* Being virtuous involves success—"getting it right"—but it also involves the ability to see what that right thing is, which in turn involves the appropriate desire or motivation. One way of understanding the basis for such mixed accounts is to follow Zagzebski's suggestion that Hilary Kornblith's way of organizing questions presents a most promising framework for reconciling internalism and externalism. In his "Ever Since Descartes" (1985), Kornblith presents internalism and externalism as views that can be made complementary by paying attention to the different levels of descriptive and evaluative analysis that go into epistemic evaluation.[17]

Kornblith begins by distinguishing two objects of epistemic evaluation, "appropriate processes for arriving at beliefs" and "appropriate actions for agents to take." The former object is of primarily non-voluntary processes, and the latter of voluntary actions that influence beliefs. Each of these objects of evaluation can themselves be divided, depending upon whether we adopt an objective (external) or subjective (agent's own) perspective on them. So long as we are asking only the question of how we ought, objectively speaking, arrive at our beliefs, a reliabilist answer in terms of reliable processes suffices. But we then neglect whether the belief is properly integrated into the agent's perspective. If we ask the same question from the position of the agent's own lights (background beliefs, available evidence, etc.), an internalist answer is called for; but then we neglect the issue of whether the belief is formed in a way that is actually (objectively) truth-conducive. If both questions have a claim as pertinent to a satisfactory account of justified belief, we cannot afford to neglect either one.

With respect to the second object of epistemic evaluation, Kornblith says that "An epistemically responsible agent desires to have true beliefs, and thus desires to have his beliefs produced by processes which lead to true beliefs; his actions are guided by these desires." According to Kornblith, "epistemic evaluation finds its natural ground in our desires in a way which makes truth something we should care about whatever else we may value."[18] Since he deems the two questions asked from the objective perspective to be closely dependent, we are left with three basic forms of epistemic evaluation.

Internal constraints may be understood in various ways. Reliabilists who have brought aspects of internalism about justification into their epistemologies have often done so by focussing on consideration of coherence and explanatory integration from the agent's situated perspective. This notion is implicit in what Sosa calls his "virtue perspectivism," which we may categorize as a form of what often goes in the literature as "perspectival internalism" (Schmitt, Haack). There is a needed place for a perspectival or internal coherence constraint on knowledge. But there is a sharp tension between it and the objective orientation of reliabilism: because it views reliably formed beliefs as neither necessary nor sufficient for belief sanctioned by the subject's perspective, perspectival internalism seems to ill-fit with reliabilism (Schmitt, p. 5). No wonder then that one finds such a sharp distinction between subjective and objective justification in some reliabilist thinkers like Alvin Goldman. This tension may be resolved, though, in mixed accounts that achieve a satisfactory level of stability. Greco, for instance, is at pains to argue that "In cases of knowledge, objective reliability is grounded in epistemically responsible action."[19]

There is a problem about whether responsibility-constraints can find a place in virtue reliabilist accounts, if these accounts identify the agent's perspective on belief acquisition only with "a sort of inner coherence" (Sosa) or with an agent's own standards or beliefs "about reliable belief-forming processes" (Goldman 1986). Kornblith appears correct in insisting that a responsibility or "action-theoretic" constraint on knowledge is also needed in addition to reliability and internal coherence constraints. It is needed partly in order to render reliability and internal coherence constraints consistent *with one another*. Thus Zagzebski's acceptance of and attempt to build off of Kornblith's model are intriguing. For our purposes it shows that virtue responsibilism and virtue reliabilism have a strong bond in the shared goal of developing a "mixed" externalist account of knowledge and justification. On the mixed account, the epistemic agent (1) has beliefs formed by reliable processes, (2) is cognitively well integrated and "in a position to know" because properly affected or attuned to her environment, and (3) seeks to acquire virtuous habits or dispositions (possibly both for their own sake and as a means of appropriately *basing* her beliefs on good reasons).

It should be noted in closing this section that Julia Driver and Jonathan Dancy both claim that compromise solutions are philosophically unstable. Neither wants an approach to ethical and epistemic evaluation that might be thought an unhappy amalgam of consequentialist and aretaic ideas, and again, neither wants to divide the field by taking very different approaches in the two fields. Ironically, this leads the former to a thoroughgoing consequentialist ethics (in line with process reliabilist views in epistemology), while it leads the latter to reject what he calls virtue consequentialism and to adopt "strong" virtue-theoretical views in both ethics and epistemology. It is of course tempting to play their views on the rejection of compromise solutions off against one another. But the serious point here is that the *problem of stability* is present not only for a virtue theory itself, but for mixed accounts of justification, which surely are compromise solutions to the internalist/externalist opposition over epistemic justification. This *problem of stability* deserves further examination in both contexts, that of what constitutes a sound and viable virtue theory, and that of what constitutes a satisfactory mixed account of justification.

Conclusions: From Fragmentation to Reconstruction

We have seen that there is a shared goal among virtue epistemologists to develop a mixed externalist account of epistemic justification. While the goal is shared, the methods for achieving it, we have also seen, are often a matter of dispute. I believe that through focussing on the mixed account of justification as a shared project, the specific divergences we discussed can be mediated, leading to the significant broadening and merging of research interests among those doing work in this field.

Virtue epistemology has unique advantages, relative to other approaches, as the basis for a reconstruction in philosophy. The concept of intellectual virtue usefully explains both what it means to have beliefs formed by reliable processes, and what it means for agents to be responsible and well-motivated in their acquired cognitive habits and dispositions. To the extent that a mixed account must understand subjective justification in terms of "responsibility" and "proper motivation," it relies integrally upon what used to be called the language of ethics. Therefore the development of a mixed account in epistemology is at the same time a step in the direction of the further goal of a unified theory of value across epistemology and ethics.

In its broader context, I have characterized virtue epistemology as one side of an integrated account of the human being as both reasoner and valuer. It is in this broader context of virtue theory (rather than virtue epistemology or virtue ethics, specifically) that we can bring the Fact/Value problem back into focus. Virtue theory addresses this problem by responding to the fragmented state of reason that John Dewey, a pragmatist who opposed the predominance of logical empiricism during much of his lifetime, presents in *The Reconstruction of Philosophy* as the central problem for modern life:

> The problem of restoring integration and cooperation between man's beliefs about the world in which he lives and his beliefs about the values and purposes that should direct his conduct is the deepest problem of modern life. It is the problem of any philosophy that is not isolated from that life.[20]

Restoration or reconstruction in philosophy, according to Dewey, is achieved by integration and cooperation. Integration is a theoretical concern, cooperation largely a practical one. Restoration itself is a response to perceived fragmentation. Epistemology in twentieth century Anglo-American thought has followed a path with many significant turns. Leaning upon a sharp distinction between the language of science and the language of ethics in the predominant logical empiricist tradition, twentieth century philosophers constructed an artificial divide between ethical and epistemic evaluation, a divide that it remains for the present century to bridge. The sharpness of this divide and the persuasive definitions of scientific and ethical discourse that supported it— tokens of their manner of responding to the Fact/Value problem—were often celebrated as confirmation of the scientific mind. Yet its result, in human terms, is precisely that crisis Dewey characterizes for us a fragmentation of human reason. Since Dewey's period the residual effects of fragmented reason continue to be felt through the various radical "turns" proposed for philosophers to take over the past quarter or half-century, and in epistemology specifically, through the unsustainably sharp conflicts between internalism and externalism, and between non-naturalism and eliminative or reductive naturalism.

The concept of a virtue has both descriptive and prescriptive senses, which together, if not conflated or used in an intuitionistic manner, provide normativity a "comfortable home" within a pragmatic-naturalistic account of knowledge and understanding. As I hope to have shown, contemporary virtue theory, with one leg firmly rooted in classical philosophy and the other in contemporary pragmatic naturalism, provides resources to fuel this endeavor.

Notes

1. "The approach to philosophical problems through the analysis of language is the contemporary counterpart of the epistemological or reflexive analysis of the former ["reflexive"] turn [in philosophy; thus] . . . Carnap's conception of logical analysis as the successor of Kant's tribunal of reason furnishes an even clearer example of belief in the neutrality of the analytic standpoint." John E. Smith, "The Reflexive Turn, the Linguistic Turn, and the Pragmatic Outcome," in *America's Philosophical Vision.* Chicago: University of Chicago Press, '1992.

2. Alan Gewirth, "Normative 'Science' and Positive 'Ethics'," *Phil. Review* LXIX, 69 (1960): 187-205. Hilary Putnam, *Realism with a Human Face*. Cambridge: Cambridge University Press, 1990. Also "Replies," *Philosophical Topics* 20, 1: 3247-408. Compare David Carr, "The Primacy of Virtues in Ethical Theory: Part II," *The Cogito Society,* Spring 1996: 34-40, 34.

3. Barry Stroud, "Philosophical Scepticism," in *Knowledge and Justification, Vol. II,* Ernest Sosa, ed. Dartmouth: The International Research Library of Philosophy, 1994, 177.

4. Ernest Sosa, *Knowledge in Perspective.* Cambridge: Cambridge University Press, 1991.

5. For clear statements of the relationship between virtue ethics and consequentialism, some of which can be analogized to the epistemic context, see Carr 1996 and Justin Oakley, "Varieties of Virtue Ethics," *Ratio* IX, 2, 1996: 128-152.

6. Sosa 1991, 84.

7. For an example of the charge that Aristotle's giving the moral virtues primacy over *eudaimonia* would be circular, and a critique of virtue ethics based on it, see Peter Simpson, "Contemporary Virtue Ethics and Aristotle," *Review of Metaphysics* 45, 1992: 503-524.

8. Lorraine Code, *Epistemic Responsibility.* Hanover, N. H.: University Press of New Hampshire, 1987; see also James Montmarquet's *Epistemic Virtue and Doxastic Responsibility. Lanham, Md.: Rowman & Littlefield.* Compare also Montmarquet's claim (chapter 11, this volume) that "there can be an internalist [an non-causal], teleological conception of the epistemic virtues."

9. "Furthermore, if it turns out that the ultimate end of truth and the ultimate ends of the moral virtues are all components of a life of *eudaimonia*, then the moral and intellectual virtues do not even differ in their ultimate ultimate ends." Linda Zagzebski, "Precis of *Virtues of the Mind,*" in a symposium on that text in *Philosophy and Phenomenological Research*, forthcoming 2000.

10. There is added benefit for responsibilists to loosen the definition of intellectual virtue. For if it is doubtful that the types of faculties and stable dispositions that reliabilists refer to as intellectual virtues are "active" enough to presuppose a motivational constraint, it is also doubtful that the success condition applies uniformly to all the CT virtues that responsibilists are concerned with. A looser definition, one that allows intellectual virtue to comprise both the "cognitive" and the "CT" virtues, allows a principled way to show how the requirements vary from one type to the next.

11. *Virtues of the Mind*, 338. Each of the two forms of "pure virtue theory" is granted by Zagzebski to have distinct advantages and disadvantages. The first account has more precedence in the history of philosophy; it "explain[s] the good of a virtue teleologically. Virtue is good because of its connection to the thing that is more fundamentally good" [i.e., the general or ultimate aim].

12. Christopher Hookway, "Cognitive Virtues and Epistemic Evaluations," *International Journal of Philosophical Studies* 2, 2, 1994: 211-227, 211.

13. However, while the issue of the relationship between virtues and goal seems least important to the classification of theories, one could conceivably maintain that the act/agent distinction is the most pertinent desiderata. This makes for a potentially cleaner break between virtue theory and the "modernist" consequentialist and deontological approaches. One could make out on this approach that even a theory that prioritizes virtues over rules can be "act-based." But it apparently then could not retain the idea that the "change in the direction of analysis" is a defining feature of virtue theory. So which is the better approach?

14. Ernest Sosa from "How Do You Know?," in Sosa 1991, 28.

15. Linda Zagzebski 1996, 134.

16. John Greco from "Virtue Epistemology," entry in Stanford Online Encyclopedia of Philosophy.

17. Hilary Kornblith, "Ever Since Descartes," reprinted here as chapter 4. See also his earlier "Justified Belief and Epistemically Responsible Action," *The Philosophical Review* 92, 1: 33-48.

18. Kornblith, "Epistemic Normativity," *Synthese* 94, 1993: 357-376, 373.

19. Greco from Stanford Online Encyclopedia of Philosophy.

20. For historical and thematic connections with American pragmatism and the associated idea of a "general theory of value," see my "Epistemic Virtue-Talk: the Re-emergence of American Axiology?" in *The Journal of Speculative Philosophy* X, 3, 1996: 172-198.

15

Epistemic Vice

Casey Swank

Goofus is a paragon of unreasonableness—closed-minded, averse to argument and uncertainty, unappreciative of his own fallibility, and motivated by the desire to have been right.[1] To be an unreasonable person just is to have these and/or similar undesirable traits, sometimes called epistemic vices. That is how I will use the term here. By epistemic vices, then, I mean those constitutive of unreasonableness—faults of the sort that come to mind when we imagine an especially unreasonable person (hereafter a.k.a. a Goofus).

It is better to be reasonable than unreasonable. Why, though? Just what is bad about epistemic vices: What makes them *vices*? And what distinguishes them from other sorts of vices (those not constitutive of unreasonableness): What makes them *epistemic* vices?

Bad and Epistemic vs. "Epistemically Bad"

We might first move, with others before us, from the trivial observation that

ev1   There is something specifically epistemic about an epistemic vice.

to the not so trivial conclusion that

ev2   An epistemic vice is a trait that is bad in a specifically epistemic way

—bad, as ev2's proponents would say, from the point of view of truth, or of attaining truth while avoiding error, or something like that.[2] But that would be a mistake: ev2 does not follow from ev1. If it did follow, we should have likewise to conclude that

ts2   A tall stranger is a person who is unfamiliar in a specifically tall way.

For it is of course true that

ts1   There is something specifically tall about a tall stranger.

But ts2 is false: There is nothing specifically tall about the way in which a tall stranger is unfamiliar. What makes ts1 true is not ts2 but rather

ts3   A tall stranger is a tall person who is unfamiliar.

Likewise, then, ev2 may be false: There may be nothing specifically epistemic about the way in which an epistemic vice is bad. What makes ev1 true may be not ev2 but rather

ev3   An epistemic vice is an epistemic trait that is bad.

The truth of ev3 would not by itself preclude that of ev2. (An epistemic vice might be an epistemic trait that is, moreover, bad in some specifically epistemic way.) But since ev3 does by itself entail ev1 (there is already something specifically epistemic about a bad epistemic trait), some further rationale (besides ev1) would be needed for ev2, were we to find that ev3 is true: ev2 could not then be founded, as it so often has been, upon the observation (ev1) that these are, after all, epistemic vices. If an epistemic vice is (as per ev3) a bad epistemic trait—if it is thus *already* distinguished as a specifically epistemic vice—then it is a mistake to assume (as per ev2) that there must also be something specifically epistemic about its badness. Our predecessors have confined their search for the essence of epistemic vice to the domain of "epistemically bad" qualities—e.g., truth-obstructiveness (reliabilist accounts), or deficient concern for truth (responsibilist accounts). But we need not follow them in this—not if (as per ev3) an epistemic vice is to begin with a specifically epistemic trait. So is that the case? Is ev3 true?

Apparently so. Consider the epistemic vices we observed in Goofus—closed-mindedness, aversion to argument and uncertainty, unappreciativeness of one's own fallibility, and the desire to have been right. Each of these faults is, to begin with, an aspect of what might be called one's epistemic character: Each is (roughly) an attitude, affection, or disposition whose object is some aspect of one's doxastic life—e.g., one's own beliefs, reasoning habits, or cognitive powers. And in this respect these are typical: Searching the literature for examples of epistemic virtue and vice, one finds only such traits as these—only epistemic traits.

Ev3 is further confirmed by an otherwise mysterious feature of the literature. It is widely held that truth-conduciveness is the defining mark of epistemic virtue—that it is their truth-conduciveness that makes such traits as open-mindedness and appreciativeness of one's own fallibility epistemic virtues.

So what about nosiness? Surely this is a truth-conducive trait. But it just as surely is *not* an epistemic virtue—not one of those qualities that comes to mind when we imagine an especially reasonable person. (Indeed, the combination would strike us as incongruous.) So why is this seemingly obvious counterexample never advanced?

There is evidently an unspoken understanding that, however "epistemically good" (truth-conducive or whatever) it might be, a trait such as nosiness—i.e., a nonepistemic trait—cannot be an epistemic virtue. Otherwise, the truth-conducivist conception of epistemic virtue would long since have suffered the swift and decisive "nosiness refutation." That this refutation has never so much as been considered attests to theorists' universal (but tacit) acceptance of ev3: Evidently, it has always just gone without saying that (whatever else they might be) epistemic virtues and vices are, to begin with, epistemic traits.

But it is unfortunate that the truth of ev3 has not heretofore been explicitly recognized. In consequence, the search for a satisfactory account of epistemic vice has unduly been confined to the area defined by ev2: Theorists have looked, specifically, for epistemic badness, where there might in fact be some other sort of badness. Since epistemic vices are, to begin with, specifically epistemic traits, our question is no longer what makes them epistemic (for we already know *that*), but is now, rather, what makes them vices—not what is epistemic about them, but rather what is bad about them. Having failed to appreciate this, our predecessors have mistakenly assumed that the badness in question must itself be epistemic. Unblinded by this assumption, open to previously unappreciated possibilities, we may fare better.

Indeed, once we stop asking what is "epistemically bad" about unreasonableness, and ask instead what is (just) bad about it, a new, simpler and more satisfying account will readily suggest itself. Working towards this, we have first to consider a representative assortment of ev2-based accounts (ranging through variants of both reliabilism and responsibilism). We shall see that none of these is satisfactory, and hence that we have still further cause to abandon ev2, and thus open the way to the better account just promised.

Truth-Centered Accounts

W. V. Quine and J. S. Ullian could as easily have been discussing any other epistemic vice when they observed that "The desire to have been right . . . stands in the way of our seeing we were wrong."[3] Accordingly, it might be supposed that

ev4   An epistemic vice is a trait that is truth-obstructive.

But then we should have to conclude that unnosiness (the otherwise nameless opposite of nosiness) is an epistemic vice. And of course it is not: Being unnosy does not make one a less reasonable person. As we have seen, though, it is clear that the proponents of such accounts as ev4 have always rather

Virtues and vices are context-invariant

intended their ev3-based variants. And this example poses no threat to the ev3-based variant of ev4—viz.,

> ev5   An epistemic vice is an epistemic trait that is truth-obstructive.

It poses no threat to ev5, because unnosiness is a truth-obstructive *non*-epistemic trait (nonepistemic, because its object, others' business, is not an aspect of one's doxastic life). Is ev5 correct, though?

No, it is not. Alongside Goofus, consider (his foil) Gallant. Gallant is a paragon of reasonableness—open-minded, responsive to argument, tolerant of uncertainty, appreciative of his own fallibility, and innocent of the desire to have been right. These traits appear to be more truth-conducive than their opposites. But there is no telling whether they are in fact so: For all we can tell, ours might be a demonworld—one in which closed-mindedness and the like are truth-conducive and their opposites truth-obstructive. Contemplating this possibility in light of ev5, we should have to conclude that Goofus might in fact be a model of epistemic virtue, and Gallant a model of epistemic vice. And surely this is wrong. As others have noted, our judgment that Gallant's is the better epistemic character, that he is the more reasonable person, is not hedged with any such proviso as "unless ours is a demonworld." Demons or no demons, closed-mindedness and the like are epistemic vices, and their opposites are epistemic virtues.

I want to be as clear as possible here on the significance of the demon-world scenario. Why (it will be asked) should we seek to accommodate such a bizarre world? Is an account that holds for the actual world not yet good enough? I agree that an acceptable account of epistemic vice need not accommodate every possible world. But it does need to hold for a certain range of these. Because we can tell which traits are epistemic vices, the quality that makes them vices must be one that we can tell they have. The quality we seek, the essence of epistemic vice, must therefore be one that these traits have not only in the actual world (whichever that might be), but in all those that might, for all we can tell, be the actual world. And the demonworld is one of these: For all we can tell, the Gallants of this (the actual) world might be demon victims, and the Goofuses might be demon's pets. It is to ensure coverage of the *actual* world that we must accommodate the demonworld.

Since we cannot tell whether ours is a demonworld, and yet we can tell which traits are epistemic vices, the quality we seek must be one that such traits have irrespective of demonic machinations. Actual truth-obstructiveness is not such a quality. But while closed-mindedness, aversion to uncertainty and the rest might in fact be truth-conducive, they certainly appear not to be: Demons or no demons, these vices are, let us say, apparently truth-obstructive. So perhaps we can salvage the spirit of ev5 with a simple epicycle—we can say instead that

> ev6   An epistemic vice is an epistemic trait that is apparently truth-obstructive.

Because ev6 squares with our assessments of Goofus and Gallant, it is an improvement upon ev5. There is something else, however, with which ev6 does not square—viz., the fact that the essence of epistemic vice must itself be a bad thing. But this wants explaining.

An apparently truth-obstructive trait is like an apparently unsafe drug. I might avoid taking a particular drug because it appears to be unsafe. But this does not mean that I regard apparent unsafeness as itself a bad thing. In fact I do not: There is nothing bad about apparent unsafeness per se. What I am avoiding is not the apparent unsafeness that actually is in the drug, but rather the actual unsafeness that appears to be in it. And just so, if I would rather not have a particular epistemic trait because it appears to be truth-obstructive, this would not be because I regard apparent truth-obstructiveness as itself a bad thing. What I would then be hoping to be without is not the apparent truth-obstructiveness that actually is in the trait, but rather the actual truth-obstructiveness that appears to be in it. There is nothing bad about apparent truth-obstructiveness per se.

It does seem that (among epistemic traits) apparent truth-obstructiveness is a reliable mark of epistemic vice. But even so, since there is nothing bad about apparent truth-obstructiveness per se—since it is not *itself* a bad quality—it cannot be the quality that gives a trait its badness: The viciousness of these traits might be signaled by, but cannot consist in, their being apparently truth-obstructive. So while the quality we seek, the essence of epistemic vice, might well be a concomitant of apparent truth-obstructiveness, it cannot be apparent truth-obstructiveness itself. Thus ev6 is unacceptable.[4]

Neither actual nor apparent truth-obstructiveness is the defining mark of unreasonableness. Might we be getting close, though? Consider a possibility I just mentioned—viz., that I might hope not to have a particular trait because it appears to be truth-obstructive. In that event, I would be exhibiting what James Montmarquet has called "epistemic conscientiousness"—i.e., an "underlying desire to believe what is true and to avoid belief in what is false."[5] This desire runs more strongly or purely in some than in others—and it is at least arguably less strong or pure in Goofus than it is in Gallant. Accordingly, it might be supposed that such concern for truth is the essence of reasonableness—that epistemic virtues are, as Montmarquet puts it, "forms of [epistemic] conscientiousness—ways of being conscientious."[6] Thus we might say that

ev7   An epistemic vice is an aspect of deficient epistemic conscientiousness.

—and so, e.g., that the epistemic vices we observed in Goofus are just expressions or products of this one deeper fault, a lack of concern for truth.

But that would be a mistake: Such unconcern need not be vicious, and is indeed compatible with an excellent epistemic character. Suppose Goldie has reached the skeptical conclusion that there is no telling what is and is not truth-conducive. Not being one to pursue that for which (she thinks) one can only hope, she does not endeavor to identify and follow truth-conducive paths. But even so, she has all the virtues we observed in Gallant. In Goldie's case, these virtues are clearly not products or expressions of epistemic conscientiousness—for she lacks this quality. It is not for the love of truth that she exhibits open-mindedness, appreciativeness of her own fallibility, and so forth: She just is that way. Contrary to ev7, then, epistemic vice cannot be identified with deficient concern for truth.

Still, there might be a somewhat looser connection between epistemic conscientiousness and reasonableness. Although one need not be epistemically conscientious to be a Gallant, an epistemically conscientious person (hereafter a.k.a. a truth-lover) would arguably want to be one—for Gallant's traits appear to be truth-conducive. This is how Montmarquet sees it: Epistemic virtues, he says, are those epistemic traits that "are desired by the epistemically conscientious person in virtue of their apparent truth-conduciveness under a wide variety of ordinary, uncontrived circumstances."[7] Following this suggestion, we might say that

> ev8 An epistemic vice is an epistemic trait that a truth-lover would rather not have (because it is apparently truth-obstructive).

But why, exactly, would a truth-lover (as such) hope not to have traits that are *apparently* truth-obstructive?

Because his characteristic desire is to believe what is actually true, a truth-lover has no aversion to apparent truth-obstructiveness per se (and, as we have seen, rightly so). If he hopes not to have apparently truth-obstructive traits, this is rather because he hopes to be without the actual truth-obstructiveness that these appear to have. Thus it is only conditionally that he would rather not be a Goofus: He would rather not be closed-minded, averse to uncertainty, etc.—*unless* these traits really are not truth-obstructive after all (e.g., unless ours is a demonworld).

But surely most of us would hope rather to be reasonable demon victims than unreasonable demon's pets: We would rather be Gallants with fewer true beliefs than Goofuses with more. In effect, then, ev8 tells us that what makes Goofus's epistemic traits vices is that they would be disvalued by someone whose aversion to them is not so deep and unconditional as our own—someone who, by our lights, does not really appreciate what is so bad about them. It is hard to see how we could, let alone why we should, accept such an account.

I say we would rather be reasonable demon victims than unreasonable demon's pets. Lest this be misunderstood, let me again emphasize that it is exclusively with the actual world that I am concerned here. I am not saying that we would rather be like Gallant in some remote possible world radically unlike our own. Rather, I mean that we would rather be like him here in the actual world, regardless of whether *it* is a demonworld—that our desire to be reasonable persons does not carry the truth-lover's "unless ours is a demonworld" proviso.

In support of this last judgment, consider the following scenario. Ours is in fact a demonworld (beliefs are more liable to be true as they are less reasonably held), and the demon, Verity, has just let you in on the joke. She will presently put you back under, and you will permanently forget all that she has just shown you. But first she makes you an offer.

As you are such a truth-lover, Verity can work some truth-conducive changes in your epistemic character. The new and "improved" you will be a paragon of unreasonableness—closed-minded, averse to argument and uncertainty, unappreciative of your own fallibility, and motivated by the desire to have been right. In consequence (this being demonworld), you will fare much better in the pursuit of truth than had you remained the (Gallantly) reasonable person you are today. Again, though, you will have no memory of this encounter.

So: Would you accept Verity's offer? Consider the Goofuses around you (here in the actual world). Would you be one of them? Would you become so obnoxiously unreasonable, just so as to have more true (but unreasonably held) beliefs? Neither would I. Recognizing (for this one never to be recalled moment) that it leads away from truth, we would nevertheless choose the path of reasonableness. Evidently, then, it is not for truth's sake that we endeavor to be reasonable.

"We would rather, of course, be right than reasonable."[8] Or so it is widely supposed. But mistakenly. Our response to Verity's offer shows that, should the two in fact be at odds in the actual world, we would rather be reasonable than right. Our own aversion to epistemic vice is thus otherwise founded than the truth-lover's. So the fact that *he* would rather not have these traits does not constitute a very satisfying account of their badness—a full appreciation of which evidently requires a concern for something else besides truth. And this spells trouble not only for ev8 but for truth-centered accounts in general. If the essence of epistemic vice is not to be discerned from the truth-lover's point of view, then it seems unlikely that any truth-centered account could have it right.

We have considered, and found deficient, four truth-centered accounts of epistemic vice. The badness of epistemic vices consists neither in their truth-obstructiveness (since there is no telling whether they actually have this quality), nor in their apparent truth-obstructiveness (since this is not itself a bad quality), nor in their bespeaking deficient concern for truth (since this lack is compatible with epistemic virtue), nor in the fact that a truth-lover would rather not have them (since our own aversion to them is not so conditional). This is not yet to say that ev2 is false: The essence of epistemic vice might still be some "epistemically bad" quality. But no satisfactory ev2-based account has yet been offered—and our response to Verity's offer indicates that the prospects are not good. Moreover, we saw above that (since ev3 is true) it is a mistake to assume that ev2 must be true. We have more than sufficient cause to abandon this assumption, and thus to broaden our search—to ask, not what is "epistemically bad" about unreasonableness, but rather what is (just) bad about it. In the remaining pages, I shall briefly sketch and defend an answer to this (less theory-laden) question.

A Truthless Account

When I reported that Goofus is closed-minded, averse to argument and uncertainty, unappreciative of his own fallibility, and motivated by the desire to have been right, I listed only his epistemic vices; I said nothing about the rest of his character. But, turning to this, who would not guess that he is also small, arrogant, defensive and insecure? Who was at all puzzled when I described his kind as *obnoxiously* unreasonable? When Hilary Kornblith introduces a "headstrong young physicist, eager to hear the praise of his colleagues," we know already that there will be corresponding defects in his epistemic character. We are not at all surprised when a devastating criticism "fails to make any impact on [his] beliefs."[9] Despite their preoccupation with its truth-obstructiveness, Quine and Ullian could not help but notice, in passing, that the desire to have been right is (also) vicious in a not specifically epistemic way. It is an instance, they remind us, of "the pride that goeth before a fall."[10] It is only natural that, as exemplars of epistemic vice, Montmarquet would offer the likes of Adolf Hitler[11] and "Senator Windbag . . . a pompous ass."[12]

With the foregoing examples, I mean to draw attention to a familiar but underappreciated coincidence: Unreasonable persons, persons of bad epistemic character, are also just plain bad. Epistemic vices are not freestanding. They are, rather, natural and unsurprising facets or consequences of more basic and general defects in one's personal character. How might we best account for this coincidence? The obvious suggestion is that the badness of epistemic vices *consists in* their being offshoots or manifestations of underlying personal vices. It is *because* they are natural (epistemic) symptoms of smallness, arrogance, and the like that closed-mindedness, aversion to uncertainty, and the rest are epistemic vices. My proposal, then, is that

> ev9   An epistemic vice is an epistemic trait that is a natural symptom of some more basic and general personal vice.

There is nothing specifically epistemic about the badness of these underlying personal vices. It is not for their truth-obstructiveness, or for anything like that, that we despise such traits as smallness and arrogance. So ev9 implies that ev2 is false—i.e., that an epistemic vice is not (unless incidentally) one that is bad in any specifically epistemic way. It is from the point of view of personal excellence, rather than that of truth (or the like), that it is better to be reasonable than unreasonable. Or so says ev9. But why should we accept this account?

First, a point of clarification. By personal excellence, I do not mean specifically moral excellence. By personal vices, I do not mean specifically moral ones. While some of the vices just mentioned might qualify as moral ones, some of them (e.g., insecurity) plainly do not. I would not want to say, then, that an unreasonable person is ipso facto an immoral one. But I would say that he is, in some real and significant (and nonepistemic) sense, a bad person (hence the term "personal vice"). For even if Goofus cannot rightly be called an immoral person, he is certainly a very *unattractive* one.

Against ev9, some might (even now) object that, since these are, after all, epistemic vices, there must be something specifically epistemic about their badness. But we have seen that this argument is fallacious. One might just as well argue that, since Mme. X is, after all, a tall stranger, there must be something specifically tall about the way in which she is unfamiliar. Because epistemic vices are already so distinguished by their being specifically epistemic traits, there need not be anything specifically epistemic about the way in which they are bad. Nor (to anticipate another misguided objection) does ev9 collapse the distinction between epistemic and other sorts of vices. Rather, it sees the former as symptoms—but as specifically epistemic symptoms—of some of the latter.

Meanwhile, ev9 shares none of the defects we discovered in the foregoing truth-centered accounts. Unlike ev5, ev9 squares with our assessments of Goofus and Gallant: Demons or no demons, closed-mindedness and the like are symptomatic of personal badness, and their opposites are symptomatic of personal goodness. Unlike ev6, ev9 identifies a quality that is itself bad (viz., underlying personal vice) as the essence of epistemic vice. Unlike ev7, ev9 leaves space for the likes of Goldie—i.e., for one whose epistemic character is unblemished by her skeptically induced (and therefore understandable) lack of concern for truth: Such unconcern need not bespeak underlying personal vice. Unlike ev8, ev9 does justice to the depth of our aversion to epistemic vices (evident, e.g., in our rejection of Verity's offer). Our desire not to be bad persons does not carry the "unless ours is a demonworld" proviso.

Speaking of which, no other account besides ev9 explains the coincidence we have noted between unreasonableness and nonepistemic vice. And it is especially hard to see how any ev2-based account could do this. We have to ask: If being an (epistemic) symptom of some more basic and general vice is not what makes a trait an epistemic vice, then why are bad epistemic and bad personal character so naturally correlated? Why should it work out that an epistemic trait is a natural facet, consequence, or manifestation of underlying personal badness just when it is also bad in some other way (this other bad quality then being the true essence of epistemic vice)? For ev9, the matter is simple: There is no other badness present here (unless incidentally), and thus no mysterious coincidence of independently bad qualities. A bad epistemic character, an unreasonable character, *just is* the sort that a just plain bad person naturally exhibits.

We began with the question: Why is it better to be reasonable than unreasonable? Despite the predominance of the truth-centered approach, no satisfactory truth-centered answer has come to light. Reasonableness does appear to be truth-conducive. But there is no telling whether it is in fact so—and there is nothing good about apparent truth-conduciveness per se. Concern for truth might tend to run more strongly or purely in reasonable persons. But in some of them (some of the more skeptical ones) it is hardly to be discerned. A truth-lover would ordinarily endeavor to be reasonable. But we would do so even where he would not. It would seem, then, that the value of reasonableness (and so, it should be noted, of reasonably held belief) is independent of any connection it might have to truth. It is better to be reasonable than unreasonable, not for anything having to do with truth, but because the shape and quality of one's epistemic character is determined by that of one's personal character—and it is better to be a good person than a bad one.[13]

Notes

1. As opposed to the desire to get it right. See W. V. Quine and J. S. Ullian, *The Web of Belief*, 2nd ed. New York: Random House, 1987, 133.

2. In the current literature, virtually every account of epistemic virtue and/or vice is ev2-based. Accordingly (for want of opposition), little is ever offered in ev2's defense (beyond some variant of the present quick argument from ev1). To deny ev2 is decidedly not to favor any one current approach (e.g., reliabilist or responsibilist) over others; it is rather to reject the premise common to them all.

3. Quine and Ullian, 133.

4. The foregoing argument is a variant of one I first offered in "A New and Unimproved Version of Reliabilism," *Analysis*, vol. 48, 1988: 176-77.

5. James Montmarquet, "Epistemic Virtue and Doxastic Responsibility," *American Philosophical Quarterly*, vol. 29, 1992, p. 336.

6. James Montmarquet, "Epistemic Virtue," *Mind*, vol. 96, 1987: 482-97, p. 484.

7. Montmarquet 1987, 488.

8. Quine and Ullian, 133.

9. Hilary Kornblith, "Justified Belief and Epistemically Responsible Action," *The Philosophical Review*, vol. 92, 1983: 33-48, p. 36.

10. Quine and Ullian, 133.

11. Montmarquet 1992, 332 ff.

12. Montmarquet 1987, 493.

13. For their help with various ancestors of this paper (dating to 1982), I wish to thank my wife, Mary, James Montmarquet, Linda Zagzebski, Jay Wood, Russ Pisciotta, Douglas Long, Guy Axtell, Matthias Steup, and (especially) William Lycan.

16

Phronesis and Religious Belief

Linda Zagzebski

Introduction

Hilary Putnam has argued that reason is both immanent and transcendent. It is immanent in that it is not to be found outside human language games, cultures, and institutions, but it is also a regulative idea that we use to criticize the conduct of *all* activities and institutions. We always speak the language of a particular time and place, and we think as members of a culture that exists only at a time and place, but the rightness and wrongness of what we say is not *just* for a time and a place.[1]

I think that Putnam's position is profoundly right. Unfortunately, it is much easier to state it than to form a coherent conception of reason that combines immanence and transcendence. In fact, the difficulty in doing so is demonstrated by the fact that some of the deepest and longest-lasting philosophical disputes are forms of the rift between what we might call immanentism and transcendentalism, as the upheaval in philosophy since the Enlightenment demonstrates. Even harder is to put the two aspects of reason together in a way that permits us to settle cases in which the rationality of a particular belief is in dispute. My purpose in this paper is to begin exploring the question of what reason would have to be like in order to be both immanent and transcendent, and the implications of that feature for the evaluation of beliefs. I will then propose a method to apply it to culture-specific beliefs, in particular, to religious beliefs.

Putnam makes it clear that he does not think it is just reason that has the feature of being both immanent and transcendent. The grounds for making that claim about reason apply equally to what we call the rational or the reasonable. Putnam is willing to say that these properties also are both immanent and transcendent in the sense he means. And there is a hidden implication of this position that Putnam does not mention. Rationality is a property that is not obviously limited to cognitive activity. In fact, I maintain, along with many others, that it cannot be, that rationality applies to our affective and motivational states and states in which the cognitive and the affective cannot be pulled apart—that is what I think an emotion is. But I am not going to argue for that today, but only want to point out that if we are going to make a fair attempt to figure out what rationality would have to be like in order to be both immanent and transcendent, we may not presume that only cognitive states are the issue. That can too easily beg the question.

An important implication of the fact that rationality is both immanent and transcendent is that neither a purely formal nor a purely substantive account of rationality will do. The more substantive an account is, the more it includes particular facts about the rational beings under discussion—almost always human beings since those are the only rational beings we are acquainted with, and these facts may vary cross-culturally. So substantive accounts can be expected to lack transcendence. For the sake of transcendence we may go the purely formal route, the route of explicating the *concept* of reason or rationality by defining it in terms of other concepts. So, for example, given that the history of the idea of rationality is closely connected with the history of the idea of truth, it is possible to define rationality solely in terms of its relation to truth. Rationality can be designated as whatever property or activity we have or do that leads us to the truth. This approach makes it an open question whether rational persons do anything in particular—for example, that they pay attention to the evidence, that they are open-minded when their colleagues (or their enemies) offer views that they don't like—whether they are even motivated by concern for the truth at all. It even leaves open the question of whether Aristotle was right that rationality is something intrinsic to human nature and distinguishes us from other animals. It also has the unfortunate consequence that the relation between rationality and truth becomes trivial—a matter to which I will return.

Instead of taking the formal approach, we can go to the other extreme. Rationality can be defined purely substantively as behavior of a certain description, such as the behavior I have just mentioned (weighing evidence, fairly evaluating the contrary views of others, and so on), without any implication of its formal relations to truth. But by leaving open the relation between rationality and truth, this route leaves it undetermined whether rationality has the theoretical interest most of us have always thought it had. After all, who cares whether we weigh evidence or not unless we think it gets us somewhere? And that somewhere is the truth. To maintain the theoretical interest in rationality, there ought to be a presumption of a connection between rationality and truth; it is precisely because we *expect* the connection that we care so much about rationality. But the interest is lost if we gain the connection by definition.

Similarly, while it is unwise to insist that very much substantive behavior is rational by definition, the concept demands that there be a presumption that certain behaviors are rational and others irrational. We assume it is irrational to believe whatever pops into your head, for example, or to engage in wishful thinking, or to take for granted that you and you alone are the final authority on the truth. That is implied by the history of the use of the idea of rationality. I think, then, that both the purely formal and the purely substantive approaches fail to respect either the immanence or the transcendence of rationality, and are not consistent with the way the concept has been used in its history. Of course, there is nothing wrong with modifying a concept from its ordinary usage, even to do so radically, but when that happens we must recognize that the question we are addressing may not be the same one that others are interested in. I hope that the question I am addressing here is one that others are interested in.

So, in my discussion today I will try to respect as much as possible both the formal properties commonly attributed to rationality and the most important substantive claims made about it in the history of discussion of what is and is not rational. I will propose three corollaries of the immanence and transcendence of reason and three constraints that I think we should respect in formulating definitions of rational belief. I will suggest a method for filling out the concept of rationality that respects both its immanence and its transcendence, and is sensitive to the constraints I will identify. It also gives us a method to settle questions about the rationality and epistemic praiseworthiness of culture-specific beliefs, including beliefs distinctive of particular religions.

The Transcendence and Immanence of the Rational and Three Corollaries

Putnam argues for the cultural transcendence of reason on the well-known grounds that denying it is inconsistent, but he puts a novel spin on that argument by claiming that cultural relativism is self-refuting for the same reason that methodological solipsism is self-refuting. Methodological solipsism is the view that all of our talk is about our own experiences and this applies to everyone, so while the methodological solipsist treats her own talk solipsistically, she grants that others do the same. The problem, of course, is that she cannot maintain this consistently. If all of her words are used solipsistically she cannot say that others do the same thing. To avoid inconsistency, Putnam says, the methodological solipsist must be a real solipsist. She must deny that there is any *you* other than what she constructs out of her own experiences. Real solipsism is not self-refuting, Putnam says, but it is nonetheless irrational. For the same reason, he argues, cultural relativism, the analogue of methodological solipsism, is self-refuting, but cultural imperialism, the analogue of real solipsism, may not be. However, Putnam adds, it is self-refuting in *our* culture since we treat norms of rationality in a way that is inconsistent with the view that rationality is whatever is accepted by our culture. An epistemically imperialist culture that did have such a view could avoid inconsistency, but it would still be irrational for the same reason real solipsism is irrational. Such a culture would lose the ability to critique itself.[2]

My argument for the transcendence of rationality is simpler than Putnam's. I do not attempt to identify a formal problem with immanentism, but to call attention to the fact that it is incompatible with a major substantive position on the nature of rationality in the history of the use of the concept, namely, that whatever rationality is, it is something all humans share. I have already said that I take this to be one of the substantive constraints on the concept of rationality. Aristotle also thought that rationality sets us apart from other animals. That may or may not be the case, but I think it is indisputable that rationality is something that humans have *qua* human. So while I do not insist that no non-human animals are rational, I do insist that all normal humans are rational. And this is not just an empirical claim because it is not purely contingent; I think it is part of what we *mean* by rationality that it is connected with our humanity.[3] What is rational is in principle recognizably rational by all rational beings, which means all humans, even those outside one's cultural community. To be rational is to be able to talk to other persons and to make oneself understood, no matter who those persons are. This is the sense in which rationality is transcendent. It is what permits us to communicate with one another and to form a human community that transcends the individual communities we inhabit.[4]

Because we are rational we must face the limits of self-trust. For the same reason, it is because we are rational that we must face the limits of trust in our culture, our social group, our religious community. I am not denying that self-trust in some degree and in some sense is rational, in fact, rationally required. And similarly, trust in our culture or religious community is rational and required for the same reason. But we know that individuals can go astray and be irrational in belief or action, and so can cultures. We must all answer to the court of the best human judgment, not just the judgment of our like-minded peers.

So rationality is transcendent, but it is also immanent. The ideally rational person is not a person who believes only what someone outside of any culture would believe. And while this point may be obvious, it has taken some hundreds of years for its moral to sink into the discourse of English-speaking philosophers. Rationality is something we all share as humans, but even though there is no *particular* culture that all humans have, it is nonetheless true that all humans have culture. No human thinks in a way that is not embedded in a culture. So the idea that a belief is rational only if it passes norms of reason that are independent of all culture misunderstands the sense in which rationality derives from what humans are like *qua* human. In fact, it is to attempt to make the ideally rational human a non-human. The problem, then, is to understand the rationality of beliefs that are distinctive of individual cultures without ignoring either the transcendence or the immanence of reason. I suggest we aim to understand normative judgments, whether about the normativity of acts or the normativity of beliefs, in a way that avoids the twin problems of solipsism, and the illusion of detached, disembodied, disencultured reason.

Let me now turn to three corollaries of the transcendence and immanence of reason. In discussing transcendence I mentioned a principle that I will call the *Rational Recognition* principle (RR):

> RR   If a belief is rational, its rationality is recognizable (in principle) by rational persons in other cultures.

Given the Aristotelian assumption that rationality is part of human nature, this principle has the consequence that if a belief is rational, its rationality is in principle recognizable by all other normal humans. I believe this principle is true, but it is unhelpful in its present form since too much needs to be packed into the qualification "in principle." For the vast majority of the beliefs of everybody, no matter how impeccably rational the belief is, there is undoubtedly somebody somewhere who is incapable of recognizing its rationality even though that somebody is human and more or less normal. We will therefore need to modify the principle once we have settled on the other criteria we want in an account of rationality.

The immanence of rationality suggests the *Culture Sensitivity* principle (CS):

> CS   The beliefs of one culture are prima facie as justified as the beliefs of any other culture.

This principle wisely reminds us to avoid epistemic imperialism. Given that rationality is connected with what makes us distinctively human, and given that culture is distinctively human, it follows that culture is not in conflict with rationality. Culture is not an aberration of nature; it is a good thing. And if it is really a good thing, it must be a good thing even when it results in conflicting beliefs in different cultures. That is hard to accept, and not only for alethic realists like myself. It is hard to accept because when persons in culture *A* assert *p* and persons in culture *B* assert *not p*, the members of both cultures experience that as a conflict, and they experience conflict as far from a good thing. Rationality moves us to attempt to resolve conflict whenever possible. Cultural relativism is one way of attempting to resolve the conflict by interpreting the claims of cultures *A* and *B* in such a way that the conflict disappears. It is important to see that relativism would not exist if there were not a perceived conflict to be resolved, and the relativist, like every rational person, tries to resolve it. My point here is not about the content of the relativist's claim, but about the place at which it appears in the human predicament. The relativist's way is subsequent to the perception of conflict in belief; it is not given prior to the experience of perceived conflict and the recognition of its undesirability. Of course, the relativist's way out is in conflict with the way of others such as those who claim that the conflict must be resolved by arguing it out—and that conflict also must be resolved. The deeper fact about rationality that this reveals is that it is a dictum of rationality to attempt to resolve conflict between rational persons. This leads to the third corollary, the *Need to Resolve Conflict* principle (NRC):

> NRC   It is rational to attempt to resolve putative conflicts of beliefs between cultures.

The *Need to Resolve Conflict* principle is required because the *Culture Sensitivity* principle and the *Rational Recognition* principle do not explain why members of cultures *A* and *B* experience tension when culture *A* accepts *p* and culture *B* accepts *not p*, and why this tension is an expression of their rationality. The *Culture Sensitivity* principle tells us that when *A* says *p* and *B* says *not p*, the members of *A* and *B* are prima facie equally rational in their beliefs, and the *Rational Recognition* principle has the consequence that the members of *A* and *B* are capable of recognizing that fact. But rational persons in *A* and *B* do not let it rest, at least not when *p* is something one or both cultures care about (and the caring itself can be rational). They want to resolve the conflict between them, whether it is by the relativist route, or the absolutist route, or some other. I think, then, that the *Need to Resolve Conflict* principle is one of the deepest principles of rationality.

Three Constraints

So far I have argued that Putnam is right that rationality is both culture-immanent and culture-transcendent, and I have proposed three corollaries of these two features. Next I want to propose three constraints on any acceptable account of rationality, each of which involves the formal properties of rationality. The first is demanded by the enormous theoretical interest in connecting rationality with truth; the second and third are internal constraints, relating the formal and substantive features of rationality. There are no doubt other constraints that come from the substantive properties of rationality. For that I would take very seriously work by those people engaged in the empirical study of human behavior, including cross-cultural comparative studies. So I am by no means suggesting that the constraints I am proposing are exhaustive.

Let us first look at what I call the *alignment problem*.[5] How is rationality connected with truth? This problem arises out of the formal interest I have already mentioned in connecting rationality with truth. The problem is, we think rationality should be closely connected with truth, but we also think we are cheating if it is gained too cheaply. Rationality cannot be connected with truth trivially, by definition. This leads to the first constraint: *Rationality should put us in the best position to get truth, but it should not come too easily.* I have already mentioned one way in which the alignment problem is solved too easily, and that is when rationality is defined as whatever leads to truth. There are versions of the popular theory of reliabilism about rationality or justification that have this defect. Putnam himself makes the alignment problem too easy, but he does so by making the definition go the other way. He defines truth in terms of rational acceptability rather than rationality in terms of truth.[6]

In contrast, evidentialists (here I'm thinking of Locke, W. K. Clifford, and a number of mainstream American epistemologists) make the alignment problem too hard because they identify two distinct epistemic goods that are included in rationality—believing on evidence and believing in a way that is truth-conducive—but there is no prima facie reason to think that they are connected. We cannot be sure, then, that when they talk about rationality, they are talking about a real phenomenon at all. Another way of making it too hard is to give a relativist account of rationality and a realist account of truth. This is an extremely common view in American intellectual culture, and it is tempting. I am tempted by it myself. To see why it is so tempting and also what the problem is, let us take an example. Suppose we are considering nine cultures with conflicting beliefs on the origin of the world. If all nine are established, respected views with a long history, an elaborate literature, and many adherents, how can we deny that all nine are rational? But if their beliefs are mutually conflicting, at most one succeeds at getting the truth. This is a very common move, but it breaks the desired connection between rationality and truth. That is because on this approach, the likelihood that our culture-specific beliefs are rational is very high (in fact, nine in nine), whereas the likelihood that they are true is very low (less than one in nine). I find this an undesirable consequence in spite of the fact that this move has obvious attractions. (Let me say that it is also, in my opinion, the most serious objection to the realist conception of truth, and it is one that I've never seen addressed, but I'm going to leave that aside.) By making truth culture-transcendent and rationality culture-immanent, this approach tries to have it both ways. The attraction is understandable, but unfortunately it does not work as long as there are numerous incompatible beliefs from culture to culture about the same thing. It is just too easy for them all to be rational and too hard for any of them to be true. The problem is avoided if it turns out there really are not very many differences among cultures after all, and some observers have, of course, claimed just that (e.g., John Hick). Notice that this position, like the others we have considered, arises from a more basic recognition of conflict and a rational desire to resolve it. This supports my earlier claim that the *Need to Resolve Conflict* principle is one of the most basic principles of rationality.

The second constraint is that it is not the content that makes a belief rational or irrational. I am not denying that the content of some beliefs might be such that no person could arrive at them rationally, but I am proposing that even in those cases, it is not the content per se that makes the belief irrational, but the way in which the belief is formed or maintained. For example, suppose that I believe that the satellite dish on my neighbor's roof is really a UFO. That belief is very likely irrational, but I am claiming that it is not irrational simply *because* it is the belief that UFOs have landed on my neighbor's roof. It is irrational because I did something I shouldn't have done in arriving at that belief, or else I didn't do something I should have done in arriving at that belief. The fact that it is not the content per se that determines rationality is suggested by the fact that we think that rational persons continue to have rational beliefs when their beliefs change. This leads to our second constraint on an account of rationality: *Rationality is not determined by the content of a belief.*

This constraint does not mean that certain beliefs cannot be privileged. There is nothing wrong with saying that whatever rationality is, it is not compatible with the rationality of the belief that denying the antecedent is valid. But there are two important points here. One is that there are serious limits to the beliefs in this category. The privileged beliefs may not call into question the normativity of rationality itself, nor the facts about rationality that we started with, for example, that normal humans are rational, that they are capable of recognizing the rationality of others, that the beliefs of other cultures are prima facie rational. So the privileged beliefs may not be ones that support cultural imperialism or solipsism.

The second important point about the privileging of beliefs is that any such beliefs have a feature that prevents circularity: we may not use the theory to defend their rationality. This gives us the third constraint: *Any beliefs taken to be benchmarks of a theory of rationality cannot be defended by the theory itself.* Let me take an example from ethics to make the point. Suppose we agree that no acceptable ethical theory may have the consequence that it is morally right to torture people for fun. We then formulate our theory, and, as planned, it has the consequence that it is seriously wrong to torture people for fun. But what we may not do, if asked why such torture is wrong, is to say that it is ruled out by the theory. The price we pay for making certain moral principles or beliefs benchmarks of any acceptable theory is that we may not justify the beliefs on the basis of the theory. That, of course, is usually an acceptable price since nobody is likely to question these beliefs if they are properly chosen; that is, indeed, one of the reasons we chose them. Similarly, we may decide that no acceptable theory of rationality may have the consequence that it is rational to believe that my mind is the only one in existence, or that I am the only rational being in existence, or that my culture is the only rational one in existence, but then we may not use the theory to justify the judgment that these beliefs are not rational. Consequently, we must choose them carefully.

Phronesis

I am now going to propose a way of defining rationality that we can use to determine the rationality of culture-specific beliefs. I have suggested principles and constraints with which any acceptable account of rationality should comply, but they do not give us a determinate direction in which to proceed. And, as I have said, those scholars working on empirical studies of the way humans form and maintain beliefs may have other constraints to add. But I think we have enough to make a start.

There are not many ways to go about defining something when you don't pretend to know what it really is. But there is one way that was used both by Aristotle and, in a completely different context, by some contemporary philosophers of language. In the seventies Saul Kripke and Hilary Putnam proposed a way of defining natural kind terms that became known as the theory of Direct Reference. According to this theory, a natural kind such as *water* or *gold* or *human* should be defined as whatever is the same kind of thing or stuff as some indexically identified paradigm instance. For example, they proposed that gold is, roughly, whatever is the same element as *that*, water is whatever has the same chemical structure as *that*, a human is whatever is a member of the same species as *that*, and so on. In each case the demonstrative term "that" refers to an entity to which the person doing the defining refers directly, usually by pointing. Obviously, these definitions require an experiential basis, in fact, a shared experiential basis. One of the main reasons for proposing definitions like this was that Kripke and Putnam believed that often we do not know the nature of the thing we are defining, and yet we know how to construct a definition that links up with the nature that it has. We may not know the nature of gold, and for millennia nobody knew its nature, but that did not prevent people from defining "gold" in a way that fixed the reference of the term and continued to do so after its nature was discovered.

I am not proposing that rationality is a natural kind, but it is interesting to see that the same indexical procedure was used by Aristotle in defining *phronesis*, or practical wisdom. Aristotle has quite a bit to say about what the virtue of *phronesis* consists in, but he clearly is not confident that he can give a full account of it. And what is more important for my purposes here, he thinks that fundamentally, that doesn't matter because we can pick out persons who are phronetic in advance of investigating the nature of *phronesis*. The *phronimos* can be defined, roughly, as a person *like that*, where we make a demonstrative reference to a paradigmatically good person. So Aristotle assumes that we can pick out paradigmatic instances of good persons in advance of our theorizing.

I propose that we use the same procedure in defining rationality. There is an important metatheoretical consideration that supports this move. A theory of rationality, like an ethical theory, is a theory about an existing human practice or set of practices. We call something rational or irrational as part of our practices of evaluation of beliefs, acts, and persons. Theory must connect to the practice; otherwise, it is not a theory *of* the practice at all. Ethicists do this all the time in justifying ethical theories. Certain particular judgments of value or moral correctness that come directly out of the practice are accepted pretheoretically and become gauges of the validity of any theory. I have already mentioned one example, that it is wrong to torture people for fun. Other such judgments might be that Jesus Christ was a good person, that the judicial punishment of the innocent is bad, that so and so was a courageous person, and so on. Any ethical theory that is incompatible with these judgments not only fails to be a correct theory; it fails in a more radical way. It fails to be a theory of ethical practices at all. In other words, if it is not wrong to intentionally torture another for fun, we don't know what "wrong" means, and we are not talking about ethics.

The rational and irrational, like the right and wrong, are imbedded in practices of evaluation from which particular judgments arise. We recognize rational persons the same way we recognize good persons, and what we say *about* rationality when we decide to theorize must be compatible with our judgments about who those people are.

My proposal, then, is that rationality should be defined in relation to its paradigm instances in the same way that Aristotle defined "phronesis" and Kripke defined "water." A rational person is, roughly, a person like *that*—and we point to a paradigmatically rational person. Notice that this model can be interpreted in a way that is as pluralistic or as monistic as you like provided that it is not so monistic that there are no paradigms of rationality in all cultures, and it is not so pluralistic that they are not recognizable outside their own culture. Either extreme would be incompatible with one of the principles of rationality we started with. It is also likely that some of our paradigms will not remain fixed. We may need to use a process of reflective equilibrium between our judgments of rational behavior and our judgments identifying the paradigms. So initially a person may appear to be paradigmatically rational, and we form judgments about how to behave rationally by observing that person, but over time, as we compare that person with other paradigmatically rational persons, we may revise our judgment.

This procedure also permits us to avoid a move that I earlier said puts us in danger of begging the question, namely, assuming that rational behavior is limited to cognitive behavior, or that it puts primacy on the cognitive. It also leaves open the question of whether rational behavior is a matter of following universal principles, or for that matter, principles of any kind. It leaves open the possibility that rationality may sometimes be governed by what John Henry Newman calls the illative sense or some other sense yet unidentified. To determine the answer to any of these questions, I suggest we look at what rational persons do.

Now I would like to connect my suggestion here with previous work. I have argued at some length (in *Virtues of the Mind*) that the intellectually virtuous person is the paradigm in relation to which a host of concepts of epistemic evaluation can be defined. My motives in that work were different from the ones I have here since one of my primary concerns there was to show that there are no significant differences between the normativity of cognitive activity and belief-formation, on the one hand, and the normativity of conduct, on the other. Both are moral, both involve the emotions, and both have the same grounding in virtue. Ultimately, I argued, it is the behavior of persons with *phronesis,* or practical wisdom, that determines both right acting and justified believing, as well as one's moral and intellectual duty and the other evaluative properties of acts and beliefs. *Phronesis* has the same relation to justified beliefs as it has to right acts in a pure virtue theory, and it has the same relation to epistemically praiseworthy beliefs as it has to morally praiseworthy acts. *Phronesis* is necessary because the virtues are many, but the self is one. It is, among other things, the virtue that permits a person to mediate between and among the considerations arising from all the virtues in any given situation, and to act in a way that gives each its proper weight. *Phronesis* determines what it is right or justified or praiseworthy to do or to believe, all things considered.

Here I want to propose two principles that identify the paradigmatically rational person with the *phronimos* and which use the behavior of such a person as a way of determining the rationality or epistemic praiseworthiness of culture-specific beliefs. Even though culture-specific beliefs are not transcendent in their content, they may be transcendent in the qualities of mind out of which they arise. Intellectual virtues are qualities that are culture-transcendent, or, at least, they are as close as we are going to get to transcendent qualities in the normative realm. So even though I am not suggesting that all cultures place equal value on open-mindedness, intellectual fairness, thoroughness, and attentiveness, or intellectual courage and autonomy, these traits *are* the ones that make cross-cultural dialogue possible. Putnam himself hints at something like this in his discussion of the way reason transcends culture in its regulative use. He mentions "a just, attentive, balanced intellect," and he goes on to emphasize the importance of discussion and communication, criticism and impartiality, all of which are intellectual virtues, although he does not give them that name.[7]

I propose that what is rational is what would or might be believed by a person of a certain sort in the circumstances in question. The *sort* of person is trans-cultural since there are *phronimoi* in all cultures, but the circumstances may be such that they only arise in a single culture. Let me suggest, then, two principles of rational belief—a weaker principle of rational permissibility, and a stronger principle of rational praiseworthiness:

Principles of Rational Belief (PRB)

PRB1   S's belief p in culture C is rational just in case a person with *phronesis* outside culture C might believe p if she were in S's circumstances in culture C. To say that the *phronim_* might believe p is just to say that it is not the case that she would not believe p. Of course, this principle applies to *phronimoi* within S's culture as well as to those without.

PRB2   S's belief p in culture C is epistemically praiseworthy just in case S's belief p is virtuously motivated, and a person with *phronesis* outside culture C would characteristically believe p if she were in S's circumstances in culture C.

These principles of rational belief permit us to give the needed modification of the *Rational Recognition* principle, as promised. It is not useful to make the standard of rational recognition all rational humans if rationality is used in the generic sense in which all humans are rational. The problem is not that such a principle is false; it is just that it has to be qualified too much to be useful. Instead, the standard of recognition should be persons who are exemplars of ideal rationality, and I have suggested that that is persons with *phronesis*. So if a belief is rational, its rationality must be recognizable by persons with *phronesis* outside the cultural community of the believer. This means that the *phronimos or phronim_* outside the community should see that he or she might have the same belief if he or she were a member of that community.[8] That is, for any belief *p*, and person *S*, if *S* is rational in believing *p* , then a *phronim_* outside of *S*'s cultural community might believe *p* if she were in *S's* community and circumstances, and the *Rational Recognition* principle says that the *phronim_* herself is capable of judging that to be the case. *S's* belief *p* is rational in the stronger sense only if a *phronim_* outside of *S*'s cultural community would characteristically believe *p* if she were in *S's* community and circumstances.

PRB respects the *Rational Recognition* principle (RR). The *Rational Recognition* principle is useful to persons who wish to test the rationality of their own culture-specific beliefs provided that they are able to recognize *phronimoi* outside their own culture. It is quite likely that they can do this in many cases since the qualities that make a person a *phronimos* are qualities that make him stand out. To be a *phronimos* is, in part, to be recognized as a person of good judgment. The *phronimos* is a person who is imitated and his judgment consulted. Such qualities are probably among the easiest for persons on the outside to recognize.

PRB respects the *Culture Sensitivity* principle (CS) since it presupposes that there are *phronimoi* in all cultures. This principle makes two forms of cultural imperialism prima facie unjustified. One is the view discussed by Putnam that rationality is defined by what my culture believes. The second is the more common view that my own culture is prima facie more rational than all others even though the rationality of others is not ruled out by definition.

PRB respects the principle that rationality gives rise to a *Need to Resolve Conflict* (NRC), since the *phronimoi* are the persons in whom we entrust leadership in conflict resolution (leaving aside the enormous political obstacles that may need to be overcome). They are more careful than most of us to determine through intercultural dialogue that putatively conflicting beliefs really are conflicting before taking steps to resolve the conflict, and they do not necessarily aim to reach consensus since they also know when the differences are too great to make consensus realistic. But their ability to look at their own culture with some detachment makes them fair arbiters of disagreement. If any two persons in any two cultures can reach agreement, it is the *phronimoi* in both.

The constraint that rationality is not defined by content is respected by PRB since the *phronimos* is not identified by any particular beliefs, but by qualities of mind and character. This constraint does not prevent us from dictating that nobody counts as a *phronimos* who has certain crazy beliefs, but if we do so, the non-circularity constraint indicates that we cannot justify our judgment about those beliefs on the grounds that the *phronimos* does not believe them.

The constraint that the alignment problem must be neither too easy nor too hard is the most difficult one with which to comply. The problem is not that PRB makes it too easy to connect rationality and truth, but that it seems to make it too hard. As I have said, this is a problem faced by metaphysical realism in general. It is common to think that the alignment problem can be solved if the judgments of rational persons converge. If a range of independent investigators converge on a determinate set of beliefs, that assures the objectivity of those beliefs. So it is common to think that agreement among rational persons is aligned with truth, and it is usually added that it is hopeless to expect that this will ever happen.[9] That may be true, but I propose that we have more reason to hope that the judgments of *phronimoi* will converge than that the judgments of all rational persons will converge. Still, we have no guarantee that it will happen. I think, then, that even though the *phronesis* theory is an improvement, the alignment problem still exists.

Religious Belief

My suggestion so far has been predominantly a formal one: (1) Rationality should be defined indexically by essential reference to paradigm instances. (2) What counts as a rational belief is what such persons would or might believe in the circumstances in question. (3) The person with *phronesis* is the best candidate I know of to serve the role I have identified. (4) The immanence and transcendence of rationality and the three constraints I have discussed are particularly important in the context of a discussion of culture-specific beliefs.

Religious communities are cultures in the sense I mean in this paper. Christianity constitutes at least one culture, probably more, and so I propose that distinctively Christian beliefs be evaluated for their rationality and epistemic praiseworthiness by the principles I have given. And, of course, the same goes for other religions. But PRB is only an outline of a procedure. A number of questions need to be answered and details filled in before the principles can have any real practical value. The concept of *phronesis* is a rich one with a long history, and in part I am relying upon that history in order to supply the necessary detail, but that rich history also means that there is more than one way of explaining what the *phronimos* is. I do not think that is necessarily a problem as long as whatever account we give of *phronesis* respects the principles I've mentioned. So the immanence of rationality permits individual cultures to give their own accounts of what the *phronimos* is like, but the transcendence of rationality requires that there must be *phronimoi* in all cultures and that they must be recognizable both inside and outside their culture. I also think that these are the people to whom we turn to resolve conflict.

It seems likely that when PRB1 and PRB2 are filled out to be sufficiently useful and are applied to Christian beliefs, it will turn out that most of these beliefs are rational for most Christians and fewer of them, but still many of them, are epistemically praiseworthy. I think it will also turn out that the same principles have the consequence that many beliefs of the other major religions are also rational and epistemically praiseworthy. But as mild as these principles are, they are enough to rule out at least one belief that is common among many Christians, and I'll get to that soon.

But first, let me turn to the application of the three principles of rationality to religious beliefs. The *Rational Recognition* principle implies that we are capable of studying other religions not simply out of curiosity, but because we think we may have something to learn from them and they from us. We depend upon each other's rationality and our ability to recognize when the other is and is not being rational in the process of promoting mutual understanding and increasing religious knowledge on both sides. Cross-cultural experience and study in comparative religion both support and are supported by the *Culture Sensitivity* principle. This rules out exclusivism about the rationality of religious beliefs. The *Need to Resolve Conflict* principle suggests that we must be willing to change when we engage in cross-cultural dialogue. This process also highlights the differences between different kinds of epistemic evaluation. Not everyone agrees on the relative importance of having epistemically praiseworthy beliefs versus having true beliefs. If many persons have epistemically praiseworthy but false religious beliefs, how should others react? How should we react to ourselves when we see that we are perceived by others as having false beliefs? How should we react when we see that we are perceived as having beliefs that lack epistemic praiseworthiness, even if they are not perceived as lacking rationality? Inter-cultural and inter-religious dialogue is an important part of communication of us all as members of the human race. But I think it is important that when we engage in it, we show to others that we respect the three principles I have discussed, in particular, that we show them that we take their beliefs to be prima facie as rational as ours, and that we believe that our rationality and theirs is mutually recognizable.

Let me now turn to the three constraints. The alignment problem is the hardest, whether it applies to Christian beliefs, other religious beliefs, culture-specific beliefs, or even to beliefs that are not culture-specific. It is therefore a problem for religious belief, but it is not a *special* problem for religious belief. It is a serious philosophical problem, not a distinctively religious one. I said that I do not claim that my position solves the problem, although I think the *phronesis* proposal makes some headway. That is because there is a greater chance of convergence of belief among persons with practical wisdom than among the whole community of human persons. But I also mentioned that it would probably turn out that many beliefs of many different religions pass the tests of PRB1 and PRB2. If so, the *phronesis* proposal still permits a wider gap between rationality and truth than is desirable. Adding further principles of rationality may help us solve the problem, but I think there really is a tension within the concept of rationality between the different roles it plays in our thinking. We think rationality is our best shot at getting the truth, but we also think that members of other cultures are as well placed as we are at getting the truth. This exposes a deeper problem in the connection between the theory of rationality and the theory of truth.

The second constraint is that reasonableness cannot be determined by content. I have said that we may privilege certain beliefs as constraints on any acceptable account of rationality, but we may not privilege beliefs that call the principles of rationality into question, and the third constraint requires that any beliefs that are privileged cannot be defended by appealing to the account we then use. So there is nothing irrational in Christians taking certain specifically Christian beliefs to be privileged, but if we do so, we may not then defend the rationality of these beliefs by a theory of rationality generated in part to be compatible with their rationality. Nor may we privilege beliefs that deny the fundamental principles of rationality. So, for example, I might believe a story which, if true, would explain why I alone in the universe am rational and others are not. Similarly, a cultural imperialist might tell a story that explains why, from the point of view of their own culture, imperialism is not irrational. But solipsism and cultural imperialism are irrational even when they are justified on the basis of a story standardly believed by the members of their culture. A form of this problem can arise for those Christians who believe an interpretation of the doctrine of Original Sin according to which human rational faculties have been so severely damaged by the Fall, that the common dictates of these faculties cannot be trusted; and in addition, personal sin leads individuals to self-deception on such a grand scale that most persons cannot trust their own sense of what is rational and what is not. Such a view shares the problems of solipsism and cultural imperialism: it comes dangerously close to denying that rationality exists at all and it makes true intercultural dialogue impossible.

The principles I have proposed rule out not just specific doctrines, but also certain approaches to the rationality of religious belief. Among philosophers of religion, the work of Alvin Plantinga is very influential. In his forthcoming book, *Warrant and Christian Belief*, Plantinga proposes a model according to which the Holy Spirit directly causes the Christian to believe the Christian doctrines in the model in the basic way, and uses a process of which the believer is unaware. Such beliefs are based on nothing—not evidence, not testimony, not even experience. Plantinga argues that belief in the model is rational if it is true, and he admits that it is not rational if false. He also admits that his position has the consequence that its rationality is not recognizable from the outside. This approach is incompatible with some of the deep features of rationality that I have tried to identify in this paper.

Conclusion

Rationality is not a suspect notion even though it has sometimes been used for suspect purposes. In fact, I think Aristotle was right that it is partly constitutive of being human. The idea of rationality is more interesting if it retains both the formal connection with truth and the substantive content with which it has been most frequently associated. I have proposed the mildest account of rationality that I think is consistent with these features, but as modest as it is, it does rule out both some particular beliefs and some rather common approaches to the rationality of religious belief.

Notes

1. H. Putnam, "Why Reason Can't be Naturalized," *Synthese* 52 (1982): 3-23.

2. "Why Reason Can't be Naturalized," *op.cit.,* and *Reason, Truth, and History.* Cambridge: Cambridge University Press, 1981.

3. I think that *irrationality* is connected with our humanity also. Irrationality is not simply the lack of something else that is intrinsic to our nature. It is a positive trait, although, of course, not evaluatively positive. I have explored this topic in "Hot and Cold Irrationality," forthcoming.

4. Cf. Putnam's Principle of Communication in "God and the Philosophers," *Midwest Studies in Philosophy,* vol. XXI (Philosophy of Religion), ed. French, Uehling, and Wettstein. West Bend, Ind.: University of Notre Dame Press, 1997, 183.

5. Bill Alston suggested this term to me.

6. Hilary Putnam, *Reason, Truth, and History.*

7. "Reason and History," in *Reason, Truth, and History,* 163.

8. What a *phronimos might* believe in some circumstances that obtain only in another culture can differ from what he *might have* believed in those circumstances. If he had been born in another culture and had grown up there, he *might have* believed some proposition *p,* even though it is not the case that he *might* believe it if he were suddenly transported there today. Since it is the possession of *phronesis* itself and not the personal identity of the *phronimos* that does the work of the *phronesis* test, it is more likely that the *might have* criterion is preferable. However, this needs to be investigated much more thoroughly.

9. Bernard Williams has taken this position in a number of places. See *Ethics and the Limits of Philosophy.* Cambridge: Harvard University Press, 1985, chapter 8.

Index of Names

About the Contributors

Guy Axtell has taught philosophy at the University of Nevada, Reno, since receiving his Ph.D. in 1991. He has written articles on epistemology, philosophy of science, American pragmatism, and philosophy of religion. He is currently at work on a book entitled *Pragmatic Pluralism: Understanding Philosophical Diversity.*

Lawrence BonJour is Professor of Philosophy at the University of Washington. He is the author of *The Structure of Empirical Knowledge* (Harvard, 1985) and *In Defense of Pure Reason* (Cambridge, 1998).

Jonathan Dancy is Professor of Philosophy at the University of Reading, UK. He has written articles and books on epistemology and on moral theory. His main interests lie at the interface between these two areas. His books include *An Introduction to Contemporary Epistemology* (Blackwell, 1985) and *Moral Reasons* (Blackwell, 1993). Forthcoming are *Practical Reality* (Oxford, 2000) and an edited volume on *Normativity* (Blackwell, 2000).

Julia Driver is an Associate Professor of Philosophy at Dartmouth College. She has published articles in journals such as *The Journal of Philosophy*, *Ethics*, *Utilitas*, and *The Philosophical Quarterly*. Her book, *Uneasy Virtue*, is forthcoming from Cambridge University Press. Her main areas of research are consequentialism and virtue theory.

Alvin Goldman is Regents' Professor of Philosophy and Research Scientist in Cognitive Science at the University of Arizona. He does research on epistemology, philosophy of mind, and philosophy of the cognitive and social sciences. He is the author of *Epistemology and Cognition* (Harvard, 1986), *Liaisons: Philosophy Meets the Cognitive and Social Sciences* (MIT, 1992), *Philosophical Applications of Cognitive Science* (Westview, 1993), and *Knowledge in a Social World* (Oxford, 1999).

John Greco is Associate Professor of Philosophy at Fordham University. He is the author of *Putting Skeptics in Their Place: The Nature of Skeptical Arguments and Their Role in Philosophical Inquiry* (Cambridge University Press, 2000), and editor (with Ernest Sosa) of *The Blackwell Guide to Epistemology* (Blackwell, 1999).

Christopher Hookway is Professor of Philosophy at the University of Sheffield in the United Kingdom. His publications include *Peirce* (Routledge, 1985), *Quine: Language, Experience and Reality* (Stanford, 1988), and *Scepticism*

(Routledge, 1990). A collection of his papers on issues arising out of the philosophy of C. S. Peirce will be published by Oxford University Press in 2000 under the title *Truth, Rationality, and Pragmatism*.

Hilary Kornblith is Professor of Philosophy at the University of Vermont. He has written on topics in epistemology, metaphysics, and philosophy of language. He is the author of *Inductive Inference and Its Natural Ground* (MIT Press, 1993) and editor of *Naturalizing Epistemology* (MIT Press, 1994).

James Montmarquet is Professor of Philosophy at Tennessee State University in Nashville. His articles on epistemic virtue and related questions concerning the ethics of belief have appeared in *Mind, American Philosophical Quarterly*, and *Ethics*. He is the author of *Epistemic Virtue and Doxastic Responsibility* (Rowman & Littlefield, 1993), and is currently working on a book on action theory and moral responsibility. With his colleague, William Hardy, he has an anthology on African-American philosophy forthcoming (Wadsworth, 2000).

Richard Paul is Director of Research at the Center for Critical Thinking at Sonoma State University in California and Chair of the National Council for Excellence in Critical Thinking. He has written seven books on critical thinking and over 200 articles. His books include *Critical Thinking: How to Survive in a Rapidly Changing World* and *Critical Thinking: How to Teach Students to Survive in a Rapidly Changing World* (Center for Critical Thinking, 1993) as well as a series of books for instructors on how to redesign instruction so as to emphasize critical thinking in the language arts, social studies, and science.

Ernest Sosa is Romeo Elton Professor in the Philosophy Department of Brown University and an adjunct Distinguished Professor in the Philosophy Department of Rutgers University. He has published papers in epistemology and metaphysics. Some of his epistemology papers are collected in *Knowledge in Perspective* (Cambridge, 1991).

Casey Swank is Associate Professor of Philosophy at St. Cloud State University. His papers include "Reasons, Dilemmas and the Logic of 'Ought'" (*Analysis* 45) and "A New and Unimproved Version of Reliabilism" (*Analysis* 48).

Linda Zagzebski is Kingfisher College Chair of the department of Philosophy of Religion and Ethics, University of Oklahoma. Formerly Professor of Philosophy at Loyola Marymount University in Los Angeles, she is the author of *Virtues of the Mind* (Cambridge, 1996), *The Dilemma of Freedom and Foreknowledge* (Oxford, 1991), and articles in philosophy of religion, epistemology, and ethics. She is presently working on *Divine Motivation Theory*, a motivation-based virtue theory with a theological foundation.